THE SMUT PEDDLERS

JAMES JACKSON KILPATRICK

THE SMUT PEDDLERS

DOUBLEDAY & COMPANY, INC., GARDEN CITY, N.Y. 1960

BI^2

$5/57/61$

0392

FOREWORD

This is a book about the obscenity racket and about the law of obscenity censorship as that law has emerged from courts and legislative bodies since Anthony Comstock's day. The book attempts to report upon what Associate Justice William Douglas has termed "the battle between the literati and the Philistines," and I have approached the conflict not as a partisan but as a sort of war correspondent.

No one who has studied at first hand the fruits of mail-order obscenity, or waded through hundreds of prurient paperbacks and magazines, can remain wholly nonpartisan toward the efforts of the postal inspectors, the decent-literature committees, and other groups seeking to combat the waves of filth now pouring across America. There *is* a social evil in commercial pornography, and I am sympathetic toward the effort to combat it.

At the same time no writer or newspaperman, dedicated to the vital principles of a free press, can remain wholly nonpartisan toward the devoted labors of the American Civil Liberties Union, the American Book Publishers Council, and the many other organizations that are genuinely apprehensive about the excesses of censorship. There is a danger in censorship, too, and I believe the press ought to be guarded against it.

I should like to acknowledge my warmest appreciation to Edward L. Bier and W. J. Callahan, of Mail Fraud Investigations in the Post Office Department; the book could not have been written without their friendly and unfailing help. The views expressed in the book, of course, are entirely my own. I am also deeply indebted to Lloyd Richards, librarian of the Virginia Law Library, who cheerfully led this nonlawyer through the mazes of some four hundred cases. Kenneth Clark of the Motion Picture Association of America made available much useful material. The librarians of the Virginia State Library in Richmond, the Alderman Library of the University of Virginia in Charlottesville, and the Congressional Library provided, as always, indispensable tools for the shaping of ideas. William P. Sloane, director of the Rutgers University Press, took time from his busy schedule to engage in a thought-provoking correspondence that was of immeasurable value to me. Finally, I am indebted beyond measure to my girl Friday, Mrs. Ann Lloyd Merriman, who shared the labors of some distasteful research, typed manuscript, and held her pretty nose through six months of living through a lot of ripe things around the office.

J. J. K.

Richmond,
February, 1960.

CONTENTS

PART I

THE FACT

Take the very lowest instance, the picture postcard sold underhand, by the underworld, in most cities. What I have seen of them have been of an ugliness to make you cry. The insult to the human body, the insult to a vital human relationship! Ugly and cheap they make the human nudity, ugly and degraded they make the sexual act, trivial and cheap and nasty. . . .

D. H. LAWRENCE
Pornography and Obscenity,
Alfred P. Knopf (1930)

1. THE OBSCENITY RACKET TODAY

"Hi, Billy!"

That was the way the letter began. It was neatly typed on a half sheet of onionskin paper. In the upper left-hand corner it bore, rubber-stamped, a street address in Los Angeles.

Hi, Billy!

I believe a COMPLETELY NUDE *girl is a work of art and have many 4" x 5" photos to prove it. These feature beautiful young girls whose busts vary from large to* EXTRA LARGE.

I can make this offer for a short time only so you better order by return air mail. My sets are $3.00, $5.00, $10.00, $20.00, and $25.00. The more expensive sets contain more and better photos. Sorry, no free samples or C.O.D. You must mention this letter.

When ordering please send your suggestions for samples. This will help me to please you.

Please write even if you just say hello.

If you like the best art photos you better order all you can right now.

Sincerely,
NINA

This letter from "Nina" was my introduction to the fastest-growing racket in the United States, the racket in mail-order sex. In the summer of 1959, under the fictitious name of Billy Williams, I had responded to a dozen advertisements in nudie magazines. Within our newspaper office we had become interested in questions of free speech and due process that were involved in legislation requested by the postmaster general. The *Lady Chatterley* case was prominent in the news. What was this obscenity business all about?

All superior numbers refer to the Table of Cases, pp. 295–306.

Thus the orders from Billy Williams went out from Richmond on August 26. And so efficiently is this racket organized that Nina's letter came back to Billy by air mail, before anything else could come in—*and we had ordered nothing from a Nina at all.* In the space of a week the name of Billy Williams, of 1928 Oakdale Avenue, Richmond, Virginia, had gone on mailing lists in Los Angeles, and Nina had bought his name. Within three weeks we were receiving wholly unsolicited material from New York. Within six weeks Billy had a bid to buy action films from Copenhagen.

The obscenity racket operates now in every state in the Union, through syndicates, wholesalers, and distributors as efficiently organized as any reputable manufacturing concern. Postmaster General Arthur E. Summerfield estimates their gross mail-order revenues at $500 million a year. The Granahan Committee of the House turned up informed estimates in 1959 that the commerce in filth, considered as a whole, may reach a billion dollars a year. Between 1954 and 1959, to judge from complaints reaching the Post Office Department in Washington, the racket doubled in size. Chief Postal Inspector David H. Stephens says: "The volume today can be measured in tons." And there is every reason to believe that operations will double again in the next five years.

What is the narcotic in which these traders deal? It is raw sex, stripped of all beauty and poetry. Their purpose is to treat the sexual act as no more than the gratification of animal passions; their object is to stimulate a prurient desire for the sex without love that is lust. The marriage relationship, when it is treated at all, is a relationship to be violated; infidelity is fun, and adultery no more than a harmless pastime.

Kathryn E. Granahan of Philadelphia, who succeeded her late husband in the House in 1956, has summed up the code of the merchant of filth: "Sex is for personal enjoyment, a biological necessity like eating and drinking; a woman is a means for gaining sexual satisfaction; one man among an eager group of young women lives in a kind of earthly paradise, and love is a passion that cannot be restrained, only surrendered to. Homosexuality is enticingly presented. Basic normal principles of honesty, integrity, forthrightness, purity, respect for authority, and regard for person, life, property, are inclined to treat the dangers lightly. Professionals in the field of juvenile crime take the traffic in pornography far more seriously. J. Edgar Hoover says flatly: "We know that in an overwhelmingly large number of cases sex crime is associated with pornography. We know that sex criminals read it, are clearly influenced by it. I believe pornography is a major cause of sex violence. I believe that if we can eliminate the distribution of such items among impressionable children, we shall greatly reduce our frightening sex-crime rate."

The chief neuropsychiatrist and medical director of the Philadelphia municipal court, Dr. Nicholas G. Frignito, appeared before the Granahan Committee. Day by day he has an opportunity, as the committee pointed out, "to study and evaluate the effects of obscenity and pornography on the conduct of youthful law violators." He said:

Antisocial, delinquent, and criminal activity frequently results from sexual stimulation by pornography. This abnormal sexual gratification creates such a demand for expression that gratification by vicarious means follows. Girls run away from their homes and become entangled in prostitution. Boys and young men who have difficulty resisting the undue sexual stimulation become sexually aggressive and generally incorrigible. The more vicious delinquent or psychopathic type may become an exhibitionist, a rapist, a sadist, a fetishist. He may commit such antisocial acts as arson, pyromania, or kleptomania, which are often symbolic sexual acts.

The Philadelphia municipal court has case histories in which sexual arousal from smutty books led to criminal behavior from vicious assaults to homicide. Some of these children did not transgress sexually until they read suggestive stories and viewed lewd pictures or licentious magazines. In several instances these children were very young, varying in age from nine to fourteen years. The filthy ideas implanted in their immature minds impelled them to crime.

Sexual stimulation by printed material does not always lead to crime, but it is always an inducement to impurity and in the more suggestible individual leads to aberrant forms of sexual misconduct, incest, voyeurism, and narcissism.

Our prisons, correctional institutions, and mental hospitals are jammed with many of the unfortunates who were prey to pornography. Many may never recover their mental or physical health. Others may never have freedom.

Pornography is an instrument for delinquency, it is an insidious threat to moral, mental, and physical health. It debases the true meaning and function of sex, it leads to excessive eroticism, morbid preoccupation with sex, and it incites to immoral and antisocial activity.

Dr. Frignito is not alone among court officers in his concern. The Granahan Committee placed in its record a resolution adopted by the National Council of Juvenile Judges at their 1956 convention, in which the judges noted a growing professional realization that filthy magazines, "through their distribution to children and youth and their extensive encouragement to read them, contribute to the breakdown of the moral sense in children which today is causing an increase in juvenile delinquency throughout the nation and is often responsible for adult criminality." In 1957 Washington's venerable Judge Alexander Holtzoff, relying upon a lifetime's experience in trial work, including eleven years on the federal bench, asserted that lewd magazines "no doubt are a contributing cause to juvenile delinquency."[32] In Delaware, State Psychiatrist M. A. Tarumianz frequently has expressed his conviction that obscene materials have a seriously harmful effect upon adolescents.[180] The Kefauver Committee on Juvenile Delinquency in 1955 queried police chiefs around the nation on their opinions on the causal relationship between obscene materials and juvenile crime. Almost without exception they agreed that lewd photographs and magazines stimulate latent sexual desires among adolescents and tend to trigger serious sex crimes. One police officer could not recall a single arrest in a juvenile sex case in which quantities of pornography were not found in the offender's possession. Inspector Harry Fox of the Philadelphia police department told the Granahan Committee in 1959: "My men search all juveniles taken into custody. I wish I could lay before you the pile of obscene pictures ripped out of magazines and valued as cherished possessions by these boys. We destroy them with a lecture—but many times this can't so easily expose it, because of its very furtiveness and its sneaking cunning. So the cheap and popular modern love novel and love film flourishes and is even praised by moral guardians, because you get the sneaking thrill fumbling under all the purity of dainty underclothes, without one single gross word to let you know what is happening.

Thirty years after Lawrence wrote that essay, merchants of filth are daily capitalizing upon the same secret and furtive desires he held in such contempt. But the pornography that offended him in England and on the continent in 1930 has changed in one respect: when he wrote, the sale of "feelthy French pictures" was in the hands of amateurs; it is a professional operation now.

Over a period of months we learned of this at first hand. Billy Williams responded to Nina's letter, of course, and by first-class mail her five-dollar set of pictures turned up—sixteen photographs of nude woman, all of them in highly provocative poses. Perhaps three or four of the pictures might have qualified as art nudes. The others were ordinary snapshots of girls nude in easy chairs, on beds, on rugs. Some of them were what the trade knows as RVN's, the rear-view nudes that carry a special prurience all their own. And the twenty- and twenty-five-dollar sets, Billy was reminded, "contain more and better photos."

Intrigued by the offering from Nina, we contrived a modest and highly amateur enterprise. Billy Williams shortly was joined by a pair of unattractive brothers, "Louis and Joseph Rocco." Billy we conceived as a twenty-three-year-old bakery salesman, a high-school graduate, interested in dirty pictures, dirty movies, sexy correspondence—anything that involved a naked woman. Joseph Rocco became an effeminate, fruity sort of character, devoted to bondage pictures, male nudes (yes, these are available by the hundreds), and the more delicate and bizarre forms of erotica. Louis Rocco was created as a furtive dealer in novelties, possessed of a peculiarly distasteful yellow letterhead, whose interest lay primarily in making a fast buck on the retail sale of whatever filth he could get at a fair price. Over a period of weeks Billy and Louis and Joseph typed out their letters, responded to ads, mailed off checks and sums of cash, and week by week the appalling merchandise began to flow in. The Rocco Brothers' novelty business operated from my own home on Hanover Avenue in Richmond, served by an aged Negro postman who at first strongly disapproved of the whole affair. He suspected that my sixteen-year-old son was sending for the stuff that his experienced eye swiftly identified, through the plain envelopes, as mail-order smut, and his reproachful glances were not relieved until the local postmaster sent a confidential notice of explanation.

Our clumsy and inexpert inquiry into the obscenity racket was conducted entirely without leads or tips from the Post Office Department. The test was to involve nothing more than any reader of a nudie magazine could order on his own. Plainly, the first requirement was to obtain a supply of these magazines and to start clipping ads. These were available from the corner store. We found:

From a source in Hollywood: "Unretouched photos of gals with raised skirts."

From a source in El Segundo, California: "200 poses, only $1. Includes 50 men and women in miniature lover photos."

From a "Kristine": "Like to give me the business? Let us send you our confidential bulletin that shows all of us and explains about our really intimate photos and films. Please enclose 25 cents to help pay for this ad."

We explored the ads of a Broadway "movie club," offering "four tantalizing movies on one big reel for $9.99." In Hollywood a fictitious Nancy, associated with an equally fictitious Pat, Mary, and Louann, offered "the kind of pictures we think you want" at three dollars for a set of twelve. We were tempted by "gorgeous, superbly developed models," by "daring and different photos," and by "art photos that couldn't be published."

The magazines from which we clipped these ads cater entirely to the prurient interest of the newsstand buyer. Some of them are published in New York, some in Los Angeles; they appear at erratic intervals, like desert weeds. Some carry advertising, some do not, but in essence they are all alike: nudie pictures, nudie cartoons, pornographic fiction. A typical story, from a magazine published in the summer of 1959, purported to be the diary of a teen-age girl who develops a crush on a movie actor making a film on a Florida location. She manages to get aboard his yacht and soon has taken off her blouse, dungarees, and sneakers:

> Then Wayne came back. "I've done all the work so far," I said. "You take off my panties." And he did, and let me tell you that felt like nothing in the world, having Wayne Whitney take off my panties. I mean it was a lovely feeling, him being a famous actor and all, and so dignified besides. So he took them off, and then I began to unbutton his shirt. At the same time he unbuttoned his pants. The thing was, we didn't have much time. . . . So in a minute he was undressed too, and we lay down on the bunks. The funny thing was, even undressed, he looked pretty dignified. I guess that that takes practice. But from the way he was touching my legs and things I guess he had had a lot of practice. So we lay there for a while, him touching the smooth part of my thighs and things like that, and after a while we got down to where there wasn't anything left to do but the main event, and we did that. . . .

That is an entirely typical passage. This same magazine opened with a story of a man seducing his neighbor's nymphomaniac wife ("The bed groaned under our weight as she nestled in my arms, pressing her thigh hard against mine"). It continued with a profile of a "primitive princess" (illustrated with nine wholly nude photographs), and went on to a story of wife-swapping ("He rose and lowered his beefy weight on to her soft, heated form"). Ninety-eight pages later this issue concluded with a story of violent rape ("He seized her and drew her to him. The feel of her warm, still moist body struggling against his was unbearably exciting").

Though this magazine is marked "for adults" it is available to any customer, teen-age or otherwise, with a dollar to spend. And it was by no means the most objectionable of the publications we examined. In every instance the big attractions are the nudes—ordinarily hard-eyed young women with enormous breasts—whose aim is to provide sensuous pleasure and to arouse sexual desire. They provide a dreary parade. In a typical issue of *Spree,* for example, 57 of the 70 pages offer nudes and seminudes. An issue of *Sir Knight* scores 51 nudes in 66 pages. A publication called *Lark* provides 87 nudes in 55 pages. This doubtless is not a world's record.

The number of nudie magazines rises and falls, as one title goes out of existence and another succeeds it. Now and then a magazine that begins by catering to any old kind of sex manages to break out of the earthier atmosphere and get into a more sophisticated orbit. *Playboy* is an outstanding example. Its early issues were garden-variety dirt, but with skilled editing its young publisher, Hugh M. Hefner, greatly raised its literary level and achieved a notable success within the highly competitive magazine industry. As *Playboy's* playmates have become steadily less prurient the magazine's editorial content has improved greatly. To the astonishment of some of its old fans, *Playboy* in 1959 even waxed earnest about strontium 90. It was as if Brigitte Bardot had begun singing the works of Carrie Jacobs Bond.

From a list compiled by the Indianapolis police department an indication of the variety of these magazines may be gleaned:

Caper	*Satan*	*Scamp*
Jem	*Monsieur*	*Stag*
Sir	*Escapade*	*Follies*
Gent	*Tan*	*Jackpot*
Male	*Man*	*Nugget*
Man's Illustrated	*Man's Adventure*	*Showplace*
Hit	*High*	*Rogue*
Glance	*Girl Watcher*	*Real Man*
Swank	*Play*	*The Dude*
Ace	*G-Eyefuls*	*Cabaret*
Bronze Thrills	*Uncensored*	*Hush Hush*
Tempo	*Bold*	*Male Life*

And this three-dozen sample does not include, to be sure, *Adam, Spree, He, She, Man to Man, Zest, Mermaid, Twenty-One, Sir Knight, Plush,* or *Mr.* By the time this book appears a dozen of these will have gone out of existence and a dozen new ones will have come along. The supply of nudie pictures is inexhaustible. Scatological fiction can be bought by the ream. The customers are waiting. And at the lower levels of the trade, advertising can be had from a hundred mail-order nudie and novelty houses.

In addition to the dozens of nudie magazines half a dozen nudist magazines also tempt the curious purchaser. There is a difference.

Both nudie and nudist magazines dedicate themselves to display of the female breasts and buttocks, but the models in the nudies are professionals and the subjects in the nudist magazines are largely amateurs. The effect, remarkably, is to imbue the nudist publications with a sexual attraction that for some readers far exceeds the excitement of the nudies. There is a feeling that the naked women of the nudist magazines, lacking the grace and posture of the professional models, somehow are real people, vicariously attainable in a way that the hard-eyed strippers and starlets of *Scamp* and *Monsieur* are not. Possibly the presence of men and women together adds to the appeal.

Whatever the explanation, the sunbathing magazines hold a continuing attraction to the thumb-and-snicker adolescents who hang around newsstands, and the nudist publications sell amazingly well. During the trial of one of Postmaster General Summerfield's suits against *Sunshine and Health* some circulation figures, ordinarily closely guarded, became public; the magazine in 1956 had a mail circulation to subscribers of ten thousand copies, and a newsstand sale of thirty thousand.[186] For whatever value the fact may have, as an aid to reflection on the general condition of mankind, this circulation then exceeded the circulation of *The Reporter, New Republic, The Nation,* and *National Review.*

The nudist magazines hold themselves out as no more than reportorial and promotional publications of the nudist cult. *Modern Sunbathing,* for example, displays the seal of approval of the American Sunbathing Association; its pages are crammed with articles intended to advance the nudist movement. Pubic areas are blandly retouched in all photographs, which adds a weirdly obscene effect to the pages, but most of the subjects are posed so this airbrushed concession to morality is not required. Invariably the covers feature an especially nubile female. A typical advertisement offers for one dollar "the true inside facts about nudism, names and addresses of 100 nudist camps, eight nudist cartoons and sample of nudist product, sent by first-class mail under plain sealed cover." A response to this ad produces some entirely innocuous drawings, a couple of leaflets on visiting a nudist camp ("Rates are reasonable, and, where provided, meals are balanced and good; alcoholic beverages are expressly prohibited at all nudist parks. The presence of liquor or intoxicated persons on the grounds will not be tolerated"), and a publication entitled *Nudist Primer*. The *Primer* is a question-and-answer affair, brimful of wholesome Americanism:

Q. Is nudism a form of Communism?

A. Absolutely not. Persons known to be members of subversive organizations or sympathetic to their objectives are excluded from nudist resorts and/or membership in the American Sunbathing Society. Radicals of any sort have no place in nudist society.

The author of the *Primer* explains that nudists aim first of all at better physical health and secondly at "a determined, and successful, effort toward lifting the standards of public morality." Their conviction is, "the more nudists, the less burlesque shows, sex preoccupation, 'cheesecake' magazines, obscene literature, and sex offenders provoked by such stimuli."

The *Nudist Primer,* in short, is no more obscene than *Rebecca of Sunnybrook Farm,* and the nudist magazines, considered in some intellectual vacuum, would not appear to have as their dominant theme an appeal to prurient interest. At the same time, as the Granahan Committee concluded, the nudist magazines would have a far more convincing case "if they were limited in their circulation to those individuals who practice nudism." The magazines are not so limited, and increasingly their photographs suggest the professional model at work. As long as *Modern Sunbathing* relies for three fourths of its sales upon the newsstand pulling power of a provocatively naked female, the nudist movement's claims upon virtue, like their photographs, will demand a little retouching.

Billy Williams early launched into the business of ordering sexy motion pictures. Most of the films we received in response to ads in the nudie magazines were feeble affairs, poorly put together, often wound backward on the reels. One of the most provocative ads produced an odd four-minute film: three minutes and fifty seconds of children's magic shows, animal pictures and travelogue, with a concluding ten-second shot of an alluring dame. In time, however, unsolicited offers began to turn up for "film clubs," and responses to these invitations brought some films—for as little as six dollars—that were thoroughly obscene. I do not mean by this that the films depicted actual intercourse; I mean only that they manifestly were intended to appeal solely to prurient interest, and that they had not so much as one second's worth of socially redeeming importance. These were the tenderfoot version of stag movies. Investigations by the Post Office Department indicate that such films sell in terms of at least $200 million a year.

The size of the stag-film racket justifies more than passing attention. This is a big business and it is operated as such: circulars are well designed and competently printed; mailings come with order forms and return envelopes; most of the vendors will accept personal checks. This is a typical come-on:

Dear Friend Film Buyer:

If you've about given up hope of ever finding films that you could show with PRIDE *to your buddies . . . if you've been misled by "smart" advertising into buying movies you could show at a dowager's tea party . . . then you're going to be glad you read this folder. You'll find the ———— Club lives up to its name—that we are not an impersonal company, but a group of people who take a personal interest in giving you exactly what you want.*

What's more, we're so confident you're going to enjoy [our] films more than any you've seen, that we offer them only on free approval. That's right—you don't pay a penny until after you've seen the films and decide you want to keep them. What could be more fair? . . .

Remember, you're spending good money on adult films. So why not enjoy films that have what you REALLY *want? You can, if you'll join on a* NO-RISK *trial membership today! Send for your first On Approval Film and Free Gift now. You'll be glad that you did!*

This letter is decorated with a couple of photographs of busty girls wearing "pasties," small adhesive butterflies, stars, bows, snowflakes, or other items about one inch square, designed to cover their nipples. A G-string completes the costume. The accompanying folder holds out a promise of "three types of high-voltage party films," in which "gorgeous, shapely young models in filmy 'peek-a-boo' lace enact daring 'you are there' plots . . . use their imagination to set yours afire." There are "dynamite, prohibited burlesque films"; there are "advanced-type movies, produced for the more sophisticated collector." And these are available in a 50-foot black-and-white reel for as little as $2.50; a 16-mm. sound film, on a 200-foot reel, is $12.

These prices are within the reach of thousands of adolescents, to whom movie projection equipment is no real problem. And it does not take the magazine buyer long to discover that the circular just quoted is a tame attraction indeed. Billy Williams sent off an inquiry to one address in Hollywood. Two weeks later an answer came from a company operating under a completely different name. A note explained that the first club was "one of our associate companies." This time Billy was offered more stimulating stuff. Gone were the pasties. For twenty dollars he could buy four reels:

MARIA: *This petite blonde goddess possesses the soft blonde beauty and perfection of figure that is seldom seen even in beauty-conscious Hollywood.*

SHERRY: *This tawny-tressed teaser bears out our claim that here is one of the world's most beautiful bodies. Sherry poses without inhibition in her Laurel Canyon hideaway.*

DANIELLE: *A sloe-eyed enchantress with rare Italian beauty and a svelte, supple body.*

BETTY: *This slender, graceful brunette has a terrific build and knows it—and so will you after an exposure to this fast-moving, provocative film!*

In each case, the model was shown entirely nude. Billy ordered from this come-on a couple of films, *Advice to the Loveworn* and *Honeymoon Helpmeet*. Both films proved to be built upon the same tawdry theme that constantly recurs in these stag productions—the fight between two half-clothed or wholly nude women. Presumably there is some special sexual bang that results from the sight of a dumb blonde, with her breasts flopping, clawing aimlessly at another dumb blonde with her breasts flopping. The acting is ludicrously poor. The girls are not attractive; their appeal is nudity alone. In any event these sorry films were entirely typical of a dozen Billy ordered (and faithfully received) on a "confidential no-risk order form." He also invested in a 100-foot film of a gal with a fabulous 38-19-36 figure, whose full-page ads appeared late in 1959 in a dozen nudie magazines, but the ad proved to be merely sucker bait: the film sent from New York was not "ultra-revealing and provocative," as advertised. It was just vulgar.

Production costs of these movies are low. Often they are shot in someone's apartment. A camera, some floodlights, a few props, a couple of girls, a "director" who supervises the brief production—for two hundred dollars or less the film is in the can. Thereafter prints can be produced for pennies, and the entire cost is recouped very rapidly. The films circulate for years, continuing to produce four or six or ten dollars a print, and the nature of the racket is such that so long as the original negative is not seized and destroyed, the promoters can keep operating under one name after another. To be sure, the postal inspectors are a constant annoyance, but with a score of fictitious names and corporations, the convenience of a post-office box, and the gullibility of the male animal, the racket keeps going nicely. A $500 fine is no more than a part of the overhead, to be debited to miscellaneous expenses. And there is always a Donna, a Patti, a Dianne, or a Dolores ready to strip and flop and slap and paw for mail-order billing to the pimple trade as "Hollywood's most beautiful women—in the NUDE!"

The racket's most reliable offering, however, is not the stag film; it is the single nude photograph. There are economic reasons for this. Even the simplest motion picture demands an "actress," a "set," a cameraman, and an idea. Moreover films can be sold only to the sort of sociable customers who want to share their sex kicks, and the market—large as it is—has certain limitations. Single photographs, on the other hand, can be produced by the millions under conditions that appeal to the one-man operator. As scores of cases in Post Office files make clear, a pornographer often saves even a model fee by using his wife. A dozen flash bulbs, a roll of film, a photographic printer, a provocative ad in a nudie magazine, a rented post-office box, a mailing list—and he is in business. If the ad pulls, and the postal inspectors do not pick him up before the sheep have been sheared, a small investment can return an amazing dividend. The office overhead is small, and the negatives have a timeless value (some of the prints received in our test mailings appeared to have been made from negatives at least twenty-five years old).

From small ventures in the singles racket large operations grow. There is, for example, Tennessee's gift to commerce, Roy Oakley. Postal inspectors have a file a foot thick on Roy Oakley, and it keeps growing all the time. His one-inch ad appeared in 1959 in dozens of nudie magazines:

TERRIFIC ADULT CATALOG

Five thousand art photos. Send no money, just your name, address, and 24¢ in stamps for large 16-page illustrated catalog of adult merchandise. Art photos, pin-ups, art books, playing cards, French books, novels, etc. One of the largest of its kind.

The curious customer who sent off his twenty-four cents in stamps received his catalog almost by return mail. It was a handsome production, done up in rotogravure, bearing on its cover (along with the pictures of six naked women) a portrait shot of Oakley himself. Copyreaders on the Richmond *Times-Dispatch* desk, asked one night to guess, without hints, at the occupation of this dignified stranger, hazarded variously that the portrait must be that of a high-school principal, a funeral director, an accordion teacher, and a youth worker. Roy Oakley is in fact a professional peddler of smut, a native of Tennessee, born in 1922, onetime Marine, onetime commercial photographer, married and divorced, the recipient of a 20-per-cent disability pension from a grateful government for his diabetes. He first attracted the department's attention in 1948 with a line of vacuous pin-ups, but as his trade improved he broadened his line. An "unlawful" order against him in 1951 proved no real deterrent. By the summer of 1955 his business was flourishing. On August 11 of that year he appeared before the Kefauver Committee investigating obscene materials; he then had a mailing list of 40,000 to 50,000 names. He estimated that during one typical year he had prepared no fewer than 250,000 photographic prints of pin-ups and nudes.

On March 25, 1958, postal inspectors, convinced they had an airtight case against Oakley, raided his plant. They found one man and two women busily engaged in mailing circulars, filling orders, and posting accounts. A supply room housed thousands of photographic prints, books, magazines, and playing cards. A mail room, efficiently equipped with postage meter, might have served as a model for a tidy mail room anywhere. On July 30, 1958, a grand jury at Nashville indicted Oakley for mailing obscene matter, but a battery of defense attorneys, headed by O. John Rogge, former assistant attorney general in the criminal division of the Department of Justice, successfully maintained that the department's search had not been properly authorized. In April of 1959 the seized property was returned.

Back in business, Oakley rushed to his mail room with a fresh circular. In May of 1959 postal inspectors received a complaint that a sixteen-year-old boy in Ohio had received a new brochure from Roy Oakley:

This cute, clever, colorful catalog is one of several thousand that were seized by postal inspectors over thirteen months ago in an illegal search and seizure. It was returned to us recently through a federal court order. It is a collector's item! Save it! Treasure it! Order from it! And your order will help wage war against the bluenoses, prudes, book-burners, professional do-gooders, and self-styled cultural commissars of the world at large.

Once again the money rolled in; in Washington the complaints came rolling in also. It later developed that while he was under indictment Oakley had kept up his regular mailings; one mailing alone saw three thousand first-class letters spread around the country.

On August 26, 1959, Billy Williams sent off his twenty-four cents in stamps for an Oakley catalog. The publication arrived on September 2, a "twelfth-anniversary special" offering a bewildering assortment of prurient merchandise: French art books at three dollars an album, 101 other books of "famous art models posed in the nude," a page of novels ranging upward and downward from the Marquis de Sade's *Justine,* a lip-licking assortment of playing cards, cartoon books, *How to Make Love, Sex Facts for Women, Tales of French Love and Passion,* and, of course, the nude photo sets. These were priced at two dollars for a set of ten, and the customer could take his choice of roughly 140 models. The mailing included an order form, a return envelope, a bonus special slip, and suddenly, shockingly, a free sample of his special selections: a crisp 4″ x 5″ print of a wholly nude girl, posed on a bathroom floor, her genital area boldly exposed; and she was gazing squarely into the camera with a look far removed from the look of a gossamer art nude.

Billy Williams sent off his order, for a deck of the Wolf Pack playing cards, a copy of *Justine,* a set of run-of-the-mill nudes, and a Special Selection No. 6. Two weeks elapsed before the mail brought a terse postcard: Roy was "out of stock on some items." Another month passed by and Billy wrote a letter of complaint. Late in October *Justine* at last turned up, accompanied by the twenty prints of Selection No. 6. They were, as advertised, unretouched—clumsy, poorly posed, poorly lighted, underexposed, and overexposed—dismal examples of the photographer's art, but well adorned with visible pubic hair.

Billy complained once more that the whole of his order had not been sent. A mimeographed form letter arrived under date of November 14:

Sorry for the delay in filling your order but we have held your order expecting a large shipment of merchandise from our publisher. . . . The merchandise you ordered is in great demand. It is hard to keep our stock supplied due to our publishers which is beyond our control. We try to give prompt service and have the interest of our customers at heart. We hope you will take our situation into consideration and will be patient. . . .

The situation Billy was asked to take into consideration, left tactfully unexplained, was that Roy Oakley was at this time still under indictment for mailing obscene matter. On June 14, 1960, he was found guilty on each of ten counts, and sentenced to two years in prison.

In one highly significant respect Oakley is an exception to the usual pattern of the obscenity racket. He operates from a small town in Tennessee. Far more typical are the operators who make their headquarters in New York and California. These are the big states for mail-order pornography. Two reasons account for this. One is obvious: in New York City and Los Angeles the supply of models is almost endless; the resources of photography, advertising, and anonymous mail handling are equally advantageous; the great cities can swallow up and conceal a merchant of filth as quietly as they digest many another shady operation. A second reason was discerned long ago: in general, the federal judges of L. A. and Manhattan are far more tolerant of obscenity than their brothers elsewhere in the country. And until 1958, when postal laws were amended to permit prosecution at the point where mail is received, rather than only at the point where mail is deposited, this judicial leniency counted for a great deal.

In many instances the Los Angeles syndicates operate behind a buxom front of "girls' clubs." The pitch is always the same. Alice, Jane, Ilene, and Shirley are four starlets who "tried real hard but didn't make the movies." Now they're in business for themselves, as art and calendar models. They are lonesome. All they do is pose and write letters. And then last month Alice came up with a terrific idea:

She said, "Why should we pose for pennies, then have some character sell our photographs and films for lots of money? Why don't we start our own little 'personalized business'—and really get to know the fellows who send for our things?"

We all talked it over and agreed it would be loads of fun! We like to model (yes, we're proud of our figures), and we like to write and receive letters.

So we had this little folder made up. . . . Then we bought a mailing list of fellows whom we thought would like the intimate, revealing poses we like to do best. . . .

So Alice, the saucy brunette, and Jane, the slim, auburn-haired gal with long tapering legs, and Ilene, the petite homebody who loves to disrobe for posing, and Shirley, the bouncy type, are now in business. They offer sets of 12 photos for $3; sets of 12 slides of the girls, "as you like them," $5.95; the whole works—48 photos and 48 slides—$30. Stag movies are available of the girls from $6 to $20, and every purchaser gets a friendly, handwritten letter from the gal of his choice.

Billy Williams and Louis Rocco ordered quantities of material from these ambitious and industrious females. Most of the returns followed a familiar pattern: a set of nude and seminude photos, varying in quality from poor to fairly good, and with the photos a tentative come-on for more and better material at a higher price. Sometimes the ads would provoke no direct response at all, but after a lapse of two or three weeks an unsolicited offer would come in from a wholly different source with an explanatory reference to "your recent inquiry to one of our affiliates."

The girls' ads, plainly enough, are intended to produce one return first of all: names. Names and addresses. And when the names and addresses indicate likely prospects the bids to buy go out from Los Angeles and New York by the thousands: Judy, Vicky, Marian, Margy, Bonnie, Kay, Linda, Bettie the onetime school teacher, Eve, Ann, Sheila, Sue; a private collection of nude movies:

Hi, Fellow:

I am closing out my own nude movies which the mail-order operators termed too risky to be sold. I will sell them direct to you. . . .

Intimate glossy "collector's item" photos, action movies, real he-man movies for the artist, student, connoisseur, photographer. . . . This cuddlesome cutie will awaken every nerve, every muscle, in your body when she displays ALL her voluptuous charms right before your eyes. . . . Watching her writhing, heaving body will doubtlessly have YOU squirming quite a bit too. . . . Would you rather spend a warm sunny Sunday afternoon with a beautiful blonde or an equally beautiful brunette? Well, after you see these two play around in ALL their *natural* loveliness, you'll have a *hard time* deciding. . . . Babs is a bountifully blessed blonde. . . . When your eyes travel over every inch of her satiny-smooth body, then watch her let go with meaningful gyrations, you'll respond as Babs does. . . . Ready Redhead, Daring Darling, Cuddlesome Curves, Sultry Senorita. . . . Are you over twenty-one years old? . . . French-style art slides. . . . Our tantalizing young and beautiful girls give pleasure. . . . Six sexational slides per set. . . . Don't delay, order now. . . . Millie's Movement, Frantic Fanny, From Bed to Worse, Shocking Suzanne. . . . Tina's Torrid Torso, Daughters of Eve, Return to Nudity, or How Far Can You Go?

How far can you go? The racket will take the willing sucker for just as much as the sucker can be taken. Preying upon adolescents, curious girls, sex-hungry old men, the pornography factories will fill any order that promises a ready profit.

The only exception Billy Williams encountered to this cynical pattern came with his correspondence with a girl who might possibly, though improbably, be named Janet. At first the come-on was the same: Darlene, Cynthia, and Janet, all new to the modeling business in Hollywood, had enjoyed posing but they just didn't like the modeling business. The promoters were making all the money.

So, we just put our heads together and decided to start our own little club-business. We saved our money and hired our own photographer—and, if we do say so, our films and photographs are a lot more desirable than what you usually receive. . . .

Billy chose Janet as his new friend and dutifully sent off a get-acquainted form identifying himself as a twenty-three-year-old fun-loving high-school graduate, a bakery salesman fond of sex and dancing. He sent nine dollars for a set of twelve pictures and a 16-mm. movie. In time the material came back, disclosing a full-breasted girl in black bra and pants; with the photos came an obviously duplicated form letter in simulated handwriting:

It was certainly a wonderful surprise when I learned I was the girl you wanted for your personal model! Even tho all three of us girls are good friends, we do have a little rivalry going—especially when it concerns a fellow who sounds as interesting as you. . . .

Ever wonder, just a little, what it is that makes two people attract each other? I do. Now, I don't really know what you look like. But how important is that? Sometimes I think just a few words a person writes say so much more about what they are inside, I mean. . . .

This little club of ours is lots of fun, much better than modeling for a living. (Of course, we're still a long way from making a living at it.) You meet such characters in this town that it's a real pleasure getting to know a sincere fellow like yourself.

I hope you enjoy the things I'm sending along. I guess they aren't too revealing, but we can't be too careful. Later, when we get to know each other better, who knows—?

As a matter of fact, I will take a chance on you. That's why I'm sending along our "confidential charter member" form. I wouldn't send it, except that I think you want to see more of me!

> *Your new friend,*
> JANET

To this seductive invitation Billy responded with a warm letter and three dollars more. This produced a second set of pictures as innocuous as the first—photographs obviously taken at the same modeling session, in the same underclothes, in the same apartment—and an oddly unprovocative letter:

Well, hello again, Bill—

Gee, was it ever nice hearing from you—and so soon, too. Are you always so punctual—and in everything?

I want you to know too how much I appreciated your order. It will certainly help pay for the groceries. Say, did you know that you are quite a flatterer? I s'pose any girl likes compliments (I know I do), and especially from someone I like.

It's funny, we've only exchanged a letter or two, but I already feel that I know you quite well. Yes, you're becoming a very real person—even tho we haven't met.

Now, in answer to some of your questions, I'm twenty-three (getting old, huh?). I like swimming, long hikes in the country, and motoring (it's so nice to get away from the city once in a while). I'm crazy about dancing (even rock 'n' roll is fun, tho waltzing is my favorite). Best of all, I guess I enjoy quiet evenings—this Hollywood nite club-bing isn't for me. . . .

The other night the other girls and myself went to the Griffith Park Planetarium. It was so beautiful—all the stars—and I never felt so small in my life. The size of the universe really makes you wonder, doesn't it—about a lot of things?

> *Your new friend,*
> JANET

The ardent Billy, rather dashed by his pen pal's venture into meta-physics, attempted once more to suggest that he would be in the market for hotter, higher-priced, and more revealing merchandise, but his further inquiry was returned with a genuinely handwritten note that added up to a definite brushoff. We concluded that (a) the Hon. Otto K. Olesen, postmaster of Los Angeles, was breathing down the back of Janet's shapely neck or (b) a shrewd operator had seen through Billy's carefully composed letters. As a third possibility, (c), it may be that the gal really did like waltzes, hikes in the country, and visits to a planetarium. Anyhow no jury would have convicted her of anything but Chicago *Tribune* spelling. *Te absolvo,* Janet; it was fun while it lasted.

Our letters to European sources were something else entirely. From the very limited test mailings conducted in the name of Louis Rocco we concluded swiftly that the postal inspectors are entirely justified in their concern at foreign sources of filth. An international agreement, to which the United States are party, is designed to deter this racket, but the traffic is devilishly hard to break up. As rapidly as the Post Office Department obtains a stop order to halt the transmission of mail to one name and address in London or Amsterdam or Copenhagen, the resourceful foreign merchants come up with a fresh name and a fresh address.

An advertisement from a London address produced a come-on letter so skillfully composed that one wept for the loss to honest merchandising when "V" took up pornography:

I'm going to put my cards on the table. Over here in Europe we can get the real thing in photos, films, etc. It's not easy of course, and it takes trouble and money, but you can get it. I travel all over Europe to accumulate suitable merchandise, and for obvious reasons it's a lot easier for me to get girls to pose for the right sort of thing! Even then you don't find many girls who are attractive enough and willing to pose for these. When you do find them you have to pay plenty. . . . So there it is, my prices are a lot higher than the usual run-of-the-mill dealers' but against that you know that when you pay good money you'll get the real goods. . . .

First of all, films. A couple of weeks ago I went down to the French Riviera and managed to get some real film there. I got hold of two girls, one of them a seventeen-year-old French girl with long black hair and Bardot type figure and got her to do a film together with (and I mean together) a fabulous blonde English girl aged twenty-five who measured 49-27-38!! Sounds impossible I know, but it's true. Apart from some seminude shots to start with, all the action is with the girls completely nude! . . .

And so forth. This particular circular went on for six single-spaced pages; it wound up with various combination and bargain offers, and with a firm admonition to send American currency only: "I cannot accept cheques or money orders of any form."

Following the pattern of American operators, foreign pornographers are primarily interested, when they run a small advertisement in a nudie magazine, in obtaining names and addresses. One ad offered "direct from Europe, the very best photos of fully developed girls." A three-dollar order, in response to this ad, produced by return airmail nothing more than an envelope of bikini pin-up pictures. Two weeks later, however, from Amsterdam, came a neatly printed circular, offering for one dollar a sample color slide, a booklet giving details of uncensored books, a sample movie strip, and an illustrated catalog. A response to this circular produced a shockingly obscene package in return. The color slide disclosed a nude woman, photographed in full front view as she leaned back on a bench; her fleshy thighs were parted, and her hands were holding her labia open. Among the movies, at fifteen dollars each:

NO. 1   *Suzy longing for love—still alone—can hardly wait for her boy friend—how on earth can he resist such beauty?*

NO. 2   *Suzy could not possibly wait any longer and is now amusing herself.*

NO. 3   *Yes, Suzy rides again and how. Life is too short to be alone, and therefore she rides again.*

NO. 4   *Did you ever see two lovely girls massaging each other? Possibly you did, but this special movie shows you complete nude massage without strings.*

NO. 5   *This is Jeanette, our little dark-haired favorite. What a girl! She dislikes making her partner disappointed; she is doing all she can to make him feel one with her.*

A tightly printed circular offered passages from five obscene books. These defy quotation. It will suffice to suggest that no defender of free press, anywhere, could justify the publication and circulation of writings so willfully and wholly depraved.

These items came from a notorious syndicate that operates from a dozen addresses out of Amsterdam. In February, 1957, and again in May, 1957, the Post Office Department's general counsel obtained "unlawful" orders against the syndicate in the names of Univers and

Cosmopolite. Immediately thereafter the same operators turned up under another name, offering the same lewd films from $12.50 to $78. In 1959 they were doing business under at least three different names and addresses. A pink printed slip, enclosed with a price slip, advised the American sucker: "If your letter is sent back to you, use another name but the same address."

Our amateur investigations, conducted in the name of Louis Rocco, also turned up some shockingly hard-core items from a source in Copenhagen. Again an innocuous first mailing, in response to an ad inserted in magazines freely available in any large American city, was followed by a circular inviting the customer to get the "real thing." For twenty-two dollars the fictitious firm of Rocco Brothers easily obtained an assortment of thoroughly obscene photographs, fully revealing pubic areas of the models, plus a catalog of color slides showing male and female models wholly nude. During our correspondence with the Copenhagen house the name of the source changed three times; the address changed twice. The slickness of printing, the efficiency of mailing, and the quality of obscene materials all indicated a highly professional and well-organized factory for the merchandising of filth.

The great bulk of mail-order filth is designed to appeal, of course, to the more or less normal male animal. If his appetite for filthy photographs and movies should pall, the mail-order merchants will sell him novelties, playing cards, peephole viewers, and jigsaw puzzles. They will sell him cartoon books, joke books, postcards, and filthy novels. They will sell him erotic recordings, suggestive statuettes, and lewd chinaware. They will sell him underclothes, sex manuals, aphrodisiac recipes, comic booklets, and something called a "girl getter" (this is a page of good clean advice on how and where a man can meet girls: "Go to church! You don't have to be religious, just go!"). Ordinarily this merchandise is offered "for adults only," which is a sure-fire appeal to adolescents, and it is offered with such an array of gift certificates, bargain offers, short-time-only deals, extra-picture premiums, order forms, and return envelopes that the cash comes pouring in.

In a class by themselves are the bizarre publications that appeal to abnormal sexual appetites. Foremost among these are the bondage books and magazines, widely distributed through a New Jersey company but available from other freely advertised sources also. Here the dominant theme is not nudity but pain; the intention is to satisfy a sadistic lust that gratifies itself in the bizarre and repulsive tortures of shapely women who are tied to racks, impaled on hooks, put in chains, and shackled to ingenious and grotesque devices. Invariably the models appear in shoes with six-inch heels or in tightly laced leather boots. Sometimes they are gagged. Refinements see them wrapped in rubber blankets. Prominent in the background are whips, gouges, and ropes. Among the most popular sales items are sets of photographs depicting two girls wrestling with each other. A gross appeal to Lesbianism characterizes the storybooks.

A typical circular from a house in Canada reads in this fashion:

Painful PUNISHMENT

Sensational scenes of sadism, including a girl tightly tied to a trestle in a spread-eagle position. Girls gagged and lashed together, etc. This exceptionally fine sequence is most unusually interesting and highly prized by seekers of the exotic. This is exceptional value. Eight photos, $6.

The Lesbian publications have their corollary in a number of magazines aimed at male homosexuals, the "gays" and "queers" who live in a shadow world of their own. These offer an amazing array of photographs of men, posed wholly nude or in posing straps that fully reveal the male genitals. Just as the nudie magazines carry advertisements for bisexual smut, from sources at home and abroad, so the gay magazines carry ads from houses in London, New York, Washington, and Los Angeles. The reader with a strong stomach can pursue these ads as far as he wishes to pursue them.

Beyond the movies, the slides, the singles, the obscene novelties, the girls' clubs, and the nudie magazines, in a specially difficult field all their own, are the dirty paperback books. These present a genuinely perplexing problem to the American citizen who finds any thought of book-burning abhorrent. A photograph of a couple engaged in sexual intercourse is patently obscene; a written description of the same act may or may not be obscene. Moreover, as a matter of law, a particular book may be obscene under state law in one part of the country and not obscene under a federal postal prosecution in another.

An example may be drawn from public records in the matter of *Rambling Maids* and *Turbulent Daughters,* two novels distributed by a publishing house in Fresno, California, known as Fabian Books. Both books were found obscene in Georgia, under proceedings launched by the State Literature Commission there. In California a federal court jury, weighing the books under Title 18, Section 1461, of the United States Code, found them not obscene.

Rambling Maids deals with the adventures of two whores, Gladys and Verna, who ply their trade from California to Texas in a fantastic series of copulations with various wealthy men. Verna tells the story. By page 17 she notices that "Jim was itching at the crotch to get on Gladys." A few pages later Gladys is involved with Hank. On page 28 Verna describes her own sex act with Jim:

I untied my negligee and flung it off, causing Jim's eyes to widen desperately.

"Hurry, Jim! I can't stand it much longer! Hurry!"

He began fumbling with his clothes and I fell onto the bed, trying to keep up the trembling until he reached me. When he finally did, it was a head-first dive to my pubic area. The phone began to ring and, while I wondered who it was, I pretended that I didn't hear it.

Toward the end Jim went old-fashioned and I felt raw. He was about as savage a man as I'd ever encountered. As well as being heavily strung, he was forcefully strong and his style was poignant. I knew then why Gladys had looked so worn and haggard after a few hours with him.

A man named Tom becomes involved in the plot, if it may be called a plot, and then another man named Clark Nesbitt. Says Verna to Gladys: "I want to lay Tom like you want to lay Nesbitt." But almost any men will do: "We're looking for some firm, hard-boiled men with rape ideas." Some incredible complications follow, and more intercourse, including a prolonged act between Verna and an old man, Sam:

Sam began to squirm and twist, and I let him loose. A sizable stick had risen against his thigh and it shocked me some to see that he was so potent.

Verna decides to marry Sam in a weird conspiracy to acquire a ranch in Texas. As they drive eastward from California, sitting in the rear seat of a car driven by still another character, Sam engages in oral intercourse with Verna. The scene is described in detail.

Enough. In my own judgment, the book is wholly devoid of literary merit. It is crudely written, cheaply printed, abominably proofread. Though it carries the byline of "Betty Short," the wretched thing actually was written by one Sanford "Les" Aday, an ex-convict who served two and a half years in San Quentin, from April, 1946, to December, 1948, on a conviction for pimping and pandering. Born in 1919, Aday went to school through the eighth grade; he was engaged in the restaurant business in Sacramento for a time and later was a distributor for a bakery. In 1952 he established the Fabian and Saber books (another of his corporations is known as Mid-Tower Publishing Corporation), all at the same address in Fresno.

That such a work could be defended by any responsible person as literature may seem unbelievable, but in November of 1958, when federal authorities brought Aday to trial in Fresno before Judge Leon Yankwich, the defense was able to produce a professor of English and a respected L. A. book editor who solemnly equated *Rambling Maids* with the works of Faulkner, Hemingway, and James Joyce. In their determination to regard *no* book as nonmailably obscene these witnesses defended a point of view which doubtless they hold sincerely. The effect of their testimony was to win Aday's acquittal, to launch the defendant on a triumphant publishing spree, to boost the sales of his books (which earlier had reached a level of forty thousand copies mailed per month), and to discourage those persons who believe that commercial smut and serious writing *can* be distinguished as a matter of law.

Aday's *Rambling Maids* and *Turbulent Daughters* are typical, not exceptional, in the field of paperback filth. There are a dozen outfits that offer little but unrestrained animal copulation; their titles can be found in racks in any newsstand, flaunting their provocative covers to the customer in search of a thirty-five-cent thrill. In the course of our investigation we waded through 150 such books. At first we marked the typographical errors, because it is a proofreader's habit to do so; and we underscored grammatical horrors, because no man who writes copy can do otherwise; and at first we proposed to earmark the worst and vilest passages with a star in the upper corner of the page. But in time, numbed by the smell of sewage, we abandoned these orderly devices. This is the world of paperback pornography; on beyond it, in a realm to be discussed later, lie such erotica as *Fanny Hill,* the memoirs of Frank Harris, and the purulent draining that poured from Henry Miller in *Tropic of Cancer* and *Tropic of Capricorn.* The paperbacks have nothing to do with Ovid, or with Mark Twain, or with Benjamin Franklin, or with any of the works beloved of scholars. This is dirt. This is the sort of pornography D. H. Lawrence denounced so long ago—dirt for dirt's sake, cheap dirt, illiterate dirt, dirt that smells of defecated intelligence, dirt with one excuse for being only: *it sells.*

It sells! That is the driving motivation that Billy Williams and the Rocco brothers found behind the stag movies, the salacious magazines, the glossy photographs of girls cupping their breasts and spreading their thighs. Neither art nor science nor feeling for the loveliness of language deters these prurieurs from their self-appointed rounds. They have sex for sale. And they sell it cheap.

2. OBSCENITY CASES PRIOR TO 1915

In one sense there is nothing especially new in all this.

"In the forty-one years I have been here, I have convicted persons enough to fill a passenger train of sixty-one coaches, sixty coaches containing sixty passengers each, and the sixty-first almost full. I have destroyed 160 tons of obscene literature."

That was Anthony Comstock speaking, late in his life. The honest Anthony, who could not have counted the felons in his train without acknowledging the last coach not perfectly filled, has been terribly maligned by the generations that have come after him. Like Thomas Bowdler, who preceded him by almost a century, Comstock gave his very name to his enemies. The sturdy, barrel-chested man with the forked beard died in September of 1915, but "Comstockery" and "the Comstocks" live after him. The evil that men do. . . .

This Caesar was born in New Canaan, Connecticut, in 1844, one of ten children whose mother died when Anthony was ten. Reared in the strict disciplines of a staunch Congregationalist household, he carried his moral precepts with him as a volunteer in the Union Army in 1863. He served an uneventful eighteen months in Florida, later to be remembered by Inspector Comstock chiefly for the depravity of his tent mates; he prayed incessantly for them. Released from service, he returned to Connecticut, worked for a time as a clerk in a New Haven store, then moved to New York. There he spent those forty-one years filling the seats in his imaginary train, totting up the ounces and pounds of seized obscenity, an avenging, square-jawed angel, commissioned by the Lord and by the Post Office too, Anthony Comstock, may it please the court, secretary of the New York Society for the Suppression of Vice.

It is easy to mock this moral guardian today. When he achieved the enactment of the obscenity law that, much amended, still governs the mails nearly a century afterward, Queen Victoria had been on the throne for thirty-six years and still had twenty-eight to reign. Many of the things that seemed obscene to Comstock in the 1880's surely would offend few persons in our more sophisticated time. This was the period, as a Canadian court remarked not long ago,[159,1] "when legs of tables were actually draped and rather stricter females never referred to gentlemen's legs as such, but called them their 'understandings.'" We do not fear the devil and his works today quite as the Great Reformer feared them then.

"I have one clear conviction," wrote Comstock, "that Satan lays the snare, and children are his victims. His traps, like all others, are baited to allure the human soul."

He saw "light literature" as no more than "a devil-trap to captivate the child by perverting taste and fancy." He hated pool halls, lotteries, gambling dens, half-a-dime magazines, and lewd newspapers:

> If a man goes about removing swill and slops he is called a scavenger. If a person goes about selling diseased meats, decaying fruits, or watered milk, he is at once handled severely by the press of the land. Let a man be discovered throwing a barrel of Paris green or arsenic into Croton reservoirs, and he would be almost lynched. What name shall be applied to the newspaper that gathers up the letters of the libertine, the secret doings of the rake, the minute descriptions of revolting crimes, the utterances of lips lost to all shame, the oozing of corruption from the debauched, and then weaving it into a highly sensational story, decks it with flying colors, and peddles it out each day for the sake of money!

He hated weekly papers—"these well-constructed traps of the devil" whose fiction corrupted the innocent child.

> These stories breed vulgarity, profanity, loose ideas of life, impurity of thought and deed. They render the imagination unclean, destroy domestic peace, desolate homes, cheapen women's virtue, and make foulmouthed bullies, cheats, vagabonds, thieves, des-

peradoes, and libertines. They disparage honest toil, and make real life a drudge and a burden.

He distrusted art and literature, which so often seemed to embrace the most obscene representations of the past: "No embellishment of art can rob lust of its power for evil upon the human nature." Incorruptible, unflagging, interminably zealous, he waged a war that by the contemporary standards of his day was a popular crusade; and when he wrote in *Traps for the Young* that his Comstock Act was the outgrowth of a "vehement demand on the part of good men that rigid laws be enacted, and strictly enforced," he was accurately describing a strong sentiment of his time. By these standards Comstock ought in fairness to be judged, and by these standards much can be forgiven him.

The act that lives after him, embodying his name to this day, may be found as Section 1461, Title 18, of the United States Code. Adopted in 1873, the Comstock Act swallowed up and replaced two earlier laws of limited application. For the first time it became a felony for any person knowingly to deposit in the mails any obscene, lewd, or lascivious book, pamphlet, picture, paper, writing, print, or other publication of an indecent character. The act wrapped into a single section the works of Boccaccio and the tools of the abortionist, the great classics and those articles intended for the prevention of conception; the act brought down on Comstock's head the wrath and ridicule of those he despised as "liberals and infidels." His law continues to this day to arouse the liberal, to perplex the constitutionalist, and to harass the merchant of filth. And the political realities are that in one form or another, for good or ill, the Comstock Act will remain on the books for a long time to come.

Enforcement of the act became the responsibility, at once, of the Postal Inspection Service. This is the oldest federal law-enforcement agency; the inspectors trace their lineage directly to Ben Franklin and the first colonial postal system. The service grew up through decades in which the inspectors were surveyors, auditors, detectives, and accountants. Never a large agency, the service operates today through fifteen coordinated field divisions headed by Chief Inspector

Stephens in Washington. This is traditionally a silent service, composed of dedicated men possessed of a fierce loyalty to the public interest as that interest is defined by Congress. And if the inspectors have erred here and there, in an excess of zeal, they have done an amazingly good job—as their records of conviction make clear—of enforcing the obscenity law in keeping with contemporary community standards.

The inspectors encountered smooth going at first. They were fortunate in obtaining, in their first test case in 1873, a district court ruling upholding the constitutionality of the law. In affirming the conviction of two New Yorkers, John Bott and John Whitehead, on charges of sending through the mails a powder intended to produce abortion, a federal judge in New York held firmly that Congress had power to define contraband materials in the mail.[204] The inspectors also won, early in the game, a judicial ruling defending their use of fictitious names and decoy letters.[15] And in 1878 a unanimous Supreme Court of the United States, speaking through Associate Justice Stephen Field, approved the basic principles of the act of 1873.[88]

In this case one Orlando Jackson had been convicted in New York for mailing a lottery ticket. From his quarters in the county jail he sought a writ of *habeas corpus;* his contention was that the act was an unconstitutional violation of the First Amendment. His attorneys made a persuasive argument, that the people never had conferred upon the federal government any affirmative power to regulate public morals; in the absence of such a delegation of power, it was contended, the authority to handle mail could not be stretched into a power to say what sort of mail might be handled.

The Supreme Court would not accept this line of reasoning. The great John C. Calhoun had advanced the same arguments more than forty years earlier, in pleading that Congress could not abridge the liberty of the press by restricting the movement of circulars by mail. In the court's view the object of Congress was not to interfere with the freedom of the press, or with any other rights of the people, but only "to refuse its facilities for the distribution of matter deemed injurious to the public morals."

All that Congress meant by this Act was, that the mail should not be used to transport such corrupting publications and articles, and that anyone who attempted to use it for that purpose should be punished. . . . The only question for our determination relates to the constitutionality of the Act; *and of that we have no doubt.* [Emphasis supplied.]

It is of passing interest that the Supreme Court, in the *Jackson* case, laid down a cardinal rule that postal inspectors have respected as an article of religion ever since: *first-class mail is private.* Said the court:

Letters and sealed packages of this kind in the mail are as fully guarded from examination and inspection, except as to their outward form and weight, as if they were retained by the parties forwarding them in their own domiciles. The constitutional guaranty of the right of the people to be secure in their papers against unreasonable searches and seizures extends to their papers, thus closed against inspection, wherever they may be. No law of Congress can place in the hands of officials connected with the postal service any authority to invade the secrecy of letters and such sealed packages in the mail; and all regulations adopted as to mail matter of this kind must be in subordination to the great principle embodied in the Fourth Amendment of the Constitution.

The Supreme Court again upheld the constitutionality of the Comstock Act in another unanimous opinion fourteen years later. Speaking through Chief Justice Melville Fuller in 1892, the court thought there was "no question" that the Congress had power to ban from the mails any instrument used in the promotion of acts universally deemed wrong, "including all such crimes as murder, arson, burglary, etc., *and the offense of circulating obscene books and papers.*"[155] Again in 1913, in sustaining the validity of the White Slave Act the Supreme Court remarked in passing that "surely the facility of interstate commerce can be taken away from . . . *the debasement of obscene literature.*"[86] (Emphasis supplied.)

But though the constitutionality of the law was many times upheld in principle in this period, postal inspectors absorbed some lumps in prosecuting particular cases. Many of these early cases involved obscene letters. The first notable prosecution in this field came in New York in 1880. A United States commissioner, J. J. Allen, began his memorandum opinion:

> The defendant was arrested upon the complaint of Anthony Comstock, agent for the Society for the Suppression of Vice, upon the charge of sending an obscene letter through the mails.

In the eyes of the commissioner the letter was "evidently obscene and indecent," but there was one trouble: the Comstock Act reached only to obscene books, pamphlets, pictures, papers, writings, prints, and indecent publications. It did not, specifically, cover obscene letters. As a consequence the defendant went free, and immediately a lively controversy developed in federal district courts around the nation.

In Illinois[220] and Ohio[223] courts held that letters were writings and hence embraced within the law. An Oregon court decided first one way[240] and then another.[246] Courts in Mississippi[261] and Indiana[191] convicted; courts in South Carolina[243] and Texas[213] acquitted. At last a circuit court in Ohio, vexed by these conflicting rulings, demanded an unequivocal statement from the Supreme Court of the United States.[229] Were obscene letters unmailable? After brooding on the matter for quite some time the high court said, no, the act of 1873 did not reach to letters.[207,208]

Congress did not wait upon the court's deliberate speed. In 1888 the act was amended to include obscene letters specifically, and at first this seemed to settle the matter.[272,269] But a couple of obstinate federal judges, one in California[207] and another in Washington,[264] found themselves still unable to define what on earth Congress could have meant by a letter, and the issue was not really settled until 1894, when Oliver P. Shiras, then a district judge in Iowa, cut to the heart of the matter; the intent of Congress, he said, was neither more nor less than this—to deny the use of the mails to obscene matter.[264] A Connecticut judge concurred[239] and with a thumping pronouncement by the Supreme Court in 1896 the law as to obscene letters settled down.[9] Obscene letters are plainly forbidden today.

Postal inspectors early discovered, however, that obscenity is not to be confused with scurrility, blasphemy, or mere vulgarity. To be nonmailably obscene a thing must "tend to suggest libidinous thoughts or excite impure desires."[265] Insulting words in themselves were not enough. A Kentucky court made the same point in 1882, when an outraged merchant was charged with mailing obscene matter for dispatching this straightforward message to a customer: "Dear Sir, you are a damned scoundrel and a rascal. Respectfully, F. A. Smith." A federal judge dismissed the charge against Mr. Smith; whatever his postcard was, it was not obscene.[260]

Other courts concurred in this view. In Minnesota it was concluded that it could not be obscene to call a man a "deadbeat."[55] A South Carolina judge, in a remarkably soothing opinion, found it not unlawful to call a man no more than "a lying son of a bitch."[218] A district court in Indiana saw nothing obscene in a valentine inscribed with this tender sentiment: "You can keep this to wipe your dirty arse on."[241] A district court in Kentucky sharply distinguished between obscenity and blasphemy, in dismissing an indictment against one Moore for mailing a pamphlet, "The Virgin Mary." The article, couched in coarse and vulgar language, questioned the chastity of Mary and ridiculed the concept of the divine birth. The court found Moore's pamphlet highly distasteful and would have liked to have held it obscene, but the pamphlet was not openly lewd and lascivious and thus was entitled to circulate in the mails.[244]

Many other prosecutions for the mailing of obscene letters also died along the way,[249] as federal courts, awakening to the twentieth century with the death of Victoria and the onslaught of an occasional new idea, wet a tentative finger toward a fresh wind of intellectual freedom. In New York in 1907 the Court of Appeals wrote an opinion still widely quoted, in acquitting an anti-Catholic pamphleteer, Norman L. A. Eastman, of a charge of publishing an indecent leaflet. His publication, known as "The Gospel Worker," assailed the Roman confessional as "the open door to hell." Three members of the court, dissenting, commented that "if this paper is not of an indecent character and within the prohibition of the statute, then it is impossible to conceive of any printed matter that would be." The four-man majority, however, concluded that the pamphlet was no more than "an example of the extent to which sectarian religious animosities may lead a weak and disordered mind, for it is mere charity to consider such to be the character of the writer of the production." Blasphemous letters thus were held not to be, in themselves, obscene letters.

Letters that merely hint at an illicit sexual relationship may or may not be obscene. If such letters are merely vulgar, as a Kentucky court held as far back as 1909, they may be beyond the law's reach.[91] If an invitation to sexual misconduct is not clearly stated no basis for prosecution exists.[95] But it is plainly unlawful to proposition a woman by mail,[242,245] as a number of literate if inarticulate lovers have discovered. The point was made clear in South Carolina in 1917, when one B. P. Parish was charged with sending a letter to a young schoolteacher in which he said he had spied her and a young man "in a very funny position down at my mill last Sunday." Said the peeping miller:

You know what the school trustees will do about this if I tell them. Now I have a proposition to make you before I expose the whole thing and if I can see you and have a private talk with you I think I can keep the whole thing quiet. . . . You can come down to the mill or I will go most any place that will suit you. . . . Don't be afraid to write as no one not even my wife will know the least thing about it; will call for my mail tomorrow noon.

Bless her heart, this little lady went straight to the postal inspectors, and they forthwith clapped the bounder in jail. J. Waties Waring, who later was to become a most controversial district judge, was then assistant United States attorney at Charleston. He prosecuted vigorously, and Parish's conviction was ringingly affirmed on appeal.

On the Supreme Court of the United States, Associate Justice Willis Van Devanter consistently turned a gelid eye on persons charged with mailing obscene matter. In upholding the conviction of one Rinker he remarked in 1904 that the fine was plainly not excessive.[160] The defendant's objection on this point

loses sight of the corrupting nature of the offense and of the necessity for effectually checking the temptation to use the mails for improper purposes. The dissemination of that which makes against decency, purity, and chastity in private life is infinitely more dangerous to society than are many offenses, the authorized and commonly approved punishment for which is more severe. And no other agency is so well adapted to the inexpensive, extensive and effective dissemination of such indecent matter as are the mails.

At about the time of the *Rinker* case the federal statute was amended to embrace letters that were not only "obscene" but also "filthy," and federal judges swiftly found meaning in the new adjective.[214] Associate Justice Louis Brandeis in 1932 held that this ban upon filthy letters was a jury question,[238] though it may be doubted that a majority of today's Supreme Court would concur in this view. Unless "filthy" may be construed as generally synonymous with the sexually obscene, the term probably is too vague to meet today's hard requirements for a criminal statute in the obscenity field.[270]

In Mr. Comstock's day these niceties were not so important. In 1889 postal inspectors obtained a conviction on the mailing of a postcard in which a Tennessean referred to a former friend as no more than a "radical."[215] In the same court one Olney was found guilty of violating postal laws for inscribing a mild complaint by postcard to the editor of his local paper: "You can take your paper and Democracy and go to hell with it."[250] By 1958, however, the rule on postcards had come to parallel the rule on other mailings: a suggestion of sexual obscenity must be present. This was the ruling of a Kentucky court in convicting a Pennsylvanian who had mailed nineteen lewd postcards to a woman, recalling publicly the days in which they had been "shacked up." This crude phrase, said the court, went "substantially beyond the customary limits of candor."

Most of the postal inspectors' cases, in the early days of the Comstock Act, were devoted to larger matters than obscene letters and lewd postcards. Then as now the yardstick for measuring nonmailable matter was a rubbery sort of guide, and the line between actionable obscenity and innocent scurrility never stayed fixed for long. One of the more famous cases of this early period arose in Kansas, when a truculent editor at first was convicted under the Comstock Act for mailing copies of the Burlington *Courier* containing this lovely example of the lost art of vituperation:

About the meanest and most universally hated and detested thing in human shape that ever cursed this community is the red-headed mental and physical bastard that flings filth under another man's name down on Neosho Street. He has slandered and maligned every Populist in the State, from the Governor down to the humblest voter. This blackhearted coward is known to every decent man, woman and child in the community as a liar, perjurer and slanderer, who would sell a mother's honor with less hesitancy and for much less silver than Judas betrayed the Saviour. . . .

He is a contemptible scoundrel and political blackleg of the lowest cut. He is pretending to serve Democracy and is at the same time in the pay of the Republican party. He has been known as the companion of Negro strumpets and has reveled in the lowest debauches. . . . His soul, if he has a soul, is blacker than the blackest shades of hell. He is the embodiment of treachery, cowardice, and dishonor, and hasn't the physical nor moral courage to deny it. He stands today hated, despised, and detested as all that is low, mean, debased, and despicable. We propose to have done with the knave. . . .

The Supreme Court of the United States, in a 5-4 decision, concluded that this admirable dissertation was "exceedingly coarse and vulgar," but found that it contained nothing to corrupt and debauch the public morals. Dan Swearingen, the Kansas editor, went free.[189] Other publications were not so fortunate. The *National Police Gazette* fell under state proscription in Philadelphia in 1889, when a jury—instructed to go only by "the articles marked in red ink in the paper"—convicted a newsstand dealer of selling obscene matter.[46] The United States Supreme Court, by a 7-2 vote in 1896, upheld the conviction of Lew Rosen, publisher of an illustrated paper called *Broadway*. Responding to a decoy letter, Rosen had mailed a copy of the "Tenderloin Number" of his paper to a postal inspector in New Jersey. On several pages appeared drawings of a nude female identified, in a regrettable perversion of the mother tongue, as a "tenderloineuse." The drawings, depicting "different attitudes of indecency," had been covered with lamp black "that could be easily erased with a piece of bread." The trial court had sentenced Rosen to thirteen months at hard labor, on instructions asking the jury to determine only whether the Tenderloin Number "would suggest or convey lewd and lascivious thoughts to the young and inexperienced." Associate Justice John M. Harlan remarked approvingly that "in view of the character of the paper, the test prescribed was quite as liberal as the defendant had any right to demand."[164]

Broadway was the sort of picture paper that Anthony Comstock hated. Such magazines were devil-traps, foul and loathsome, produced to lead children into the hands of Satan, and he fought them relentlessly all his life. Nor was he to be deceived by a pose of physical culture. In 1908 even Bernarr MacFadden, the onetime ninety-pound weakling, fell under post office guns: his magazine, in the eyes of a federal judge, was "suggestively lewd and bad, [and] none the less so because of the alleged reforming and corrective purpose in overlaying it."[105]

Mr. Comstock was less successful in his assaults against classical literature. Grudgingly the Great Reformer might concede that "the wit and genius of past writers is of value to the student," but in his heart he was convinced that a Boccaccio ought to be preserved, if at all, only in Italian, and then only on a few locked shelves. In English Boccaccio was a menace:

> Many of these stories are little better than histories of brothels and prostitutes. . . . How often are found, in these villainous stories, heroines, lovely, excellent, cultivated, wealthy, and charming in every way, who have for their lovers married men; or, after marriage, lovers flock about the charming young wife, enjoying the privileges belonging only to the husband! How often does the young wife in these accursed stories have a lover more wealthy and accomplished than the one to whom she has plighted her love! Clandestine meetings are described, and plots and conspiracies to put the husband out of the way are not infrequent.

In the light of these views it was to be expected that in 1894 when it appeared that the Worthington Company in New York was going out of business and might make available for public auction a torrent of classical filth, Mr. Comstock descended in holy wrath. He wanted the sale stopped. But the Supreme Court of the State of New York struck a blow for common sense, and got in a good backhanded slap at Mr. Comstock, in dismissing his suit. Among the firm's assets, it was noted, were a dozen titles that the vice hunter regarded as immoral literature. These included Payne's edition of the *Arabian Nights,* Fielding's *Tom Jones,* the works of Rabelais, Ovid's *Art of Love,* the *Decameron* of the despised Boccaccio, in English, God forbid; the *Heptameron* of Queen Margaret of Navarre, the confessions of Rousseau, *Tales from the Arabic,* and *Aladdin.*

The receiver for the Worthington Company wanted to sell the books —they were all "choice editions," richly bound, and were in every way "specimens of fine bookmaking." Mr. Comstock objected. Judge Morgan J. O'Brien's pointed opinion merits quotation at some length:

It is very difficult to see upon what theory these world-renowned classics can be regarded as specimens of that pornographic literature which it is the office of the Society for the Suppression of Vice to suppress, or how they can come under any stronger condemnation than that high-standard literature which consists of the works of Shakespeare, of Chaucer, of Laurence Sterne, and of other great English writers, without making reference to many parts of Old Testament Scriptures, which are to be found in almost every household in the land. The very artistic character, the high qualities of style, the absence of those glaring and crude pictures, scenes, and descriptions which affect the common and vulgar mind, make a place for books of the character in question, entirely apart from such gross and obscene writings as it is the duty of the public authorities to suppress.

It would be quite as unjustifiable to condemn the writings of Shakespeare and Chaucer and Laurence Sterne, the early English novelists, the playwrights of the Restoration, and the dramatic literature which has so much enriched the English language, as to place an interdict upon these volumes, which have received the admiration of literary men for so many years.

What has become standard literature of the English language— has been wrought into the very structure of our splendid English literature—is not to be pronounced at this late day unfit for publication or circulation, and stamped with judicial disapproval, as hurtful to the community. The works under consideration are the product of the greatest literary genius. Payne's *Arabian Nights* is a wonderful exhibition of Oriental scholarship, and the other volumes have so long held a supreme rank in literature that it would be absurd to call them now foul and unclean. A seeker after the sensual and degrading parts of a narrative may find in all these works, as in those of other great authors, something to satisfy his pruriency. But to condemn a standard literary work, because of a few of its episodes, would compel the exclusion from circulation of a very large proportion of the works of fiction of the most famous writers of the English language.

There is no such evil to be feared from the sale of these rare and costly books as the imagination of many even well-disposed people might apprehend. They rank with the higher literature, and would not be bought nor appreciated by the class of people from whom unclean publications ought to be withheld. They are not corrupting in their influence upon the young, for they are not likely to reach them. I am satisfied that it would be a wanton destruction of property to prohibit the sale by the receiver of these works, for if their sale ought to be prohibited the books should be burned— but I find no reason in law, morals, or expedience why they should not be sold for the benefit of the creditors of the receivership. The receiver is therefore allowed to sell these volumes.

This degenerate and lascivious judgment left Mr. Comstock indignant—he often was left indignant by the depravity of judges—but he stayed too busy to remain indignant for long. Though he received no federal pay as a postal inspector until late in life, the traffic in mail-order pornography constantly absorbed him; and when he was not roaring off on a magnificent raid against some gambling hell or lottery den he was contriving fictitious letters against purveyors of filth. The techniques that he relied upon are essentially the techniques relied upon by postal inspectors today; the techniques of his adversaries are essentially unchanged also. Merchants of filth, said Mr. Comstock, work *systematically*. He and R. W. McAfee of St. Louis, agent of the Western Society for the Suppression of Vice, warred upon the smut peddlers through an astounding variety of fictitious names,[75] and the pornographers switched their own names as rapidly. The notorious Charles Conroy, who inflicted on Comstock a knife wound the reformer bore to his grave, operated at various times under the names of Dexter, Taylor, Colby, Hart, Carleston, Durphy, Labin, Scribner, Depau, Scott, Marsh, Kirke, Appleton, Manning, Evans, Burt, and Cook. And interestingly, the smut peddlers even in Comstock's time hit upon the device of school directories as a source of names for their mailing lists. "No institution of learning ought to furnish these scoundrels a directory," Comstock pleaded. "None should be printed while this danger exists."

Photographic processes of course were less efficient in Comstock's day, but even so a number of prosecutions involved the sale of single photographs.[76] Among Comstock's cases in 1884 was a prosecution against August Muller for selling some French photographs of nude women, said to be copies of paintings hung in the Salon de Paris. One of the paintings recently had been exhibited publicly at the Centennial Exhibition in Philadelphia. The key legal point involved Muller's effort to prove through expert witnesses that the pictures were not intended to be obscene but were intended to be works of art.[137]

"It does not require an expert in art or literature," said the New York appellate court, "to determine whether a picture is obscene or whether printed words are offensive to decency and good morals. These are matters which fall within the range of ordinary intelligence, and a jury does not require to be informed by an expert before pronouncing on them. . . . The issue was not whether in the opinion of witnesses, or of a class of people the photographs were obscene or indecent, but whether they were so in fact, and upon this issue witnesses could neither be permitted to give their own opinions, or to state the aggregate opinion of a particular class or part of a community. . . . The question whether a picture or writing is obscene is one of the plainest that can be presented to a jury, and under the guidance of a discreet judge there is little danger of their reaching a wrong decision."

Anticipating what many judges were to say later, the New York court declared it evident that "mere nudity in painting or sculpture is not obscenity." Only a false delicacy and mere prudery would condemn all nudes as obscene. Neither would the court approve any test by which the mere capability of suggesting impure thoughts might cause a book or a picture to be banned; to the excessively prurient mind almost anything might be capable of suggesting impure thoughts. The motive of the artist might be argued as a proper test of obscenity, and so might the circumstances of publication or sale be considered; but in the end all that mattered was the jury's verdict: was the picture obscene *in the jury's opinion?*

This same pragmatic point of view, which holds that the juror is always right, prevailed in the West in 1906, when postal inspectors filed a memorable case against a Utah lawyer, Richard B. Shepard. Little by little Shepard had become the moving spirit behind a book company specializing in works of erotica. He read these books, bought them, and traded in them, and when he received a courteously formal inquiry from one G. G. Latimer in Denver, inquiring for a number of erotic books, Shepard willingly mailed his catalog. In the course of time Latimer, who happened to be chief clerk of the Denver Division of Post Office Inspectors, found himself investing in *The Amorous Adventures of a Japanese Gentleman,* and corresponding avidly for a copy of *Fanny Hill.* When at last the inspectors cracked down Shepard futilely pleaded entrapment, but the Eighth Circuit Court brushed the defense aside; this technique had been approved so often by the courts "as to place the practice beyond the field of discussion."[222] The classical nature of Shepard's erotica notwithstanding, a jury sentenced the defendant to prison for thirteen months at hard labor.

It is a long jump from the investigations of Comstock, McAfee, Latimer, and others, a half century ago, to the genuinely systematic pornographers of our own time, but the leap will disclose few essential changes. Today's smut peddlers are technically better equipped: film is cheap, and photographic paper is cheap; Victoria is dead, and Hollywood is crowded with full-breasted starlets; the ingenious mind of the pornographer has contrived salacious novelties that did not exist during the long life of Anthony Comstock. But the essential commodity of the merchants of filth has not changed at all. They still are selling sex—cheap, degraded, and often unbelievably perverted sex—and they reap fantastic profits.

3. THE WAR ON OBSCENITY TODAY

TESTIMONY OF MARY DOROTHY TAGER, BALBOA, CAL.
(Before a subcommittee of the United States Senate; questions by committee's counsel and by Senator Kefauver)

MR. BOBO: Mrs. Tager, would you state your full name and your address and where you are presently living for the record?

MRS. TAGER: Mary Dorothy Tager, 2100 Ocean Boulevard, Balboa, California.

MR. BOBO: Mrs. Tager, have you ever been engaged in a mail-order business of sending photos and other things through the mail?

MRS. TAGER: Yes, sir, I have.

MR. BOBO: At what time did you begin in this business?

MRS. TAGER: Well, I would say sometime later in 1948, and I was active in the business up, oh, until sometime in 1951.

MR. BOBO: And under what trade name did you operate this business?

MRS. TAGER: Well, actually under several. We operated under Stand-Out Products, Novel Arts, T & R Sales. They are the main names we operated under. We also operated under, oh, many hundreds, I guess, of fictitious names.

MR. BOBO: In this business what was the merchandise which you sold, Mrs. Tager?

MRS. TAGER: I sold nudes, straight nudes, nothing pornographic, consisting of slides, black and white films, 8- and 16-mm., 50-, 100-, 400-foot reels.

MR. BOBO: In these nudes which you sold, many of them were in various suggestive poses. Would you mean by the fact that they were not pornographic that they might not be considered under the present laws pornographic?

MRS. TAGER: Well, no. Personally I don't consider a picture of a nude woman as pornographic. I think it definitely depends on the way the woman is posed. . . .

MR. BOBO: Did you sell these particular nudes and novelty cards through the United States mail?

MRS. TAGER: Yes, sir.

MR. BOBO: How would you secure the names of customers to whom you were sending this?

MRS. TAGER: Well, there are many sources. Of course magazine advertising is one of the main sources of your names. There are many ads appearing even today in magazines or comic books, which are more or less a come-on actually for nude-picture buyers. So over a period of time from the replies you get from these various magazines you accumulate a very large mailing list.

MR. BOBO: Do you buy these mailing lists from other persons, from the publishers of so-called legitimate magazines?

MRS. TAGER: Yes, that can be done. That can be done.

MR. BOBO: Do you know the names of any of the magazines in which your advertisements have appeared?

MRS. TAGER: Yes, there are many. I mean, in all of the girlie magazines they have appeared in.

MR. BOBO: You speak of girlie magazines. You are speaking of what type of magazines?

MRS. TAGER: Well, you have got *Pic* and *See* and *Hit* and *Miss* and *Male* and *Man* and all that.

MR. BOBO: That type of publication?

MRS. TAGER: All that type of magazine.

MR. BOBO: If I sent in an order to you from one of these magazines and enclosed my ten dollars—

MRS. TAGER: Yes.

MR. BOBO: Would I get a letter of inquiry back as to my age or would I get the strip photos or whatever other merchandise you had to sell?

MRS. TAGER: Well, no. When you place an ad in a magazine— of course I am going by my own experience; what some of the others do might be entirely different. When an ad is placed in a magazine and you, perhaps, answer the ad, you send me a dollar. Well, naturally, for that dollar you are not going to get nudes. You get four pin-up pictures. Your name is kept on file, and in order for me to keep or try to keep children out of my files, I would send them a letter of inquiry as to their age, and I would get that letter of inquiry back from them before I would attempt to send them any of these advertising pieces for nudes.

MR. BOBO: The original was just a come-on?

MRS. TAGER: That is right.

CHAIRMAN KEFAUVER: Well, when you would finally send the real thing, the nudes, did you send those through the mail?

MRS. TAGER: Yes, sir.

CHAIRMAN KEFAUVER: You said that you tried to keep the age of children or secure it for a while. Did you give up that effort?

MRS. TAGER: I did because I would, oh, several would come back to me in a handwriting that you could more or less tell that it wasn't a grownup's handwriting, and on the coupon the age might be marked as twenty-six or thirty; so I finally felt that—I mean, it was kind of a useless cause, so I dropped it.

MR. BOBO: Did you receive mail from quite a number of people of the young age?

MRS. TAGER: There were quite a few. There were quite a few. . . .

That testimony was taken before the Senate Subcommittee to Investigate Juvenile Delinquency on June 18, 1955. The witness, Mary Dorothy Tager, had broken with the smut racket following her divorce from her husband, Louis Tager. Earlier the Tagers, in association with Roy J. Ross, had operated one of the largest factories on the West Coast. Mrs. Tager told the committee that their individual mailings varied from twenty thousand pieces to "a couple of hundred thousand—even more." Their gross revenues, she said, at the peak of their operation, averaged three thousand dollars a day; it was a million-dollar-a-year business, a thoroughly professional and efficient undertaking. In the course of a couple of years, Mrs. Tager confessed, they used possibly two hundred different addresses. Their custom was to rent a post-office box, mail their circulars, and wait two weeks for returns to come in. Then the orders would be filled from a central office on Ventura Boulevard, and that particular name and box number would then be abandoned. At the height of their operation, they had a payroll of more than fifty typists and mailers. The color slides of nudes that cost them 16½ cents were sold for three dollars. Fifty feet of black-and-white film, obtained for sixty-five cents, sold for four dollars. And the volume of their business reached such a level that the post office at Encino, used for their principal mailings, was raised from a fourth-class post office to a second-class post office.

The material sent out in the Ross-Tager operation was not hard-core obscenity; it was the sort of borderline pornography that causes such great difficulty in enforcing state and federal laws. A tolerant judge in a Los Angeles district court impatiently dismissed obscenity charges against Ross and Tager in March of 1954, and an eighty-count indictment against them in Kansas, where their mailings had reached a number of juveniles, fell in 1952 on a jurisdictional objection. The Kansas decision, incidentally, led to the change in postal laws in 1958, by which prosecution for the mailing of obscene materials may now be maintained not only at the point of mailing but also at the point of receipt.

In a quiet office at the Post Office Department in Washington the record of Ross and the Tagers now lies interred among case histories on thousands of investigations. These are the headquarters of Mail Fraud Investigations within the Chief Inspector's Bureau, headed by a soft-spoken veteran of many years in the postal service, W. J. Callahan. Directly in charge of obscenity work is slim, wiry Edward L. Bier. He has the walk and build of a welterweight boxer, and his filing cabinet mind is an inexhaustible storehouse of facts on the obscenity racket. Bier's chief lieutenant is another veteran of the postal wars, an amiable and artful detective whose real name is Harry J. Simon. Under two hundred other names he is one of the obscenity racket's most tireless customers. His decoy letters, mailed for him by postmasters from coast to coast, have placed him on mailing lists beyond number, and the day seldom passes that he does not receive some circular under one fictitious name or another.

The merchants of filth are well aware of this tactic, of course, and frequently go to great lengths, involving weeks or months of a feeling-out correspondence, to make certain that an apparently *bona fide* customer is not in fact a postal inspector under a bogus name. Few of them, however, have approached the protective scheme worked out by Albert J. Amateau, the wiliest fish that ever swam in Harry Simon's sea.

Inspector Simon first encountered Amateau in June of 1956, when a circular fell into his hands from ARA Productions, Inc., of Los Angeles, soliciting remittances of ten dollars each from a "selected clientele" as an annual membership fee in a Certified Buyers' Registry. Customers accepted for this exclusive registry, among whom were said to be 350 persons scattered over the country, received advance descriptions of "items of unusual personal interest." No sales were made to anyone not on the registry.

Having an abiding concern for "items of unusual personal interest," Simon judiciously selected a likely test name, and in the guise of Wesley B. Saroka of Ellensburg, Washington, wrote to ARA Productions and requested full details. Within a few days the Ellensburg postmaster forwarded to Simon in Washington a fresh circular that had arrived for Mr. Saroka, accompanied by a neatly printed application blank. This form called not only for the name, address, and occupation of the applicant but also for the names, addresses, and occupations of two references.

Simon was intrigued. Through the postmaster back in Ellensburg he arranged for two responsible businessmen, a Ford dealer and an insurance man, to attest the existence, good character, reliability, and discretion of the mythical Wesley B. Saroka, whom he turned into an oversexed public accountant, and off to California went Wesley's ten-dollar membership fee.

"Shortly thereafter," Inspector Simon recalls, "a reply was received to the effect that ARA Productions could find no record of ever having sent an invitation to a Mr. Saroka in Ellensburg, Washington, to become a member of the Certified Buyers' Registry. A reply was requested on Mr. Saroka's letterhead."

The obliging Simon arranged for a job shop to run off some elegant letterheads, and on this stationery an apologetic note went off to ARA Productions. Mr. Saroka had received the original invitation many months before but never had gotten around to filling it in. And because Simon thought his character references might also be checked out, he alerted them for an inquiry from California. Sure enough, the two Ellensburg businessmen were queried. Simon provided letters to be returned to California, attesting the prudence and good credit of a character he was beginning to grow rather fond of.

This did it. Wesley B. Saroka finally won a place on the Certified Buyers' Registry and began receiving circulars and "evaluations" describing these items of unusual personal interest in which he might invest. The circulars, however, were in crude code, and had to be deciphered from a code book provided with the acceptance of his application. One motion picture, offered at $115, was described in this fashion:

#33 Nugg uvoleotain "Bobuz Sattur"
Uzieng, buotafel, brenuttu bobuz sattang fir babuz if ggadiggur; gghum fozzur luovoes, fumolu endrussus ti bozzu. Fozzur till, uzieng, hendsim, hoaruz ond mescelor; hu ruterns himu, serprasus zzu ggimon nokud an zzu bozzu. Hu andecus hur ta uzauld. Ggimon hos buoetafelluz farmud bizus, smoll farm bruosts and napplus. . . .

This was translated, rather obviously, as:

#33 New Evaluation "Baby Sitter"
Young, beautiful, brunette baby sitter for baby of widower; when father leaves, female undresses to bathe. Father tall, young, handsome, hairy and muscular; he returns home, surprises the woman naked in the bath. He induces her to yield. Woman has beautifully formed body, small firm breasts and nipples. . . .

The description continued with a detailed account of the couple's "thrilling action and very exciting contortions," complete with many close-ups and unusual angle shots. Simon did not have time to respond to this evaluation before a cryptic note came in from ARA Productions: "For obvious reasons we must discontinue previous code. Future evaluations will come in this [new] code. Please! Keep it safe and strictly confidential. New offers in this code will not be sent until acknowledgment is received in sealed envelope. Just write 'Received' and sign."

The new code was as crude as the old. Mr. Saroka was invited to buy a movie.

#34. 18 st6r4 b8h7nd 18 st6r4.—J6 7* ch9rL84 9r8 b5s dr7v8r b5dd78s. J6 d9t8s B81-/4, 18 b895t7f5L br5n81-/ 2% 18 d7sp9tch8r's 68-/7c8, 2h7L8 ch9rL84 m9k8s 9 d9t8 8% G8n78, 18 fL9m7ng r8d h89d 2% p94rdd-/. J6 7* ch9rL84 kn62 9 h89v8nL4 pL9c8 2% 18 23-/ds. J6 t9k8s B81-/4 18r8 6n s5nd94 6% 9 P7c-N7c. . . .

And this was translated as:

#34. The story behind the story.—Joe and Charley are bus driver buddies. Joe dates Betty, the beautiful brunette in the dispatcher's office, while Charley makes a date with Genie, the flaming red head in payroll. Joe and Charley know a heavenly place in the woods. Joe takes Betty there on Sunday for a picnic. . . .

The circular went on to describe, in appalling detail, how the two couples wind up having intercourse side by side, and the two girls engage in perverted acts between themselves. Simon obtained a cashier's check for $115 and sent it off. Within ten days the film was in his hands, shipped by express from Los Angeles. It fully lived up to the evaluation.

Now extensive investigation began at the California end of the line. The post-office box of ARA Productions led postal inspectors to Albert J. Amateau, born in Turkey about 1889, an immigrant to the United States in 1910. He had been in trouble before on questionable mail-order operations, but there had been nothing to compare with the Certified Buyers' Registry scheme.

All told, more than fifteen months were spent in gathering the evidence and in reconnoitering a building at Alameda, New Mexico, where Amateau stored and printed his master negatives. These included some sixty films, all of them pitched to an unspeakable level of sexual depravity.

From their investigations postal inspectors discovered that Amateau and his wife intended to leave New York City for Europe on October 15, 1958. Two weeks before their scheduled sailing date Simon was able to fit together the last pieces of his case. On October 1 inspectors made their arrest. Amateau at first professed outraged innocence, but following his indictment in April of 1959 under Sections 1461 and

1462 he entered a plea of guilty. District Judge Harry C. Westover remarked from the bench that he often had heard, as a judge, that filthy movies were in existence, but these, he said, were beyond anything he ever had imagined. He sentenced Amateau to three years in prison, but in view of the filth merchant's advanced age the court suspended execution of all but six months of the sentence.

The racket in mail-order smut operates with a crab-grass spread; one tentacle leads to another, and this to still another, and the business is conducted under such a bewildering variety of two-week phony names that inspectors often meet themselves coming and going. One typical investigation in 1959 began with the indictment in Detroit of Burton Steiger and James S. Frew; their part of a web led to one Daniel Loewinger, who had done work for Louis Tager. The thing was all knotted up.

The names of these particular dealers mean little; they might as well be Smith, Jones, and Brown—and considering the ease with which they shifted from one front name to another, they might indeed be Smith, Jones, and Brown! But Steiger is worth a passing sentence, if only to make the point that the dealers in stag items are not crude illiterates, speaking in dese-and-dose accents. Steiger, one of the larger and better-known West Coast dealers in mail-order materials, born in 1927, was graduated from the University of Florida in 1951 with a degree in aeronautical engineering. He entered the Navy in 1954, attended Officers Training School, became a lieutenant junior grade; following his release from service in 1957 he worked briefly for North American Aviation. Then he took up the mail-order racket, operating out of a Los Angeles suburb under the name of Adrian.

Dear Friend:

I am writing to you as a person interested in collecting all types of art photography of nudes. I myself am a collector and photographer and have been collecting photos, movies, and slides over the past few years. Now I need money and am trying to sell my entire private collection. . . .

Everything is absolutely unretouched, the same type you may have purchased from England, Germany, or Denmark. Some of the shots

are of complete nudes; some are of nudes in high heels and hose or
other feminine bits of attire. . . .

The movies have good clear action, with plenty of close-ups. They
haven't been worn or scratched like lots of films you have seen at
parties. I guarantee them to be clear and sharp and not "oldies."
There's one, two, or three performers on some reels. These I have
decided to send by railway express.

The address is on the enclosed self-addressed envelope. If I don't
hear from you in about ten days, I'll assume you aren't interested,
and send this to some more on down the list. I'm hoping the first
mailing will take care of my entire collection, since obviously the
less people I contact the better.

Sincerely yours,
ADRIAN

One of Steiger's mailings fell into the hands of a Catholic priest
in Jefferson City, Missouri. Other mailings fell into the hands of
outraged parents across the country. And because several of the
circulars from Steiger and Frew happened to wind up at about
the same time in Detroit, the Post Office Department sought and
obtained an indictment against both of them there in June, 1959.
Also indicted was Harold Steiner, who had taken over a Filmfare
Company from one Abe S. Toberoff. Steiger pleaded *nolo contendere*
and on August 17, 1959, was fined $10,000 and placed on probation
for five years. Frew, who operated as Camfield House and Saturn
Company, among other fronts, contested the indictment. The case
against him and Steiner dragged on through 1959 and early 1960
and had not been tried as this manuscript was completed. Interestingly, Louis Rocco, in Richmond, received a lengthy circular from
Camfield House on November 23, 1959, and Billy Williams received
a highly provocative circular from the Saturn Company on January
18, 1960, *while the indictments were pending*. The smut peddlers are
a brazen crew.

Within a few weeks after the indictments were returned in Detroit
against Steiger, Frew, and, later, Steiner, a man in Houston complained to postal inspectors of a mimeographed letter, signed C.
Damron, he had received on July 3 from Crenshaw Station in Los

Angeles. The letter enclosed a photograph of a nude woman exposing her pubic region to full front view. Films, color slides, and movies were offered, but for cash only: "Postal inspectors use checks and money orders as trial evidence and since this is a new list I am mailing I cannot take the chance." Investigation disclosed no record of a C. Damron.

On July 23 complaints reached the Post Office Department in Washington of similar mailings from a Dale Collins at a post-office box in North Hollywood. These were forwarded to Los Angeles. Comparison of the post-office-box applications indicated strongly that both boxes had been rented by the same person. Investigation disclosed no record of a Dale Collins.

On July 22 another post-office box in North Hollywood was rented by a woman giving the name of Carol Cooper. That same afternoon a Betty Cooper rented a box in Burbank. Within a matter of weeks postal authorities received complaints of mailings from C. Cooper and B. Cooper.

One of the B. Cooper mailings caused Harry Simon some amusement. The letter came to him under a fictitious name he had abandoned many months earlier. Enclosed was a sample photograph, with an invitation to buy more like it, provided he sent cash only: "Checks and money orders can be used by inspectors as tracers and one never knows whether an inspector is on the list or not, and as you can understand, I can afford to take no chances." The sample photograph offered a full front view of a woman, kneeling on a bed, lifting her slip or dress high above her breasts; the print had been inadequately fixed, so that it would fade before it might ever become evidence in court. Simon, who had learned this trick thirty years earlier, dropped the print in a convenient tray of hypo and wound up with a most acceptable permanent print.

Back in Los Angeles the various post-office boxes were placed under surveillance. On August 13 a relief supervisor at Crenshaw Station observed a man picking up mail from Damron's box; the supervisor caught the license number of a pickup truck in which the man left the post office, and this led inspectors to the home of Garland L. Coughtry, at Porterville, California. On the night of August 19, after watching Coughtry remove twenty-three letters from the box at Burbank, inspectors rapped on his door. Coughtry told them he was both Damron and Collins and identified the two Misses Cooper as his office girl. Between July 1 and August 15 he had mailed about two thousand circular letters; his gross sales were between seven and eight hundred dollars.

In Coughtry's office inspectors found hundreds of nude photos and extensive mailing lists. They also found in a cabinet drawer a brown envelope containing certain deposit slips in the name of Bill Prada, together with seventeen 4″ x 5″ pictures of a girl known to them as Corinne. The crab-grass operation began to jerk loose. Investigation led them to Bill Prada's real-life person, a Los Angeles printer and lithographer named Daniel L. Loewinger. Postal authorities in Washington and Los Angeles had received hundreds of complaints stemming from indiscriminate mailings of Loewinger's material. His printing plant turned out thousands of circulars for Louis Tager and other mail-order dealers on the West Coast.

A typical Bill Prada mailing began:

Dear photo film collector:

Meet Corinne. Her picture is yours free with my compliments. The picture is from the opening scene of one of the most provocative films you'd ever want for your collection—Corinne is talking to a client! Frankly, you can't call this an art film. It's too intensely human and earthy!

But before I go further, let me introduce myself. My name is Bill Prada. I operate a magazine stand at one of the big office buildings in downtown Hollywood, selling candy, cigarets, etc. However, at night is when I really make my money. I have a library of extremely interesting action films, and I show them for money at stags, smokers, vets' meetings and other men's organizations. I have quite a large clientele worked up, and I keep busy just about every night of the week. . . .

While I think of it, if you are only interested in pin-ups or art posing, these are NOT the films for you. I'm not what you would call a collector myself, so I can only presume there may be fellows that only want pin-ups, so if children, or their wife should accidentally see them, no one would be hurt.

If you're like my regular show customers, you'll really enjoy these pics and films—I guarantee. However, should they offend your taste, you can return them, and I'll promptly return your money.

When you order, be sure to state that you're over twenty-one, and please destroy this letter. Be hearing from you.

BILL PRADA

A number of Loewinger's mailings had gone to Minnesota. There both he and Coughtry were indicted, in September, 1959, by a St. Paul grand jury. In March 1960, on their pleas of guilty, each was fined $2,000 and sentenced to three years in prison.

Multiply the names of Ross, Tager, Steiger, Frew, Coughtry, and Loewinger by one thousand, and then multiply this figure by twenty different front names for each one, and some idea of the complexity of the postal inspectors' problem begins to emerge. Then imagine that many of these fronts spring into being and remain in existence only two to six weeks; consider that the mail-order dealers operate through first-class mail, which cannot be opened in transit by postal inspectors; take into account that the fines and punishments levied upon conviction for violation of postal laws ordinarily are mere slaps on the wrist—and the stubborn nature of the racket begins to appear.

Since August of 1958, however, the Post Office Department believes it has made some headway against the smut peddlers. At that time Congress amended postal laws to permit prosecution of mail-order pornographers at the point where mail is received. Earlier, when the offense was confined only to "depositing in the mail," courts construed the phrase literally: the offense began and ended when mail was deposited; and in Los Angeles and New York, centers of the obscenity racket, judges frequently viewed defendants in obscenity cases as no more than miscreant boys.

Then came the case of Charles and Mary Hall. In the summer of 1958 inspectors responded to some magazine ads in the name of Mari, offering seven sexy pin-up pictures for a dollar. "If it's all or nothing with you, then I'm just the gal you're looking for." A tentative inquiry, in the decoy name of Malcolm D. Scanlon in Idaho, brought merely borderline photos, but with these pictures came a letter suggesting that "detailed and unretouched" photos also were available. Scanlon sent seven dollars to Mari for her "no. 10 special" set of pictures; these proved to be unretouched indeed, and an accompanying letter hinted at still more to come: "I believe that I have the kind of photos that you want. . . . Good clear ones, too." For ten dollars Scanlon obtained sets 11 and 12, considerably more obscene than the pictures in set no. 10. Weeks passed, and at last, in October, the fictitious Idahoan received from the fictitious Mari some "doubles" pictures of a highly obscene nature. With these the Post Office Department cracked down.

Investigation led the inspectors directly to Mary J. Hall, twenty-nine, at Cottonwood, California. She and her thirty-one-year-old husband, and their seven children, were then living in a two-bedroom house that inspectors described as "filthy beyond description." Mrs. Hall was the subject for almost all the obscene films and pictures they sold through the mail. The two of them were indicted in Boise, the federal district where the pictures had been received, and on December 29, 1958, after the case had been returned to California on their plea of guilty, the district court at Sacramento sentenced each of them to ten years in prison.

The sentences imposed upon the Halls had a shock effect within the California division of the obscenity racket. A fine of a few hundred dollars—even a sentence of a few months in jail—may be a hazard to be risked with equanimity; a ten-year term in a federal prison is something else. A few of the known dealers in nude pictures and films apparently folded up. On the East Coast, however, business continued as usual. And on April 7, 1959, postal inspectors in New York conducted the largest raid in the history of arrests under the Comstock Act. Their target was a cluster of publishing and mail-order enterprises operated by three men, Ben Himmel, William Glanzman, and Sidney Poss.

Behind this raid were months of investigation into complaints that poured into the Post Office Department in Washington. Himmel's principal operation was in the name of Pigalle Imports. Glanzman operated under a bewildering variety of trade names: Monart, Inc., Reyelle, Derey, Viking Company, Bowery Enterprises, Glanzman Studios, Photo Features, B & R Features, Paragon Productions, French Features, Stereo Company, Topaz Company, Malmo Company, Cinemovie Club, Adanac Photo, Milimeter, Foto Features, Reel-o-Rama, Atina Company, Layne Movie Club, and Elve Company. (One of Glanzman's mailings on the letterhead of the Elve Company went to Mr. Henry C. Lodge, 275 Hale Street, Beverly, Massachusetts, inviting the recipient to order "the same type of movies you may have purchased from Denmark, Germany, or England." Ambassador Henry Cabot Lodge, to whom the letter was forwarded at the Waldorf-Astoria, was not amused; he forwarded the circular on to Postmaster General Summerfield, with a hot letter of his own.) Sidney Poss, for his part, operated as Jefferson Creations, Milco Specialties, the Master Studio of Art, Dame Features, Top Hit Enterprises, K & L Photos, Glamacolor Productions, Model Movies, Dana Associates, and First Nighter Movie Club. One of Poss's mailings went to a twelve-year-old boy; he also circularized college boys in a foreign country, resulting in a formal complaint from the government of that country.

The three of them had a flourishing traffic going. Simultaneously the department descended upon Himmel's operation on West Forty-sixth Street, Glanzman's on East Thirty-third, and Poss's on Broadway. The seized material weighed an estimated fourteen tons; it included thousands of nudie photographs, films, slides, addressograph plates, mailing lists, and the like. Three inspectors, four clerks, and two laborers worked for more than a month simply to inventory the haul. They placed the retail value of the seized material at more than $878,000, the great bulk of it in the name of Himmel. Each of the operators was indicted by a federal grand jury for violation of the Comstock Act. Their cases had not been finally disposed of as this manuscript was prepared.

Most of the traffic in mail-order sex is aimed at the more or less normal male who lusts for the more or less normal female. Vast quantities of material, however, are vended to sexual deviates, whose particular fetish is the bondage photograph in which women are depicted bound in ropes or trapped in torture devices. And as postal inspectors have discovered since Postmaster General Summerfield stepped up a campaign against pornography in the spring of 1959, an incredible commerce exists in material for male homosexuals.

Among the proceedings brought by the Post Office Department in this field is the case against John P. Palatinus, Leonard Dunn, and seven subordinate defendants who were arrested following an investigation by Washington and New York postal inspectors. The case began when an inspector received a circular through test names he long ago had abandoned in Idaho and Mississippi, advertising photographs of boys fourteen, seventeen, and nineteen years old. A test order brought pictures of a fourteen-year-old boy in tight-fitting pants, his penis and scrotum clearly outlined. Following the receipt of other material, postal inspectors made a stake-out on four locations in New York from which the Rainbow Studios and General Photo Studio were operating. In simultaneous raids on January 28, 1959, inspectors seized almost a hundred thousand photographs and drawings, almost all of a fetishistic or homosexual nature, together with binding ropes, handcuffs, heavy masks, and other props used in posing deviate pictures. A notebook, containing the names and addresses of male models, led inspectors to the apartment of a young reserve lieutenant, where a large collection of obscene photographs, two bull whips, three riding crops, three chains, seven cloth masks, five pairs of leg irons, a canvas strait jacket, and a pair of handcuffs were seized. Inspectors estimated from the evidence gathered during the January raid that Palatinus and Dunn were doing a gross business of some ten thousand dollars weekly. Their mailing lists had roughly ten thousand names.

Not all the department's cases, of course, involve large dealers. The mails are infested by hundreds of small operators also. Typical of these were Albert and Roselyn LeBail, who ran a filthy business from Milwaukee. In the summer of 1958 LeBail began selling obscene photographs of his wife to a few customers around the country, in Pennsylvania, Minnesota, Tennessee, and Illinois. Roselyn, helping the family enterprise along, struck up a correspondence with a man in Chicago, who paid her from three to five dollars for handwritten obscene letters in which she described various acts of masturbation and intercourse. In time postal inspectors uncovered their sordid traffic. On April 13, 1959, a federal court placed Roselyn on probation for three years; Albert was sentenced to ten years' imprisonment, later reduced to three years.

A still more bizarre case arose in 1958, when postal inspectors, picking up a trail developed by New Orleans police, cracked a nation-wide mate-swapping ring. Two of the principals in this operation were James G. Brock, a retired civil-service employee then living in Valparaiso, Florida, and Louis E. Stewart, a literate ex-convict who once served time in Virginia for armed robbery. At the time the case cracked open, late in the summer of 1957, Stewart and his wife were members of the Three Lakes Nudist Club, outside New Orleans. Their custom was to visit back and forth with various couples and to while away the evenings taking obscene photographs of each other. Some of the film was mailed to Brock in Valparaiso for processing. In the course of time New Orleans police descended upon the nudist camp; Stewart surrendered extensive correspondence files, and from these a fantastic tale began to take shape. The mate-swappers, known to each other as "related souls," traded partners with degenerate abandon. It appeared that members of the group lived in almost every state, in Mexico, in Canada, and in several foreign countries. Working swiftly, postal inspectors called upon "related souls" in Sacramento, San Francisco, Spokane, Norfolk, Newport News, Baton Rouge, Houston, Dallas, and New York. Among the participants were several doctors and professional men. A typical member was a serviceman in Massachusetts who mailed photographs of his wife, nude, to correspondents in Texas, Pennsylvania, and North Carolina. At the time the obscene correspondence was broken up Stewart and his wife were planning a veritable convention of mate-swapping, to which forty-five or fifty couples were to be invited, but this never came off. In September of 1958 Brock was sentenced to a year and a day in federal custody; the following December a federal court gave Stewart an eighteen-month sentence for mail violations.

These several cases, chosen at random from recent files of the Post Office Department, suggest something of the scope and nature of the traffic in borderline and obscene materials. They echo many similar cases documented by the Kefauver Committee of the Senate in its 1955 hearings, and they pose for a reporter a troublesome dilemma: how is one to write descriptively of the obscenity racket—how is he to help the reader understand the vile nature of this ugly traffic—without falling into fresh obscenity himself? It cannot be done. But the reader who wishes to dig out the Kefauver transcripts, or to go through department files, or to study the reports of New York's legislative committee on obscene material, will find on public record sufficient ugliness to convince the most skeptical of what obscenity means: children of fourteen and fifteen photographed in acts of perverted intercourse . . . women photographed with animals . . . men engaged in sodomy . . . records of sex orgies . . . reports of obscene materials seized . . . cold statistics on the astonishing profits of the merchants of filth. The Kefauver Committee heard testimony of one operator who traded in two million lewd photographs a year. Inspector Roy Blick of the Washington Metropolitan Police told of a dealer whose card file of five hundred negatives was indexed by the type of perversion depicted. The closely printed pages tell of an Illinois dealer who maintained a fleet of trucks to keep his distributors in supply. The record contains a chart of one operator's salesmen, neatly pin-pointed from Syracuse and Utica to Birmingham and Atlanta. And since the Kefauver Committee completed its investigations the racket in obscene materials, by the grim estimate of the Post Office Department, has roughly doubled. The department made 136 arrests and obtained 112 convictions under obscenity statutes in 1954; in 1960 the department made 389 arrests, an increase of 23 per cent over the preceding year.

The federal government's weapons against this traffic are few in number, though three different agencies are concerned in enforcement of obscenity laws. Customs officials, under the Treasury Department, have authority to seize obscene materials sought to be imported into the United States. The FBI, under the Justice Department, enforces Title 18, Sections 1462 and 1465, which prohibit the transportation of obscene materials by express, or otherwise, in interstate commerce. The postal inspectors bear the largest load in enforcing the basic law against mailing obscene materials and in warring upon the obscenity racketeers through "unlawful" orders and the impounding of mail under 39 U.S.C. 259a and 259b. This latter statute, 259b, permits the Post Office temporarily to impound the mail of a suspected racketeer; it is intended to freeze the hit-and-run operator in his tracks, so that he has no time to reap the harvest of a one-shot circularization of a large mailing list. As soon as an administrative complaint is filed, the department can move in with an impoundment proceeding; the person to whom such mail is addressed may call at his post office and pick up letters and packages not connected with the suspected enterprise, but other mail is held until the formal proceeding under 259a is completed. If a hearing establishes the obscenity of the operation, the department follows through with an "unlawful" order. This directs the local postmaster to intercept mail directed to a proscribed individual or company, except for letters that may be identified on their face as not relating to the obscene enterprise; the intercepted mail is held for twenty-four hours, and then returned to the senders stamped "unlawful." In practice an order under Section 259b often is countered by the filing of a petition for an injunction against the Post Office Department, to prevent the proposed impoundment; and because of the speed with which the racket operates—every day counts in a hit-and-run circularization—the department frequently has found itself forced to trial on the merits of a suspicious operation before a complete case can be worked up. If an injunctive proceeding is successful, and impounded mail must be released, the racketeer becomes indifferent to any subsequent "unlawful" order that may be entered against his ABC Company; by that time he has made his haul and has switched to an XYZ Company, at a different address.

In addition to its powers under the "unlawful" and impounding statutes the Post Office Department can exert some influence on the mails through its control over the granting of second-class-mail privileges to periodicals. This control is far less effective than ordinarily is thought. During the administration of Postmaster General Robert E. Hannegan, in the famed *Esquire* case, the department attempted to establish a requirement that magazines, to be eligible for second-class privileges, must not only not be obscene but also must contribute something affirmatively toward public education or enlightenment. This effort failed, and when some years later the department found itself unable to prevent the mailing of a nudist magazine it became apparent that the statute governing second-class mail offers a feeble weapon in the war upon obscenity.[113] The department still has power to withhold a second-class permit, when a permit originally is sought, on a publication ruled obscene at the outset; but once a magazine has established its frequency of publication, proved the existence of a circulation list, and obtained a permit, there is little that can be done. It is widely believed that the granting of a second-class permit implies some sort of approval by the department of a magazine's contents in perpetuity; this is not true. The magazine that sends out an acceptable issue in January may mail an obscene issue in February, but this does not mean its permit can be revoked for an issue in March; the government, if it wishes, can prosecute the publisher for his February issue, but postal authorities cannot assume that future, unprepared issues of the magazine will be, in the department's view, also obscene.

The department's most effective weapon remains the weapon forged by young Anthony Comstock in 1873. Many times amended, this statute, the substance of which is now to be found in Section 1461 of Title 18, declares "every obscene, lewd, lascivious, indecent, filthy, or vile article, matter, thing, device, or substance" to be nonmailable matter. The statute also covers devices "intended for preventing conception or producing abortion." And it covers "every written or printed card, letter, circular, book, pamphlet, advertisement, or notice of any kind giving information, directly or indirectly, where, or how, or from whom, or by what means any of such mentioned matters, articles, or things may be obtained or made." Any person convicted of knowingly mailing such nonmailable matter may be punished on first offense by a fine of up to $5,000 and a prison term of as much as five years; second offenders risk double these punishments.

The provisions of Section 1461 relating to the mailing of advertising circulars have come in for much attention in recent years. One of the cardinal characteristics of the obscenity racket, as hundreds of thousands of suckers have discovered by now, is that ordinarily the circulars and come-on advertisements are far sexier and more provocative than the delivered items themselves.

As far back as 1876, only three years after the basic Comstock Act had been adopted, a federal district court in New York indirectly laid down some law on circulars in refusing to dismiss an indictment against one Edward B. Foote.[219] The charge against him was that he had sent out a notice, by first-class letter, offering obscene materials for sale. Though Foote's principal defense was that the federal law did not specifically proscribe the mailing of obscene letters (this was before the act was amended to take care of the point), the court's decision went to a larger consideration. The purpose of the postal statute, said the court, is "to prevent the mails of the United States from being the effectual aid of persons engaged in a nefarious business, by being used to distribute their obscene wares." It is not the form in which the matter is mailed, *"but the character of the matter itself,* which fixes the criminality of the act." (Emphasis supplied.)

The Supreme Court of the United States impliedly accepted this point of view almost twenty years later, in affirming a year-and-a-day sentence imposed upon one William Grimm.[75] Postal Inspector McAfee, using the improbable name of Herman Huntress, wrote to Grimm in St. Louis: "A friend of mine has just showed me some fancy photographs and advised me that they could be obtained from you. I am on the road all the time, and am sure many of them could be sold in the territory over which I travel. How many different kinds can you furnish?"

Grimm responded by sending a price list, quoting a price of $2 a dozen or $12.50 per hundred, and McAfee ordered some photos. The pictures, "conceded to be obscene," turned up in the mails, and McAfee promptly obtained an indictment. To Grimm's protest that he had been trapped, the court replied that McAfee had not induced Grimm to commit any crime, but merely had inquired whether certain photographs were available from him. It would have been easy enough for Grimm to say no, but "the law was actually violated by the defendant; *he placed letters in the post office which conveyed information as to where obscene matter could be obtained. . . ."* (Emphasis supplied.)

The Supreme Court's ruling in the *Grimm* case was relied upon shortly thereafter in Chicago, where postal inspectors won a conviction against Anthony L. De Gignac and his partner for sending out circulars advertising "pictures of nude women, too obscene, lewd and lascivious to be here described." The defendants were proprietors of the Mills Novelty Company and, as such, vendors of the old

Quartoscope machines, in which the gay blades of 1900 could see twelve stereopticon pictures for one nickel, the twentieth part of a dollar. The Seventh Circuit Court of Appeals held the circulars were distributed for a prohibited purpose, and upheld a sentence finding the defendants guilty and sentencing them to a year in the Cook County jail.[52]

The same circuit renewed this position thirty years later, when in 1932 it affirmed the conviction in Chicago of one Ira O'Neal.[114] The evidence against him and a confederate was that they had mailed a circular reading in part:

Dear Sir:

I only hope that this letter is not addressed to some Kid as Kids often write for this type of merchandise and their parents get hold of it and make things bad for us. . . . I have a good line of merchandise that if we were in some barnyard together we could express our views on each item. This is not a magazine gyp concern, as I do not advertise in magazines as they are always under investigation.

Here's my list of Hayloft Favorites: Too high for minors to buy. The most beautiful Photos in the world of Girls and Men together, posed in Action, and boy are they a Wow at $5.00 per dozen. . . .

Single Photos postcard size of girls alone, $3.00 per dozen. Beautiful. . . .

Last but not least, "Carts," short for cartoon books. I have Tillie and Mac, Jiggs, Boob, Moon, Dumb Dora and others. These books . . . are not the cheap variety. Price $1.00 each; $10.00 per dozen.

O'Neal and his co-conspirator—who incidentally were doing business from a Vincennes Avenue address in the name of Pierre Balzac—got two years in the penitentiary.

The most significant case of recent times, dealing with the mailing of obscene circulars, arose in Pennsylvania in 1955. Postal inspectors obtained an indictment against Jay Hornick and Jesse Traub, doing business as the Burlesque Historical Company, for sending out some nine thousand circulars advertising:

Sex-sational
for the
FIRST TIME
All Revealing
Color
Photographs
of
BURLESQUE QUEENS

These "actual photographs" promised to bring out "every charm of the Female Form Devine [*sic*]" in the "SEXIEST OF POSES," and if this did not prompt the sucker to bite, a second mailing promised "NATURAL BEAUTY IN FULL COLOR—BETTER THAN THE MARILYN MONROE CALENDAR." It was stated that the pictures "cannot be sent through the mail—'Nuff said?"

District Judge Rabe Ferguson Marsh observed succinctly that the circulars "capitalize on a human trait to sample forbidden fruit."[227] The appellate court agreed:

> We have no doubt that the whole tone of both these advertisements gives the leer that promises the customer some obscene pictures. Indeed, it has been held that under this section the announcement itself is not required on its face to promise obscene material if that is its purpose. But here the represented nature of what the customer is to receive is, we think, too clear for argument. . . .
>
> The statute does not say that the advertisement must be true or that the information must be accurate. What is forbidden is advertising this kind of stuff by means of the United States mails. We think that the offense of using the mails to give information for obtaining obscene matter is committed even though what is sent in response to the advertisement is as innocent as a Currier and Ives print or a Turner landscape.

The circulars, said the court, were "tainted by the sender's objective." That was sufficient for conviction.[228]

The *Hornick* decision was relied upon by a district court at Dayton, Ohio, the following year, in convicting one John Fugate, of

Xenia, Ohio, on an indictment charging the mailing of an estimated two hundred thousand circulars over a period of eleven months. Some of Fugate's circulars had been addressed to a fourteen-year-old boy; others had been addressed to an Earl K. Southerland, who turned out to be, not surprisingly, none other than Postal Inspector Harry J. Simon. These various mailings, in the names of Star Photo, the Surprise Shop, Bush Sales, National Sales, Starco, and Males Book Company, all undertook "to give information as to where and how obscene and indecent pictures (or publications) might be obtained."

Counsel for Fugate attempted to argue that the obscenity and indecency of the pictures and publications in themselves would have to be determined. Judge Lester L. Cecil brushed this objection aside:

Such a theory has no legal merit. If obscene and indecent matter can be barred from the mails, there is no reason why Congress cannot take the additional step and bar advertising which would lead to the acquisition of such material, whether through the mails or otherwise.

Obscene and indecent pictures or literature such as is described by the statute debase the public morals. The Government of the United States does not want to be, and should not be, an agency to promote the distribution of such degrading literature.

Fugate's various circulars, said the court, "would be repulsive to any normal, reasonable person and would whet a lustful appetite in any person whose desires led him in that direction." The whole tone of the advertising matter, in the court's view, "cries out as an appeal to lust and what is base in man." Judge Cecil found nothing funny in one of Fugate's circulars, describing "photos out of this world," which wound up with this punch line: "Yes, when it comes to sex, these are really innocuous." If Fugate truly had wanted to explain to his prospective customers that his merchandise had no sex appeal, the court said, he could have done so in a simple manner: "One way would have been to omit the reference entirely." In brief, "it is what is advertised and not what is supplied that determines the violation of the statute."

Two years later, in 1958, Federal Judge Irving R. Kaufman, in

New York, took a wholly opposite view. Ignoring the *Fugate* decision entirely, he commented coldly that *Hornick* "had no predecessors and no progeny." In dismissing a proceeding against Joseph P. Schillaci, doing business as the Regal Art Company, Judge Kaufman indicated that he felt a circular alone was not enough; the obscenity of Schillaci's films, slides, and photographs should be determined. (This was a more charitable treatment, incidentally, than Schillaci had received less than six months earlier, when the Post Office slapped an "unlawful" order on his mail in Los Angeles. Then, a federal judge had ruled that Postmaster Otto Olesen was "not unreasonable" in suspending Schillaci's mail.)

Just a month after the *Schillaci* decision in New York, on November 19, 1958, another district judge in New York took a more sympathetic view of the Post Office Department's war on the smut merchants. The department's judicial officer had ruled some circulars of Glanzman's Monart, Inc. were in themselves obscene and hence unmailable and in violation of Section 1461; the company sought an injunction against New York's Postmaster Robert K. Christenberry to prevent him from carrying out the departmental ruling.

Judge Sylvester J. Ryan denied the injunction and upheld the department's action.[71] Monart's circulars advertised "artistic nude photographs, color slides and motion pictures, for the convenience of students of photography, commercial artists, painters and sculptors." Yet the whole tone of the circular belied this apparently wholesome and educational venture. There was nothing artistic here. Said the court: "The Post Office Department is not required to sit idly by and lend itself as an instrument for the commission of a crime, when matter proscribed as nonmailable is offered for mailing."

A month later in a similar suit brought by Glanzman against Christenberry, involving still another mailing, Federal Judge Edward Jordan Dimock heartily concurred in Judge Ryan's view in the *Monart* case. He found that these circulars also were designed deliberately to appeal to prurient interest, and ruled them nonmailable.

These various decisions were brought together in December, 1959, by District Judge Frederick Van Pelt Bryan, who in July had won national recognition for his opinion refusing to uphold Postmaster General Summerfield's ruling against *Lady Chatterley's Lover*. This time Judge Bryan thought the department was on considerably sounder ground in cracking down on Sidney G. Poss, whose Camerart Studios had been raided the preceding April.[149]

In an effort to strengthen the *Hornick* doctrine, the department had not charged directly that Poss's circulars were obscene or that the material to be sent to purchasers in response to his advertisement was obscene. The department's charge was rather, in the language of *Hornick,* that the whole tone of the circular "gives the leer that promises the customer some obscene pictures." Poss's advertisement offered motion pictures, stills, and slides of female nudes "to help you develop your latent creative ability." The circular, Judge Bryan noted, "contains photographs of sixteen completely nude ladies in various provocative and suggestive poses."

> The photographs prominently feature the breasts of the posed nudes so as to focus attention on them. Each "model" is given a rather showy and presumably glamorous name. There is an attempt to conceal one portion of the anatomy only. Such concealment as there is has nothing to do with modesty but is rather designed to suggest and provoke. On the frontispiece of the circular there appears a man with a camera seemingly taking a picture of the only concealed portion of the anatomy of one of the models.

> The prospective purchaser is invited to order his movies, stills, or slides by the name of the model he prefers. He also may order a pocket movie viewer or a folding slide viewer with wallet "which you can keep in your pocket," for handy "on the spot" viewing. It is noted that "you must be over twenty-one to order."

> Most of the text has implications similar to those in the language representing that each movie features "a different model in a varied assortment of unretouched front, side, and back views" and asking that the customer "open up and see for yourself how our nude movies, photos and color slides will help you."

There was no question in Judge Bryan's mind that this circular met the sweeping tests of *Hornick* and *Fugate,* but these cases had antedated the *Roth* decision of 1957 (to be reviewed in the following chapter), and the court doubted that a mere promise to supply obscene material any longer would support a prosecution—*unless the promise itself were couched in an obscene fashion.* This seemed to him the case here: "In the circular at bar, there is little doubt that the publisher's purpose is to appeal to the salaciously minded. No one could be naïve enough to suppose that these photographs have anything whatever to do with 'art.' The circular does not contain any 'ideas of redeeming social importance.' Nor has it the slightest vestige of literary or artistic merit." With these comments Judge Bryan invited the department to bring a fresh proceeding against Poss, charging not that the circular merely gave information where obscene matter could be obtained, but rather that the circular in itself was obscene matter.

The effect of these various rulings in the influential district court of New York, in the *Monart, Glanzman,* and *Poss* proceedings, apparently is to leave the Post Office Department in a good position to prosecute on circulars themselves, without going to the obscenity of the actual merchandise. True enough, the broad scope of *Hornick* has been somewhat compressed—a mere promise, or the simple suggestion of indecency, may not suffice. But if a circular willfully appeals to prurient interest it becomes nonmailable matter in itself, and the department may proceed under Section 1461.

The first conclusion that a student arrives at, in any inquiry into the obscenity racket and the law of censorship, is that few difficult questions of law or public policy would be presented if the problem involved only hard-core pornography of the sort D. H. Lawrence himself denounced. Not even the most advanced defender of individual liberties contends that a merchant of filth should be free to use the United States mails for shipping the sort of depraved motion pictures sold by an Albert Amateau. Society surely has power to prevent the public display of photographs depicting actual acts of intercourse and sexual perversion.

But hard core items constitute only a part, and the least troublesome part, of this entire field. The great difficulty lies in determining, as a matter of law, what is obscene. For nearly a century courts in the United States and England have grappled with various definitions, in an earnest effort to reconcile the powers of society with the rights of the artist and writer. Out of this continuing process of refinement a new concept has begun to evolve; fresh ground rules are being laid down. Citizens' groups and members of legislative bodies may wish to know where the law has been, and in general where it stands now, if they would plan fairly and effectively on means of pursuing the elusive figure of obscenity in the years ahead.

PART II

THE LAW

Obscenity is an indefinable something in the minds of some and not in the minds of others, and it is different depending upon the individual's taste, occasion, background and time. It is not the same today as it was yesterday or will be tomorrow.

JUSTICE LOUIS I. KAPLAN
Court of Special Sessions, Richmond County, New York,
in People v. Richmond County News, 170 N.Y.S. 2d 76 (1958)

1. THE ROTH-ALBERTS CASE

SAMUEL ROTH, PETITIONER, V. UNITED STATES OF AMERICA	On Writ of Certiorari to the United States Court of Appeals for the Second Circuit
DAVID S. ALBERTS, APPELLANT, V. STATE OF CALIFORNIA	On Appeal from the Superior Court of the State of California, Los Angeles County, Appellate Department

[June 24, 1957]

Mr. Justice Brennan delivered the opinion of the court:

The constitutionality of a criminal obscenity statute is the question in each of these cases. In *Roth,* the primary constitutional question is whether the federal obscenity statute (18 U.S.C. 1461) violates the provision of the First Amendment that "Congress shall make no law . . . abridging the freedom of speech, or of the press. . . ." In *Alberts,* the primary constitutional question is whether the obscenity provisions of the California penal code invade the freedoms of speech and the press as they may be incorporated in the liberty protected from state action by the Due Process clause of the Fourteenth Amendment. . . .

With that paragraph the Supreme Court of the United States, late in June of 1957, embarked upon one of its landmark decisions.[166] Any inquiry into the law of obscenity must sooner or later reach the *Roth-Alberts* decision; all roads lead up to it; now fresh paths descend from it. The court's majority opinion makes certain flat assertions and lays down certain definitions, in language so positive and unequivocal that state and local authorities reasonably may rely upon these pronouncements for some years to come. The dissenting opinions, especially Harlan's, raise some profound constitutional objections that must be regarded with sober respect. These several opinions, coupled with the majority and minority opinions handed down the same day in the case of *Kingsley Books* v. *Brown*,[90] bring together almost a century of statutes and judgments in the field of obscenity law. And because this field of the law is so long and so broad, it has seemed appropriate to use excerpts from *Roth-Alberts* as a sort of frame in which to fit a leisurely and discursive review of some of the cases that led to Mr. Justice Brennan's opinion that June afternoon.

> *Roth conducted a business in New York in the publication and sale of books, photographs, and magazines. . . .*
> *Alberts conducted a mail-order business from Los Angeles. . . .*

The two defendants whose separate cases were to be merged for decision by the Supreme Court came from widely different backgrounds. Samuel Roth, born in Poland about 1894, came to the United States as a ten-year-old boy. He settled in New York and by his early thirties had embarked upon a flourishing business in the sale of erotic materials. At first he dealt in the smutty vest-pocket novelties that identify the mere peddler of pornography; later he began to concentrate upon the mail-order sale of books and on the publishing of nudie magazines. Some of the books that he sold in this period now are regarded as classics; ironically Roth's first conviction under obscenity laws was for the sale of a work of classic Hindu erotica, his second, in 1930, was for sale of James Joyce's *Ulysses*. He received a six months' suspended sentence on the first charge, sixty days in a Philadelphia jail on the second. But many of his books were not classics at all. In 1936 he was sentenced to three years in a federal prison for the sale of seven obscene books; ten years later he was again convicted for the sale of obscene works, and this time sentenced to two years in jail.

By the early 1950's Roth was again out of jail and doing business at his same old stand, on the eighth floor of a loft building at 110 Lafayette Street in New York. From this headquarters Roth and a fifteen-man staff managed to keep the mails flooded with provocative circulars and questionable merchandise. Nothing deterred them. In the course of a few years postal authorities harassed Roth with six fraud orders, nine "fictitious" orders, and eleven "unlawful" orders, but these were all in the day's work. He operated at various times under at least sixty-two front names: Seven Sirens Press, Gargantuan Books, Gargoyle Books, Book Gems, Falstaff Books, Paragon Books, and many others. In time he learned the ways of postal inspectors so well that he once sneered that their decoy orders were paying his postage bill. Articulate, literate, shrewd, Roth knew how to operate right on the border line between the barely mailable and the probably obscene.

Sometime in 1953 Roth began to step up his activities sharply. Growing bolder, he enlivened his salacious circulars with sarcastic cracks at the Post Office Department; he fell into a noisy feud with Walter Winchell; he boosted his mailings until he could boast to the Kefauver Committee of a mailing list of forty thousand names. Over a period of a few years he sent out ten million pieces of mail. Some of his circulars went to children in orphanages and prep schools, to an eight-year-old boy in Iowa, to a fifteen-year-old girl in Pennsylvania. His only regret was that these mailings to juveniles represented a wasted expense for postage.

A smart tactician, Roth played deliberately upon the sympathies of liberals and intellectuals who instinctively oppose censorship. He undertook to describe his *American Aphrodite* as a serious literary magazine; in one open letter to the postmaster general, he piously invoked some great names and some great ideals to defend his operations:

For my part every form of censorship is a book-burning, and in my time book-burning has been done, not by the common hangman, but by a common paperhanger. Early in this century Theodore Dreiser, one of the acknowledged literary giants of all time, was attacked in a thousand pulpits as an indecent writer, and the paperhanger burnt his books along with those of Heine. In some areas

*of this country, the teaching of simple facts of reproduction to young
people is regarded as if it were instruction in depravity. These are
all symptoms of the same disease—pride of office—usually coupled
with a dirty mind. . . .*

*Our language, the language of Chaucer and Shakespeare and Ben
Jonson, of Thomas Jefferson, of Clay and Daniel Webster and
Henry Adams, is the source of our power as a people. From it sprung
the Magna Carta and the Common Law. As my part of this great
tradition I want freedom of speech as a publisher. . . .*

Pretty words. But at 110 West Lafayette Street these splendidly
Miltonian concepts embraced very little of Chaucer and Shakespeare
and Ben Jonson. Samuel Roth's racket was in advertising books in the
sexiest possible terms, whether or not the books were sexy in themselves, and in spreading prurient bait wherever he could find fish to
bite. One of his many brushes with the Post Office Department came
in 1948, when the New York postmaster obtained an injunction to
prevent Roth from mailing three different books—*Self Defense for
Women, Bumarap,* and *Waggish Tales from the Czechs.* The charge
on the first two books was fraud: Roth had advertised them as
obscene, and in fact they weren't; the charge on the third was simple
obscenity.

Early in 1949 the United States Circuit Court of Appeals for the
Second Circuit, not without some soul-searching, upheld the injunction.[165] The court had no special trouble with the fraud orders ("the
standards of fraud are at least somewhat clearer than those of obscenity"), but the three judges were uncertain about the ninety-six
"waggish tales" offered by Roth at ten dollars a copy.

"Our task is not made easier," said the court, "when we discover
them to be American-made or shared smoking-room jests and stories,
obscene or offensive enough by any refined standards and only saved,
if at all, by reason of being both dull and well known."

But after mulling the matter over, the court concluded that it
"perhaps is not unreasonable to stifle compositions that clearly have
little excuse for being beyond their own provocative obscenity, and
to allow those of literary distinction to survive." In any event the court
could find no gross abuse of the postmaster's discretion, and the

orders were permitted to stand. Circuit Judge Jerome N. Frank, who recently had joined the court, filed what he politely called a concurring opinion, in which he dissented eloquently from his brothers' view. His objections and reservations are reviewed in a later chapter.

By the spring of 1954 Roth again was in trouble with postal authorities. He was indicted on eight counts of violating obscenity laws, but the following year these charges were abandoned in favor of a twenty-six-count indictment covering the mailing of obscene pictures, photographs, magazines, and books. In January of 1956 Roth went to trial on this indictment. Skilled attorneys offered psychological testimony to prove the harmlessness of smut; they offered the Bible in evidence as a book equally as obscene as some of Roth's mailings, and drew parallels with matter published in *Life* magazine. A jury, not impressed, found Roth guilty on four counts. The court imposed a fine of $5,000 and sentenced the defendant to five years in prison.

Roth promptly noted an appeal. The court denied bond, but even in jail as he awaited appellate proceedings Roth kept his business going: Post Office Inspector W. N. Nelson, who had led the successful fight against Roth, received a circular under one of his test names. It came from 110 Lafayette Street, and it offered, in a plain envelope, a hot and intimate number: *Sexual Conduct of Men and Women*.

Once again the Second Circuit Court affirmed, and once again Judge Frank dissented at length.[165.1] His colleagues, speaking through Chief Judge Charles E. Clark, plainly were disturbed by the constitutional objections raised by Roth's attorneys. Their impulse, supported by personal opinions, was to declare the postal statute void; they were troubled by the serious problems that arise when works of literary value may be banned from the mails. But in Roth's case they concluded at last:

> no such issues should arise, since the record shows only saleable pornography. But even if we had more freedom to follow an impulse to strike down such legislation in the premises, we should need to pause because of our own lack of knowledge of the social bearing of this problem, or consequences of such an act; and we are hardly justified in rejecting out of hand the strongly held views of those with competence in the premises as to the very direct

connection of this traffic with the development of juvenile delinquence. We conclude, therefore, that the attack on the constitutionality of this statute must here fall.

Roth's attorneys set to work preparing their petition for *certiorari* to the United States Supreme Court.

Meanwhile on the West Coast a case gradually had been taking shape against David S. Alberts. Born in 1922, Alberts had matched Roth in industry if he had lagged behind him in eminence. His lively trade as a dealer in obscene materials led him to a sixty-day jail sentence, under state law, in June of 1950, and to a token fine, under federal law, in October of the same year. Put on probation for three years, he emerged unrepentant, and in tandem with his attractive wife, Violet Evelyn Stanard Alberts, entered upon a large-scale operation. Under the name of Male Merchandise Mart, Alberts soon was selling smut by the ton. He maintained a central office on Melrose Avenue and a warehouse on Santa Monica Boulevard. He operated as APR Industries, Paragon Enterprises, Film Fare Company, Falcon Sales, Bachelor's Den, House of Armond, Rarepix, and Sailor Jock's. By the spring of 1955 his operations were averaging seven hundred incoming letters a day; his own expenses for postage amounted to almost a thousand dollars a week. A Los Angeles police lieutenant, in testimony before the Kefauver Committee, placed Alberts' gross business in this period at forty to fifty thousand a month, all of it in sales of filthy books, bondage pictures, and prurient photographs. In June of 1955 the municipal court of Beverly Hills found him guilty of lewdly keeping for sale obscene and indecent books, in violation of the California penal code. Alberts was fined $500, sentenced to sixty days in prison, and put on probation for two years. Challenging the constitutionality of the state law, he too appealed. Two years elapsed, and the day at last arrived, in the paneled chambers of the Supreme Court in Washington, when Mr. Justice Brennan began reading the opinion that concerns us here:

The dispositive question is whether obscenity is utterance within the area of protected speech and press. Although this is the first time the question has been squarely presented to this Court, either under the First Amendment or under the Fourteenth Amendment, expressions found in numerous opinions indicate that this Court has always assumed that obscenity is not protected by the freedoms of speech and press.

A consideration of this "dispositive question" requires at the outset a restatement of an elementary principle of constitutional government: In terms of federal powers the Constitution both authorizes and prohibits; in terms of state powers the Constitution prohibits only. The Congress may enact only those laws that the Constitution authorizes it to enact, and it may not enact those laws that the Constitution prohibits it from enacting. So far as the states are concerned they draw their powers not from the Constitution but from their inherent sovereignty: they may enact any laws the Constitution does not prohibit them from enacting. Thus, any examination of federal statutes relating to obscenity must inquire into two questions. First, does the Constitution delegate such a power to the United States? Second, does the Constitution prohibit such power to the United States?

In a consistent stream of decisions, dating back to the *Jackson* lottery case,[88] earlier mentioned, the Supreme Court has found no difficulty in answering the first question affirmatively. The Constitution delegates power to the United States "to establish post offices and post roads"; it also delegates power to the United States "to regulate commerce with foreign nations and among the several states." Accompanying these specific delegations of power is the authorization vested in the Congress "to make all laws which shall be necessary and proper for carrying into execution the foregoing powers."

However, these affirmative delegations of power are subject to one firm prohibition: "Congress shall make no law . . . abridging the freedom of speech or of the press." In reconciling the positive and the negative, federal courts have found it necessary to dig deeply into the precise wording of the First Amendment. It will be noted that the commandment is that the Congress must not *abridge* freedom. The verb is to be narrowly construed. In general the courts take the view that laws may not be passed which prevent the exercise of free

speech; *but laws may be passed that punish its abuse.* Long ago
Blackstone put it this way:

> The liberty of the press is indeed essential to the nature of a free
> state; but this consists in laying no *previous* restraints upon pub-
> lications, and not in freedom from censure for criminal matter
> when published. Every free man has an undoubted right to lay
> what sentiments he pleases before the public; to forbid this, is to
> destroy the freedom of the press; but if he publishes what is im-
> proper, mischievous or illegal, he must take the consequences of
> his own temerity.

The important point to be gleaned from this trend of opinions is
that freedom of speech and freedom of the press are no more absolute
rights than any other constitutional rights are absolute rights. To
some degree these vital rights of the individual are subject to restriction by society as a whole. There is nothing novel in this doctrine.
Long ago a federal district court in Kansas summed up the law in a
couple of opinions twice convicting a stubborn newspaper publisher,
Moses Harmon, of mailing obscene material.[224,225] His paper, *Lucifer,
the Light Bearer,* was a singular publication. The particular issue that
brought its fall from grace was dated February 14, E.M. 291, which
is to say, the 291st year of the Era of Man. In the Kansas court,
however, it was still February 14, 1890, and the court was not inclined to agree that Harmon's platform of "perfect freedom of
thought and action for every individual" embraced a perfect freedom
to discuss the sexual relationship. The offending issue was especially
free in this regard. In declaring the issue nonmailable, and upholding
Harmon's conviction, the court said:

> It is a radical misconception of the scope of the constitutional pro-
> tection to indulge the belief that a person may print and publish,
> *ad libitum,* any matter, whatever the substance or language, with-
> out accountability to law. Liberty in all its forms and assertions in
> this country is regulated by law. It is not an unbridled license.
> Where vituperation or licentiousness begins, the liberty of the
> press ends. While the genius of our institutions of government
> accords the largest liberality in the utterance of private opinion,

and the widest latitude in polemics, touching questions of social ethics, political and domestic economy, and the like, it must ever be kept in mind that this invaluable privilege is not paramount to the golden rule of society, *sic utere tuo ut non alienum laedas*— "so exercise your freedom as not to infringe the rights of others or the public peace and safety." While happily we have outlived the epoch of censors and licensors of the press, to whom the publisher must submit his matter in advance, responsibility yet attaches to him when he transcends the boundary line where he outrages the common sense of decency or endangers the public safety.

From this approach to the law two broad (and sometimes fuzzy) classifications in the field of obscenity legislation have developed. There are, first, those laws that propose to lay down some form of prior restraint upon publication; in general these have been held unconstitutional. There are, second, those laws, such as Section 1461 under which Roth was convicted, that propose to punish the abuse of free speech; in general, but with many qualifications, these laws have been sustained.

Congress has undertaken to enact only two laws that attempt to impose any sort of prior restraint upon publications that may be obscene. One is the statute that permits the Post Office Department, through an "unlawful" order, effectively to prevent the mailing of matter regarded as fraudulent or obscene. The other is the statute that vests some discretion in the Post Office Department in the granting of permits for second-class mail privileges. Both statutes have been touched upon earlier and will not be reviewed extensively here.

The constitutionality of the "unlawful"-order statute was upheld by the Supreme Court as early as 1904, in a case involving a scheme of the "Public Clearing House" in Chicago.[150] This was an elaborate tontine affair, in which a League of Equity sought members at three dollars a head. Those who paid their initial fee and stayed with the game for five years at dues of a dollar a month looked forward to splitting a melon accumulated from the defaulted payments of those who dropped out. Chicago's Postmaster Frederick E. Coyne found the operation fraudulent and entered an order blocking all mail addressed to the promoters. They sought an injunction, which was denied them, and the case went to the Supreme Court.

The court found no difficulty in sustaining the law. There is no absolute right to mail, said Associate Justice Henry B. Brown; Congress has power to say what may be carried and delivered in the mails, and this power to classify mail embraces a power "to forbid the delivery of letters to such persons or corporations as, in its judgment, are making use of the mails for the purpose of fraud or deception or the dissemination among its citizens of information of a character calculated to debauch the public morality."

This view was reaffirmed by the court in 1922, over the dissenting opinions of Associate Justices Holmes and Brandeis, in approving an "unlawful" order filed by the postmaster general against a patent-medicine house in Chicago.[97] The defendant was circularizing Organo Tablets, good for nervous weakness, general debility, sexual decline or weakened manhood, urinary disorders, sleeplessness, and a run-down system. The court was not especially concerned with deciding whether the tablets were "entirely worthless as a medicine." There was some conflict on this point. But the court found it entirely clear that the tablets were so far from constituting the panacea described in the circulars as to perpetrate a fraud upon the public. The defendants were prevented from using the mails for this purpose.

Holmes and Brandeis, dissenting, objected to this form of prior restraint. The Organo circulars impressed Holmes as letters, neither more nor less, and as such protected by First Amendment guarantees of free speech. In his view the damage to potential buyers of the tablets was of far less importance than the damage done to individual freedom. Since then courts repeatedly have cautioned the department against arbitrary orders under administrative statutes.[70,98,273]

Today the Post Office Department exercises its power to prevent the dissemination of matter by mail with a discreet hand. While many "unlawful" orders are entered against foreign distributors of obscene matter, without formal hearings, such orders against domestic dealers usually see all the protective clauses of the Administrative Procedures Act invoked in a defendant's behalf. In any contested case there must be a judicial finding of obscenity, with full reliance upon due process of law, before the publication of any matter by mail may be prohibited.

The revocation or denial of a second-class mailing permit, as an instrument of prior restraint by the Post Office Department, has encountered much criticism in the courts and is today a largely discredited and ineffective procedure. In the first significant case going to the department's powers in this regard, however, the statute was upheld.[206] This was in 1921, when the Supreme Court by a 7-2 vote upheld an edict of Postmaster General Albert Burleson denying second-class mailing privileges to the Milwaukee *Leader,* a Socialist newspaper, on the grounds that the paper regularly had published during the spring and summer of 1917 matter "in violation of the Espionage Act." What was this material? The paper had described the war as unjustifiable and dishonorable, as a capitalistic war, and as a plot of a plutocratic and autocratic government; moreover the paper had denounced the draft law as unconstitutional, arbitrary, and oppressive, and had criticized the Congress as a rubber-stamp body devoted to "Kaiserizing America."

A majority of the court interpreted these strictures not merely as the expression of opinion calculated to obtain repeal or modification of particular laws, but rather as expressions intended to encourage actual violation of laws. This "willful attempt to cause disloyalty and refusal of duty in the military and naval forces" was more than the majority could stomach in the name of a free press. Burleson's order was found "amply justified."

Justice Brandeis delivered a long and powerful dissent, in which he denied flatly that the postmaster general had authority, in the absence of a judicial proceeding, to deny any newspaper second-class privileges *merely upon his own opinion* that the newspaper had violated the Espionage Act. Brandeis conceded the right of the postmaster general to refuse specific items of mail offered for delivery, but a blanket order denying all future issues of a newspaper a privileged postal rate was something else entirely. Such a power would make the postmaster general "the universal censor of publications."

Holmes agreed. Granted, he said, that the postmaster general could refrain from forwarding particular issues of a publication; the postmaster general could not issue a general order "that a certain newspaper should not be carried because he thought it likely or certain that it would contain treasonable or obscene talk." The United States may give up the Post Office when it sees fit, said Holmes, "but while it carries it on, the use of the mails is almost as much a part of free speech as the right to use our tongues; and it would take very strong language to convince me that Congress ever intended to give such a practically despotic power to any one man."

The rule of the majority prevailed, however, as an influential statement for nearly twenty-five years. Then came the *Esquire* case, one of the most famous and least understood censorship cases of recent years, and the Milwaukee *Leader* rule was abandoned.

The *Esquire* case[82] involved the same sort of basic proceeding—a denial by the Post Office Department of second-class mailing privileges. Contrary to widespread belief *Esquire* was not prosecuted as an obscene publication, nor was any effort made to bar it from the second-class mails for lewdness. At the time Postmaster General Hannegan descended, Congress had laid down specific conditions governing various classes of mail. One of these conditions extended second-class privileges only to magazines "originated and published for the dissemination of information of a public character, or devoted to literature, the sciences, arts, or some special industry . . ." What Hannegan held, as to *Esquire's* issues of January through November, 1943, was simply that the magazine did not meet the requirements thus established. He therefore revoked *Esquire's* second-class privileges, and the magazine, seeing a $500,000 annual subsidy in danger, promptly sued to have his order set aside.

A unanimous Supreme Court, speaking through Justice Douglas, strongly upheld the magazine's point of view. Hannegan had attempted to take the position that magazines do not have to be fully obscene in order to be denied second-class privileges. It was sufficient, he felt, if the dominant tone of doubtful publications reached such a level of vulgarity that plainly "they are morally improper and not for the public welfare and the public good." A publication, said Hannegan, is bound to do more than merely refrain from disseminating obscenity if it wishes to retain second-class privileges: "It is under a positive duty to contribute to the public good and the public welfare."

The court would not accept this construction of the postal laws. To permit a postmaster general to decide what contributes to the public good, said Douglas, would be to grant the postmaster general a power of censorship. "Such a power is so abhorrent to our traditions that a purpose to grant it should not be easily inferred."

Looking back to 1879, when the classification act had been adopted, Douglas found no evidence of intention on the part of Congress to vest the Post Office Deparment with censorial powers. To be sure, the Congress had sought deliberately to foster and to subsidize periodicals devoted to "literature, the sciences, arts, or some special industry," but there was nothing to suggest that the naked fiat of the postmaster general was to determine the nature of literature.

"A requirement that literature or art conform to some norm prescribed by an official smacks of an ideology foreign to our system," said Douglas. "To withdraw the second-class rate from this publication today because its contents seemed to one official not good for the public would sanction withdrawal of the second-class rate tomorrow from another periodical whose social or economic views seemed harmful to another official. *The validity of the obscenity laws is recognition that the mails may not be used to satisfy all tastes, no matter how perverted.* But Congress has left the postmaster general with no power to prescribe standards for the literature or the art which a mailable periodical disseminates." (Emphasis supplied.)

From these and other pronouncements of the Supreme Court we may conclude that the "prior restraint" powers of the Post Office Department lie somewhere between the highly circumscribed and the almost nonexistent.[183] The United States mail (and by extension, the interstate express and rail lines,[163] and the ships and planes from abroad) are vital instruments of distribution, hence of publication. Blanket orders, prohibiting the use of these media will be sanctioned only where free access is provided to judicial process, and not always then.

The states and cities have experimented far more widely than the Congress in adopting laws imposing forms of prior restraint upon speech and press. Prior to the adoption of the Fourteenth Amendment, and for many years thereafter, nothing in the United States Constitution prevented them from doing so. The First Amendment was plainly limited in its application; it said that *"Congress* shall make no law . . ."* But by a piece of judicial exploration, not perfectly appreciated to this day, the Supreme Court discovered that the prohibitions laid upon Congress by the First Amendment were imposed upon the states by the Fourteenth; questions of obscenity censorship by prior restraint today must be considered without relevance to state or federal imposition. The most familiar exercise of prior restraint under color of state law is to be found in the field of motion-picture censorship, to be considered separately later.

The general principles here under review were set forth on the West Coast more than sixty years ago in a California case that arose when an enterprising theatrical producer, W. R. Dailey, saw an opportunity to capitalize upon a prominent murder trial then in progress in San Francisco.[51] He proposed to stage a play, *The Crime of a Century,* based squarely upon the trial. Counsel for the accused went to court and obtained an injunction to block the enterprise.

Dailey appealed to the Supreme Court of California and there won a solid decision authorizing him to proceed—*at his own risk.* The production of a play, said the court, is as much a form of free speech as the publishing of a newspaper. And because no daily journal in San Francisco might be enjoined, in advance of publication, from commenting on the trial, no proposed drama could be enjoined either. "The right of the citizen to freely speak, write, and publish his sentiments is unlimited," said the court, "but he is responsible at the hands of the law for an abuse of that right. He shall have no censor over him to whom he must apply for permission to speak, write, or publish, but he shall be held accountable to the law for what he speaks, what he writes, and what he publishes. *It is patent that this right to speak, write, and publish cannot be abused until it is exercised,* and before it is exercised there can be no responsibility." (Emphasis supplied.)

The court went on to quote Blackstone: "To subject the press to the restrictive power of a licensor, as was formerly done before and since the Revolution of 1688, is to subject all freedom of sentiment to the prejudices of one man, and make him the arbitrary and infallible judge of all controverted points in learning, religion, and government."

The court also quoted Story: "Liberty of the press . . . is the right to publish without any previous restraint or license; so that neither the courts of justice *nor other persons* are authorized to take notice of writings intended for the press, but are confined *to those which are printed.*" (Emphasis supplied.)

These great principles of free press apply to publications that may be obscene, just as they apply to publications that may be merely foolish, contumacious, or scandalous. And because these principles are not widely understood, many persons who are shocked by the nudie and girlie magazines regularly inquire why such magazines can't be driven out of existence once and for all. How is it that *Adam,* for example, can keep on publishing month after lascivious month?

An answer to this question, and it is a most vital and important answer, can be found in what is known simply as the *Near* case.[111] To those of us who live by freedom of the press, and do reverence to this ideal, the *Near* case is of surpassing meaning. And anyone who would try to understand the law of obscenity, and to comprehend how this law can be made to work consistently, must first understand the *Near* case.

J. M. Near is a sorry figure around which to build a great ideal. He was a publisher and editor in Minneapolis thirty-odd years ago, the proprietor of a hate sheet known as the *Saturday Press.* He was a pathetic fellow in some respects, warped, full of bitterness, tormented by consuming hatreds, convinced that a Jewish plot threatened Minneapolis.

"It is Jewish men and women—pliant tools of the Jew gangster, Mose Barnett, who stand charged with having falsified the election records and returns in the Third Ward. . . . Practically every vendor of vile hooch, every owner of a moonshine still, every snake-faced gangster and embryonic yegg in the Twin Cities is a JEW. . . . I simply state a fact when I say that ninety per cent of the crimes committed against society in this city are committed by Jew gangsters. . . . It is Jew, Jew, Jew, as long as one cares to comb over the records. . . . I have withdrawn all allegiance to anything with a hook nose that eats herring. . . ."

In various articles and editorials in the fall of 1927 Near publicly charged that the city administration was controlled by Jewish gangsters, that the chief of police was guilty of gross neglect of duty, that the county attorney was conspiring with the hoodlums, that a member of the grand jury was in sympathy with gangsters, and so on. At last the city and county officials brought suit, under a state law, to have the *Saturday Press* permanently suppressed as a "malicious, scandalous and defamatory newspaper," and as such a public nuisance.

Convicted in the state courts, Near appealed to the Supreme Court of the United States, and in June, 1931, Chief Justice Charles Evans Hughes wrote the opinion that set Near free and affirmed in great broad strokes the principles of press freedom.

What the court held—and it is a ruling for which free men may be forever grateful—is that, within certain very narrow limits, there can be no prior restraint upon publication. In general the liberty of the press is to be unrestrained, provided, however, that men must always be responsible for its abuse. Hughes quoted from James Madison:

"Some degree of abuse is inseparable from the proper use of everything, and in no instance is this more true than in that of the press. It has accordingly been decided by the practice of the states, that it is better to leave a few of its noxious branches to their luxuriant growth, than, by pruning them away, to injure the vigor of those yielding the proper fruits."

Hughes went on to say, for his own part, that the importance of Madison's approach had not diminished over the ages. "While reckless assaults upon public men, and efforts to bring obloquy upon those who are endeavoring faithfully to discharge official duties, exert a baleful influence and deserve the severest condemnation in public opinion, it cannot be said that this abuse is greater, and it is believed to be less, than that which characterized the period in which our institutions took shape. . . . The fact that the liberty of the press may be abused by miscreant purveyors of scandal does not make any the less necessary the immunity of the press from previous restraint in dealing with official misconduct. *Subsequent punishment for such abuses as may exist is the appropriate remedy,* consistent with constitutional privilege." (Emphasis supplied.)

Hughes acknowledged that there are times when prior restraint may be permissible; freedom of the press, he made plain, is not absolute. In wartime, for example, a newspaper might be enjoined against publication of the dates of transport sailings or the number and location of troops. Also, *"the primary requirements of decency may be enforced against obscene publications."* The security of a community may be protected against incitements to riot and the overthrow by force of orderly government. The constitutional guaranty of free speech, he said, quoting an earlier case, does not "protect a man from an injunction against uttering words that may have all the effect of force."

But apart from these strict and narrow limitations the right of any man to publish what he pleases, *provided he is liable for the consequences of his acts,* is not to be disturbed. If a man publishes libel he may be sued for libel. If he publishes obscenity he may be prosecuted for that offense. But suits and prosecutions must come after the fact, and not before.

Regrettably the towering principles of the *Near* case were written into the Supreme Court *Reports* by the narrowest possible margin— 5-4, with Butler, Van Devanter, McReynolds, and Sutherland hotly dissenting. They felt that Minnesota had power permanently to suppress a publication as malicious and defamatory as Near's *Saturday Press;* their objection was that suits for libel took too long to be tried and that meanwhile the offenses could be compounded. They felt that the First Amendment embraced no more than a liberty to publish "what is true, with good motives, and for justifiable ends." They thought it "fanciful" to suggest that anything might be wrong with enjoining the further publication of a newspaper judicially determined to be a public nuisance.

Hughes' great doctrine now is fairly well embedded in the law of this republic. With few exceptions no prior restraints may be placed upon speech or press, nor may government attempt by such devices as oppressive taxation to drive a publication out of existence.[76] What are the permitted exceptions? The law recognizes two areas in which prior restraints validly may be imposed—first, when the *content* of speech or publication would constitute a clear and present danger to society, and second, when the *form* of speech or publication would impose unfairly upon society's rights to peace and good order.

The first of these exceptions may best be represented by the undoubted power of the government to prohibit publication of troop movements, military codes, and other highly restricted material in time of war. Another example would be a community's power to enjoin publication of material that patently might start a run on a bank. Such laws go to content. In the second field of exceptions, going to the form of speech or publication, a community validly may impose reasonable and nondiscriminatory restrictions upon the use of public streets and parks. When a group of eighty-eight members of Jehovah's Witnesses formed themselves into a single-file line of marchers through the streets of Manchester, New Hampshire, to the inconvenience of everyone else, a unanimous Supreme Court in 1941 sustained their conviction for parading upon public streets without a license.[50] However, an ordinance to compel every person to obtain a permit before distributing "literature of any kind" was found to strike at the very foundation of free speech and thus was void.[100] But a closely divided court in 1949 approved an ordinance of Trenton, New Jersey, prohibiting sound trucks that emit "loud and raucous noises."[94]

There is one keenly significant case, however, touching upon this process of state-imposed prior restraint, that may well be reviewed at this point. This was the case that wound up as *Brown* v. *Kingsley Books,* decided on the same day that *Roth-Alberts* was decided, in which the high court upheld a New York statute that since has been widely considered as a model for injunctive proceedings in the attack of other states upon obscene books. The case can be traced to some laconic testimony before the Kefauver Committee, in which a twenty-eight-year-old printer by the name of Eugene Maletta was called to the stand:

CHAIRMAN KEFAUVER: Did you print *Nights of Horror?*

MR. MALETTA: I refuse to answer that question under the Fifth Amendment, that it may tend to incriminate me, Senator.

He was preceded by an even more laconic witness by the name of Eddie Mishkin:

MR. BOBO: Mr. Mishkin, is it true that you own the Times Square Book Bazaar, the Little Book Exchange, and the Kingsley Book Store, located in the Times Square area of New York City?

MR. MISHKIN: I refuse to answer under the immunity provisions of the Fifth Amendment to the Constitution.

CHAIRMAN KEFAUVER: Where were you born?

MR. MISHKIN: I refuse to answer.

MR. BOBO: Do you import any pornographic material from foreign sources?

MR. MISHKIN: I refuse to answer.

CHAIRMAN KEFAUVER: We are not getting anywhere here. How old are you, Mr. Mishkin?

MR. MISHKIN: I refuse to answer.

These uncommunicative witnesses did not wish to discuss an appalling piece of pornography, *Nights of Horror,* that in 1954 had been offered for sale in a series of paperback booklets at several shops in the Times Square area. Earlier that same year, following a report from a special legislative committee, New York had amended its obscenity law to provide a new weapon in the form of injunctive relief. The modified law, of interest to civic groups and public officials throughout the country, permits a city attorney or county prosecutor to sue for an injunction against any person who may be about to sell or distribute

any book, magazine, pamphlet, comic book, story paper, writing, paper, picture, drawing, photograph, figure, image, or any written or printed matter of an indecent character, which is obscene, lewd, lascivious, filthy, indecent, or disgusting, or which contains an article or instrument of indecent or immoral use.

The statute requires a trial on the merits of the petition within one day after a summons is served. If a court concludes that the suspected matter is in fact obscene, the sheriff is to destroy the material.

Operating under this new law, New York's corporation counsel descended upon the Times Square bookshops with a petition for an injunction to stop them from selling *Nights of Horror.* The defendants bitterly assailed the constitutionality of the statute as a denial of their rights of free press. They contended that an injunctive procedure is essentially a prior-restraint procedure, and they argued at length that any sort of prior restraint is prohibited.

The Supreme Court of New York County, speaking through Judge Matthew M. Levy, handed down a lengthy opinion, bristling with citations, in which the court firmly upheld the new injunctive procedure.[26] Judge Levy's task was made easier, the jurist confessed, by the manifest obscenity of these publications: "If ever there could be found appropriate applicability for Section 22-a, this case emerges as the perfect example of what the Legislature has sought to curb."

> The booklets in evidence offer naught but glorified concepts of lustful and vicious concupiscence, and by their tenor deride love and virtue, invite crime and voluptuousness, and excite lecherous desires. There is no true dissemination of lawful ideas—rather is there a direct incitement to sex crimes and the sordid excrement of brutality. . . . These books are not sex literature, as such, but pornography, unadulterated by plot, moral or writing style.
>
> *Nights of Horror* is no haphazard title. Perverted sexual acts and macabre tortures of the human body are repeatedly depicted. The books contain numbers of acts of male torturing female and some vice versa—by most ingenious means. These gruesome acts included such horrors as cauterizing a woman's breast with a hot iron, placing hot coals against a woman's breasts, tearing breasts off, placing hot irons against a woman's armpits, pulling off a girl's fingernails with white-hot pincers, completely singeing away the body hairs, working a female's skin away from her flesh with a knife, gouging and burning eyes out of their sockets, ringing the nipples of the breast with needles. . . . Sucking a victim's blood was pictured; and so was pouring molten lead into a girl's mouth and ears; and putting honey on a girl's breasts, vagina and buttocks—and then putting hundreds of great red ants on the honey. Sodomy, rape, Lesbianism, seduction prevail. . . .

Judge Levy commented, in evident distress of spirit, that he would refuse to ban the books if he could find in them anything which indicated "the slightest effort to contribute to our culture or knowledge."

"I would not want or (if I could avoid it) permit this court to become a licensor, a censor, a book-burner."

But the volumes before the court, he said, "are so totally lacking in merit, and so obviously pornographic in intent, that their banning poses no threat to freedom of expression in literature or otherwise." The public has a vital interest in shielding the immature mind, of whatever age, from pornography; and if ordinary criminal statutes are ineffective, injunctive relief may be sought to prevent the sale of pornography in the first place. The New York Legislative Committee had found that "the reading of these publications contributes to juvenile delinquency, stimulates sexual desire, lowers standards of morality, and interferes with the normal development of sexual tendencies in both adolescents and adults." Congressional committees had reached the same conclusion. In the light of his own everyday observation of "the shocking rise of juvenile delinquency and sex crimes," Judge Levy thought the evidence abundantly supported public pleas for the suppression of lewd publications.

"All these indicate such a clear and present danger of substantive evils that, as a judge, I cannot ignore the cry unless the Constitution says I must. I do not find that it does."

Judge Levy's opinion was appealed, of course, and in April, 1956, the Court of Appeals of New York handed down a decision that has come to constitute something of a landmark in the law of prior restraint. In a long and carefully documented opinion Judge Stanley H. Fuld upheld the injunctive procedure and ruled that New York's law did no violence to freedom of the press.[24]

Here the court emphasized that injunctive relief validly may be sought only against *published* works; future issues of magazines, or prospective books, may not be enjoined. Further, the process must be conducted at every point through the established judiciary; there can be no "imprimatur of a censor."

In this particular case the books were "indisputably pornographic, indisputably obscene and filthy," and the defendants admitted it. Their sole defense was freedom of the press. But the right of free expression, ruled the court, is not an absolute right, and society has power not only to punish persons who actually sell and distribute obscene materials but also to prosecute by injunction those persons about to sell and distribute such material.

Once again the booksellers appealed, this time to the Supreme Court of the United States. The high court, speaking through Associate Justice Felix Frankfurter (with Chief Justice Earl Warren and

Associate Justices Douglas, Black, and Brennan dissenting), upheld their conviction by a 5-4 vote.[90] For persons who believe strongly in states' rights Frankfurter's pronouncements carry special weight, for he went out of his way to affirm the power of the states to punish those who would "exploit a filthy business." The Supreme Judicial Court of Massachusetts had made this plain in 1917: "[Obscenity statutes] are well within one of the most obvious and necessary branches of the police power of the state."[41] The Superior Court of Pennsylvania had affirmed state powers strongly in convicting one John Nicholas Donaducy in 1950 for publishing an obscene magazine, *The Tipster,* in Erie: "There is no merit in defendant's contention that his conviction violates the Federal Constitution. The right of the several states to prevent and punish the publication of obscene writings cannot successfully be disputed."[43] Such decisions were typical of an unbroken series of cases over a long stretch of time, said Justice Frankfurter, in which "it has been accepted as a postulate that 'the primary requirements of decency may be enforced against obscene publications.' " The State of New York, he said flatly, "can constitutionally convict appellants of keeping for sale the booklets incontestably found to be obscene."

In proceeding against the merchants of filth are states and localities to be restricted to piecemeal prosecution, sale by sale, of a book or magazine judicially found to be obscene? A majority of the court thought not; the states may resort "to various weapons in the armory of the law." If a state chooses to proceed by criminal prosecution of a newsstand operator, or by injunctive relief, "it is not for us to gainsay its selection of remedies."

Is there an element in this of censorship by prior restraint? The majority acknowledged that from one angle of judicial vision this might be so, but "the phrase 'prior restraint' is not a self-wielding sword, nor can it serve as a talismanic test." Under some circumstances a measure of prior restraint may be valid; under the New York law full protection is accorded the bookseller against whom an injunction is sought: he is assured a prompt trial on the merits of the publications in question, and because the proceeding is against the specific book or magazine, and not against the bookseller in person, criminal punishment lies only for later contempt of an injunction.

Three separate dissenting opinions accompanied the majority's ruling in the *Kingsley* case; these are important for the light they shed upon the views of individual members of the court.

Chief Justice Warren objected flatly to the business of putting a book, and not the bookseller, on trial. He said:

> It is the manner of use that should determine obscenity. It is the conduct of the individual that should be judged, not the quality of art or literature. To do otherwise is to impose a prior restraint and hence to violate the Constitution. Certainly in the absence of a prior judicial determination of illegal use, books, pictures and other objects of expression should not be destroyed. It savors too much of book-burning.

Justice Douglas, joined by Justice Black, went further than Warren in denouncing the New York procedure. In his view the statute "gives the state the paralyzing power of a censor." Douglas and Black agreed that the law permits a temporary injunction to issue *ex parte*— without an opportunity for the bookseller to be heard—and even though a hearing must be promptly given and the issue of obscenity promptly determined, "every publisher knows what awful effect a decree issued in secret can have."

> We tread here on First Amendment grounds. And nothing is more devastating to the rights that it guarantees than the power to restrain publication before even a hearing is held. This is prior restraint and censorship at its worst.

The two justices had still another objection. An injunctive procedure brought against a book under state law, and ultimately upheld by the highest state court, has the effect of banning sale of a particular book throughout an entire state. Black and Douglas objected:

> The judge or jury which finds the publisher guilty in New York City acts on evidence that may be quite different from evidence before the judge or jury that finds the publisher not guilty in Rochester. In New York City the publisher may have been selling his tracts to juveniles, while in Rochester he may have sold to professional people. The nature of the group among whom the tracts

are distributed may have an important bearing on the issue of guilt in any obscenity prosecution. I think every publication is a separate offense which entitles the accused to a separate trial. Juries or judges may differ in their opinions, community by community, case by case. The publisher is entitled to that leeway under our constitutional system. One is entitled to defend every utterance on its merits and not to suffer today for what he uttered yesterday. Free speech is not to be regulated like diseased cattle and impure butter. The audience (in this case the judge or the jury) that hissed yesterday may applaud today, even for the same performance.

The high court's opinion in the *Kingsley* case, to repeat, was a 5-4 decision. The validity of an injunctive approach to obscene works, under the supreme law of the land, thus hangs upon the personal convictions of the next judge who may have a hand in writing the supreme law of the land in this field of the law. Meanwhile the approach holds judicial approval. If New York's Section 22-a may be viewed as a form of prior restraint, then this is a form of prior restraint under color of state law that other states may wish to emulate. It is an exception. Not many such exceptions have won court approval. State laws permitting the prior censorship of motion pictures, for example, under any sort of licensing plan, are anomalies—they do not fit under the exceptions as to form, and their content scarcely offers a clear and present danger to rank with the publication of troop movements in wartime.

Laws dealing with subsequent punishment for speech or publication, as distinguished from prior restraint upon speech or publication, are severely circumscribed also. Here again a rough division can be made in terms of form and content. The man who scatters leaflets by airplane cannot plead rights of free press in defense against anti-littering laws; mass picketing may be punished under criminal laws because of the intrusion this represents upon the superior rights of a community; and the right of free speech of course does not embrace a right to lie under oath, in violation of perjury laws. Under the heading of "content," laws may be sustained that impose criminal punishments in two general areas: the first involves speech that jeopardizes public safety; the second, speech that involves public decency.

The Supreme Court summed up these few exceptions in 1942, in unanimously upholding the conviction of a Jehovah's Witness, Walter Chaplinsky, for violating a New Hampshire law against "offensive" speech in public.[34] Chaplinsky had publicly referred to a city official in Rochester as a "God-damned racketeer," and to the town government as "Fascists or agents of Fascists." These were "fighting words," said the court, and not defensible as an exercise in free speech or free religion. Such rights are not absolute "at all times and under all circumstances."

> There are certain well defined and narrowly limited classes of speech, the prevention and punishment of which have never been thought to raise any constitutional problem. *These include the lewd and obscene,* the profane, the libelous, and the insulting or "fighting" words—those which by their very utterance inflict injury or tend to incite an immediate breach of the peace. It has been well observed that such utterances are no essential part of any exposition of ideas, and are of such slight social value as a step to truth that any benefit that may be derived from them is clearly outweighed by the social interest in order and morality. [Emphasis supplied.]

In recent years the Supreme Court has made it clear that public safety or public order must in fact be actively jeopardized if a criminal conviction is to be sustained under laws inhibiting free speech. This was not always the case. In the early days of the Republic several members of the high court individually sustained the iniquitous Sedition Acts of 1798. As recently as 1915 Holmes himself sustained the conviction of a Washington state newspaperman, Jay Fox, for publishing an article that tended merely "to encourage or advocate disrespect for law."[61] And in 1919, in a famous case, Holmes upheld the conviction of a Socialist agitator, Charles Schenck, on a charge of promoting insubordination in the armed services in World War I; it was in this case that Holmes' often quoted comment appears, that the Constitution does not protect a man "in falsely shouting fire in a theater and causing a panic."[168] Since the Schenck case, however, few convictions or proscriptions in this field have found judicial approval. Two years after *Schenck* a federal district judge in Cleveland granted an injunction to the Dearborn Publishing Company to prevent the mayor of Cleveland from suppressing a weekly paper for publishing anti-Semitic articles. The mayor felt the articles "would tend to create religious and racial dissensions, and have a tendency to create breaches of the peace," but the federal court would not agree that any real danger to public safety was present. Neither was there anything "indecent, obscene, or scandalous" in being publicly anti-Semitic; and if the paper libeled any individual that individual could find remedy in a civil suit.

This is not to suggest that newspapers are immune from the obscenity laws. They are not. As far back as 1897 the Supreme Court sustained a two-year prison term imposed upon a Chicago editor for permitting the publication of ads from prostitutes, inviting gentlemen to come for "baths" and "massages."[56] In California an editor went to jail for attempting to mail a copy of his paper which included an article, "Ripe and Unripe Women."[231] In Michigan the publisher of a Finnish newspaper ran into serious trouble for publishing obscene photographs.[194] In Oklahoma one Hobart Coomer went to jail for sixty days for publishing a "Free Love Edition" of the Sayre Social Democrat, in which he asserted bravely that "women are human beings" and not merely "a multiplication table for the human species."[49] In Cincinnati in 1914 the publisher of The Owl, a sort of post-Edwardian Confidential, was convicted for mailing an issue containing an obscene article describing the amours of a "merchant prince" for his long-lost niece.[21] In New York in 1917 the prosecution of a somewhat similar publication led to the conviction of Alexander L. A. Klauder; his offense rested in reporting the libidinous activities of a libidinous priest who had seduced a young female, assaulted a married woman, and left one parish with a helpless pregnant girl behind him.[235] Klauder's report of the holy father's orgies, assignations, and scandalous associations in the Tenderloin and at a mountain resort was more than a district court felt inclined to tolerate: "If this is not lewd and obscene, what is?"

A few newspapers managed to win not guilty verdicts in this period. A West Virginia publication got off when an indictment was found to be defectively drawn, charging the paper with describing an assignation of a local citizen "with a noted prostitute, stark naked in the bushes,"[212] and in Richmond in 1912 Judge Edmund Waddill, Jr., returned a notable opinion, still frequently quoted, upholding the right of the *Evening Journal* to publish and mail an accurate account of a salacious rape trial in his court.[232] Judge Waddill approved the power of the Post Office Department to determine "the manner and method" of carrying the mails, and "to exclude therefrom what may be considered injurious to the public morals," but at the same time "a large discretion must exist in the publisher, who generally acts through others, and most frequently under great stress in the matter of time." Otherwise both newspapers and magazines frequently found their mailings successfully blocked and their editors and publishers subjected to indictment and prosecution. Law was law, and pulp obscenity was an imposition upon the public not to be accepted.

It was not until a decade after Holmes' opinion in the *Schenck* case that his doctrine of "clear and present danger," there enunciated, began definitely to emerge. Then the Supreme Court, with McReynolds and Butler dissenting, refused to approve a California law that made it a misdemeanor to fly any red flag "as a symbol of opposition to organized government, and as an invitation and stimulus to anarchistic action."[182] Speaking for the majority, Hughes found no clear and present danger in a symbol. In 1937 the court by a 5-4 division refused to permit the conviction of a Negro Communist organizer, Angelo Herndon, under a Georgia law making it a felony to incite others to overthrow of government by force.[84] Here the evidence was that Herndon had extorted his Negro followers to "banish capitalists from the earth" and to unite in a revolution after which white property would be confiscated across the Black Belt "for the benefit of Negro farmers." The court majority concluded that Herndon's appeal, inflammatory and offensive as it was, still was not really likely to incite anyone to immediate insurrection. In quite recent years the high court has adhered to this view in refusing to sanction the punishment of Communists for merely teaching, as distinguished from immediately and actively inciting, the overthrow of government by force.

This digression will now wander back in the general direction of Samuel Roth and David S. Alberts, who were left sitting on the edge of some indented type back on page 86. If some of the foregoing discussion has seemed remote from the law of obscenity censorship it is not in fact remote. Obscene writings and publications are part of the press, for all that they may be obscene, and the thought here has been to suggest that the Constitution generally frowns upon laws that either inhibit or punish the operation of the press. Censorship by prior restraint is severely limited; laws that permit subsequent punishment for speech or publication, where public safety and order may be jeopardized, also lie barely beyond the scope of First Amendment protections. One classification only remains for review: these are the laws, state and federal, that provide *subsequent punishment* for the publication of material that may offend public decency. May obscene speech be defended as an exercise in free speech, and thus as speech that is protected under the Constitution?

In *Roth-Alberts* the Supreme Court answered that question with a flat and unequivocal no. Examining the early history of the First Amendment, the court noted that ten of the fourteen states that comprised the Union in 1792 had in their own state constitutions guaranties of freedom of expression, but these guaranties plainly were not intended to protect every utterance: thirteen of the fourteen states simultaneously had laws against blasphemy or profanity or both. The object of the First Amendment was to permit *the unfettered interchange of ideas* for the purpose of bringing about political and social changes desired by the people. That is still the object and purpose of the First Amendment today:

> All ideas having even the slightest redeeming social importance —unorthodox ideas, controversial ideas, even ideas hateful to the prevailing climate of opinion—have the full protection of the guaranties, unless excludable because they encroach upon the limited area of more important interests. But implicit in the history of the First Amendment is the rejection of obscenity as utterly without redeeming social importance. . . . *We hold that obscenity is not within the area of constitutionally protected speech or press.* [Emphasis supplied.]

In that brief sentence lies the great significance of the *Roth-Alberts* decision in terms of constitutional law. Obscenity is beyond the scope of free speech and free press.[37,170,171] It is therefore irrelevant whether the effect of a particular writing is merely to produce lewd *thoughts,* as distinguished from lewd *actions;* it is not necessary to prove a causal relationship between obscene publications and actual anti-social conduct. All that is required is to prove that a given work is in fact obscene.

And what, pray, is meant by "obscene"? *As a matter of law,* how is the adjective to be construed? Here the Supreme Court tackled the second great point of *Roth-Alberts:*

> The early leading standard of obscenity allowed material to be judged merely by the effect of an isolated excerpt upon particularly susceptible persons. *Regina* v. *Hicklin* (1868) L.R. 3 Q.B. 360

One day in May, 1867, Henry Scott, a respected metal broker in Wolverhampton, England, undertook to sell a certain pamphlet. Scott was an active member of an anti-Catholic society, the Protestant Electoral Union, which had as its purpose the election of men to Parliament who would "expose and defeat the deep-laid machinations of the Jesuits, and resist grants of money for Romish purposes."

To further the society's aims the gentleman offered at a shilling a copy, "The Confessional Unmasked," a pamphlet "showing the depravity of the Romish priesthood, the iniquity of the confessional, and the questions put to females in confession." The Watch Committee of the borough, regarding the booklet as obscene, arranged to have Scott arrested; a police officer seized 252 copies of his pamphlet, and the case came on for trial at the quarter sessions.

Justice Benjamin Hicklin (and an associate not identified in the court reports) had no trouble deciding the case against the militant Mr. Scott. The pamphlet had been put together from the writings of such theologians as Peter Dens and Liguori; a good part of it was in Latin; at least half of the material was at most controversial or casuistic. But the remaining half dealt with impure and filthy words, acts, and ideas, and in the view of the court this served to make the whole work obscene. The pamphlets were ordered destroyed.

The defendant appealed to the recorder's court, and here he found a more sympathetic forum. The recorder agreed that, yes, "The Confessional Unmasked" was probably obscene, but he thought Mr. Scott's heart was pure: he had sold his pamphlet only with the very best motives, "to protest against those teachings and practices which are un-English, immoral, and blasphemous." The defendant had not *intended* to be obscene; he had not published dirt for dirt's sake, as later judges were to construe the law of obscenity; he merely had exercised his right of free speech to criticize a religious denomination. His object was honestly to expose what seemed to him the evils of the Roman confessional, and that object he had carried out honestly. So the recorder ordered the pamphlets restored, and the prosecution dismissed.

The Crown appealed, and such is the procedure of English law that the resulting opinion of the Court of Queen's Bench is styled *Regina* v. *Hicklin*.[159] This is the beginning of contemporary law on obscenity; and the student who would track his way through this swampy and uncertain field must start on April 29, 1868, when the Rt. Hon. Sir Alexander James Edmund Cockburn, joined by Sir Colin Blackburn, Sir John Mellor, and Sir Robert Lush, considered the case against Mr. Scott, reversed the recorder's decree, and restored the decision of Justice Hicklin.

Many of the arguments that were to be heard over the next ninety years were presented to the Court of Queen's Bench that April day. The defense insisted, for one thing, that Scott's pamphlet as a whole was not obscene; only parts of it, at most, were obscene. The defense insisted that Scott had acted with good intentions. The defense argued that "The Confessional Unmasked" was surely no more offensive than many classic works or medical works permitted to circulate without objection. And to all of this the court listened with courteous attention but with some occasional rude interruptions.

"We have considered this matter," said Chief Justice Cockburn in the end, "and we are of opinion that the judgment of the learned recorder must be reversed." It is quite clear, said the court,

that publishing an obscene book is an offense against the law of the land. It is perfectly true . . . that there are a great many publications of high repute in the literary productions of this country the tendency of which is immodest, and, if you please, immoral, and possibly there might have been subject-matter for indictment in many of the works which have been referred to. But it is not to be said, because there are in many standard and established works objectionable passages, that therefore the law is not as alleged on the part of this prosecution, namely, that obscene works are the subject-matter of indictment. . . .

At this point, we may imagine, Chief Justice Cockburn drew a long breath, for he then laid down the definition that was to be quoted a thousand times in subsequent years:

and I think the test of obscenity is this, whether the tendency of the matter charged as obscenity is to deprave and corrupt those whose minds are open to such immoral influences, and into whose hands a publication of this sort may fall.

That is the *Hicklin* rule. By this yardstick the Court of Queen's Bench measured Scott's anti-Romish pamphlet and found the pamphlet wanting. The pamphlet was plainly obscene—that is, it was "calculated to produce a pernicious effect in depraving and debauching the minds of the persons into whose hands it might come"—and Scott's righteous intention was of no consequence: "The law says, you shall not publish an obscene work. An obscene work is here published, and a work the obscenity of which is so clear and decided that it is impossible to suppose that the man who published it must not have known and seen that the effect upon the minds of many of those into whose hands it would come would be of a mischievous and demoralizing character."

Chief Justice Cockburn made the point, to be made many years later, that the manner of distribution is important in weighing obscenity. A medical treatise, he had remarked during the oral argument, would not be subject to indictment, even though it might be, in a certain sense, obscene, because it would circulate only among those whose education would be benefited by it. But in this case Scott had sold his pamphlets indiscriminately on the corner, in an effort to prevent the public from falling into the clutches of the Pope, "when the probability is, that 999 out of every thousand into whose hands this work would fall would never be exposed to the chance of being converted to the Roman Catholic religion."

"I think the old sound and honest maxim, that you shall not do evil that good may come, is applicable in law as well as in morals," said the court, "and here we have a certain and positive evil produced for for the purpose of effecting an uncertain, remote, and very doubtful good."

Other members of the court concurred with the Chief Justice. Sir Colin added that Parliament had taken pains to exempt classic works, such as Shelley's *Queen Mab,* from further prosecutions "instituted merely for the purpose of vexation and annoyance." Indictments based upon the sale of recognized classics would not be proper. Neither did the court have any intention of inhibiting free speech: there "is nothing illegal" in Catholics and Protestants denouncing each other. "But I think it never can be said," Sir Colin added, "that in order to enforce your views, you may do something contrary to public morality; that you are at liberty to publish obscene publications, and distribute them amongst everyone—schoolboys and everyone else—when the inevitable effect must be to injure public morality."

This, then, was the *Hicklin* case, the *Hicklin* rule of 1868, the standard, as Brennan acknowledged, that was approved for so many years. And though *Hicklin* now has been discredited, the thoughtful reader may wish to make a mark in the margin or to turn down the corner of a page. There is merit in *Hicklin;* there is much merit here. If obscenity laws make sense at all, they make sense, in part at least, in terms of "particularly susceptible persons." Early decisions in the United States repeatedly accepted this view.

The first significant American decision came eleven years later, when Circuit Judge Samuel Blatchford, sitting in New York, in 1879, wrote his long opinion in *United States* v. *Bennett.*[203]

The defendant, Deboigne M. Bennett, had been convicted under Section 3893 of the United States Code for mailing an obscene booklet, "Cupid's Yokes, or, The Binding Forces of Conjugal Life." He contended that the act was unconstitutional; Judge Blatchford considered the point and dismissed it. Bennett contended that Anthony Comstock had no right or authority to persecute him; the argument was brushed aside. He argued that the booklet as a whole was not obscene; the appellate court upheld the trial judge's instruction that obscene excerpts were sufficient. It was objected that the indictment failed to set out the whole of the booklet; Judge Blatchford, citing many authorities, said this was unnecessary. The defense insisted that Bennett had not *intended* to be obscene; "the object with which this book is written is not material." Bennett said he was deprived of freedom of the press; said the trial court, in instructions approved by Judge Blatchford: "Freedom of the press does not include freedom to use the mails for the purpose of distributing obscene literature, and no right or privilege of the press is infringed by the exclusion of obscene literature from the mails."

Point by point Judge Blatchford upheld the *Hicklin* rule, and laid it down as the law in the United States: an obscene publication is one that tends "to deprave and corrupt the morals of those whose minds are open to such influences, and into whose hands a publication of this sort may fall." Further, "the *general* scope of this book is not the matter in hand, but the question is, whether *those marked passages* are obscene or indecent in character." (Emphasis supplied.)

The federal courts have come a long way since Bennett's conviction was upheld. Our purpose now is to trace the theme defined by Brennan in convicting Roth and Alberts. Decisions since the *Hicklin* ruling, he said, have rejected it and substituted a five-point test. And the first of the five points is this:

Whether to the average person . . .

"*The average person . . .*" This was one of the two great departures of *Roth* from the mossy monuments of *Hicklin*. Earlier the yardstick measured the effect on susceptible persons—"those whose minds are open to such influence, and into whose hands a publication of this sort may fall." It was a stretchable sort of yardstick, capable of measuring a conviction here and an acquittal there, but for nearly half a century American judges dutifully laid the rule alongside the evidence and judged accordingly.[266] Thus in Missouri in 1881 a defendant was convicted for mailing a medical tract that might have been approved for doctors and medical students but was highly improper when "spread broadcast among the community, being sent through the mail to persons of all classes, including boys and girls."[209] The same position was taken by the Missouri court a few years later when a Dr. Clark was found guilty of mailing a treatise on venereal disease; he too contended his tract was not obscene—or at least no more obscene than some of the writings of Suetonius—but the court ruled tartly that Suetonius was not on trial. The important thing was that the pamphlet might excite sensual desires "in the minds of those persons into whose hands they might come," including the young, the immature, the ignorant, and "those who are sensually inclined."[211] This same year a Philadelphia newsdealer was convicted for selling the *National Police Gazette:* its articles might suggest "impure and libidinous thoughts in the young and inexperienced."[46] Lew Rosen, publisher of *Broadway,* drew thirteen months' imprisonment in 1896 on jury instructions to determine if his paper "would suggest or convey lewd thoughts and lascivious thoughts to the young and inexperienced." Justice John M. Harlan's approving comment, quoted earlier, bears repetition in this context. "In view of the character of the paper, as an inspection of it will instantly disclose, the test prescribed for the jury was quite as liberal as the defendant had any right to demand."[164] In 1908, in the Bernarr MacFadden case,[105] the test again was the harm his *Physical Culture* might do to "the young, to whom the magazine is particularly addressed."

The rule prevailed on into the twenties. In 1924 the Supreme Court of New York County weighed *Casanova's Homecoming* and delivered a short sermon in the process:

The future of a nation depends upon its youth. . . . Just as it is of national concern and interest to protect their health, it is equally important to protect our youth against the corruption of their morals, so that we may do everything within governmental power to afford them physical, mental, and moral virility, and not have their development arrested in these respects during the formative period.

Three years later another New York decision, this one involving an attempted production of *The Captive* at the Waldorf Theater, again saw a tight censorship upheld.[99] The action of the play, said the court, *"might* give to *some* minds a lecherous swing, causing corruption of the moral tone *of the susceptible members of the audience."* (Emphasis supplied.)

This was the *Hicklin* rule carried to its limits of assumption, hypothesis, and possibility. Some reaction set in, as we shall see in a moment, but the rule itself stubbornly survived. One of the most notable prosecutions of this period came in New York early in 1929, when bookseller Donald S. Friede was charged with selling Radclyffe Hall's *The Well of Loneliness*.[129] The book carried a preface by Havelock Ellis; it was accompanied in court by the endorsements of literary critics both in England and in the United States. The magistrate's court was ready to concede that the book had literary merit, but this was beside the point: it was not the court's function to judge literary values but to interpret the penal law. On this point the court thought the testimony of literary experts inadmissible.

Here was the story of a Lesbian, setting forth her sex experiences in some detail and seeking to idealize and extol "the unnatural and depraved relationship portrayed." The characters were described in attractive terms, "and it is maintained throughout that they be accepted on the same plane as persons normally constituted, and that their perverse and inverted love is as worthy as the affection between normal beings and should be considered just as sacred by society." Said the court:

> The book can have no moral value, since it seeks to justify the right of a pervert to prey upon normal members of a community, and to uphold such a relationship as noble and lofty. Although it pleads for tolerance on the part of society of those possessed of and inflicted with perverted traits and tendencies, it does not argue for repression or moderation of insidious impulses. . . . The theme of the novel is not only antisocial and offensive to public morals and decency, but the method in which it is developed, in its highly emotional way attractive and focusing attention upon perverted ideas and unnatural vices, and seeking to justify and idealize them, is strongly calculated to corrupt and debase those members of the community who would be susceptible to its immoral influence.

Morris L. Ernst and Alexander Lindey, representing Friede, had contended strongly that the book ought not to be banned because of its possible effect on "those whose minds are open to such immoral influences," because this would measure the mental and moral capacity of the community by that of its dullest-witted and most fallible members. The court said this contention of the defense "overlooks the fact that those who are subject to perverted influences, and in whom that abnormality may be called into activity, and who might be aroused to lustful and lecherous practices, are not limited to the young and immature, the moron, the mentally weak, or the intellectually impoverished, but may be found among those of mature age and of high intellectual development and professional attainment." The New York legislature had imposed upon the courts a duty to protect the weaker members of society from "corrupt, depraving, and lecherous influences, although exerted through the guise and medium of literature, drama, or art." And there could not be any mistaking New York's public policy in this regard: less than two years earlier the Legislature had amended the state penal law to prohibit specifically the presentation of dramas dealing with sex perversion. Thus, in the magistrate's view, a prosecution based upon *The Well of Loneliness* fell squarely within the area of public policy embraced by state law and supported by the *Hicklin* rule.

Other New York courts accepted this view. In 1937 a New York appellate court upheld the conviction of a dealer in art supplies, who had sold a book of eighty-eight nudes to purchasers indiscriminately. In some of the photographs the lighting had been so arranged as deliberately to emphasize the breasts and pubic area, and these pictures had been displayed "in such a manner as to be open to view of the young as well as the old, the strong-minded as well as the weak, and particularly to those the statute was expressly designed to protect —the young and impressionable."[148] Some years later, in *People* v. *Gonzales*,[132] a New York magistrate's court echoed this statement precisely. In Brooklyn a magistrate took a "realistic approach" to the case of a candy-shop owner charged with selling obscene "strip" pictures and nudie magazines to all customers alike:

Here is a small neighborhood store serving the families of the area. It caters to high school children who come in, observe these pictures, purchase them and seek dark corners and privacy to snicker over their contents and pass the pictures around among their friends. This is a condition we may not be able to cure, but when the opportunity arises to alleviate it, it should not be allowed to pass.[128]

The Supreme Court of Missouri, in 1954, sternly held to *Hicklin* in upholding the conviction of one Becker for selling a couple of nudist magazines.[176] The defense had attempted to offer testimony from expert witnesses to the effect that the magazines were not obscene, but the trial court had correctly rejected this: "No college professor, or other expert, was required to determine whether these publications are obscene and offensive to good morals, or might arouse lustful desires, or encourage commission of crime by the susceptible man or woman, boy or girl." The purpose of the statute, in the Missouri court's view, was to protect "the morals of the susceptible into whose hands these publications may come." And a few weeks later, in California, a federal district judge, even though he decided against the government on the merits, acknowledged the power of society to control "the perverted thirsts for lust that lurk in a very few morally unbalanced individuals."[119]

Yet all along, the broad reach of the *Hicklin* rule caused deep concern among thoughtful jurists. As early as 1913 Judge Learned Hand, who then had been on the bench only four years, had occasion to try Mitchell Kennerley for mailing an obscene book, *Hagar Revelly*. The opinion he wrote still is quoted widely a half century later.[234]

The book dealt with a young woman in New York, fond of pleasure and restive under the monotony of her surroundings, who is compelled to earn a living. Her virtue is unsuccessfully assailed by a man she does not love, and later successfully assailed by one whom she does. "In order to give complete portrayal to the girl's emotional character, some of the scenes are depicted with a frankness and detail which have given rise to this prosecution."

Kennerley demurred to the indictment, on the grounds that the book was not obscene. Regretfully Judge Hand overruled the demurrer; under the precedents he had to let the case go to a jury; he was in no position, as a newcomer to the bench, to overthrow the impressive tower of the *Hicklin* rule. And because such parts of the book as pages 169 and 170 might be found obscene, in that they would have a tendency to corrupt the minds of those who concerned themselves only with pages 169 and 170 and not with the book as a whole, Kennerley was sent to the jury.

But his duty done, the troubled Judge Hand felt compelled to add three long paragraphs to his opinion, and these merit a careful reading. Here are the beginnings of the modern law of obscenity, set down in 1913 by a wise and literate man:

While, therefore, the demurrer must be overruled, I hope it is not improper for me to say that the rule as laid down, however consonant it may be with mid-Victorian morals, does not seem to me to answer to the understanding and morality of the present time, as conveyed by the words, "obscene, lewd, or lascivious." I question whether in the end men will regard that as obscene which is honestly relevant to the adequate expression of innocent ideas, and whether they will not believe that truth and beauty are too precious to society at large to be mutilated in the interests of those most likely to pervert them to base uses. Indeed, it seems hardly likely that we are even today so lukewarm to our interest in letters or serious discussion as to be content to reduce our treatment of sex to the standard of a child's library in the supposed interest of a salacious few, or that shame will for long prevent us from adequate portrayal of some of the most serious and beautiful sides of human nature. That such latitude gives opportunity for its abuse is true enough; there will be, as there are, plenty who will misuse the privilege as a cover for lewdness and a stalking horse from which to strike at purity, but that is true today and only involves us in the same question of fact which we hope that we have the power to answer.

Yet, if the time is not yet when men think innocent all that which is honestly germane to a pure subject, however little it may mince its words, still I scarcely think that they would forbid all which might corrupt the most corruptible, or that society is prepared to accept for its own limitations those which may perhaps be necessary to the weakness of its members. If there be no abstract definition, such as I have suggested, should not the word "obscene" be allowed to indicate *the present critical point in the compromise between candor and shame at which the community may have arrived here and now?* If letters must, like other kinds of conduct, be subject to the social sense of what is right, it would seem that a jury should in each case establish the standard much as they do in cases of negligence. To put thought in leash to the average conscience of the time is perhaps tolerable, *but to fetter it by the necessities of the lowest and least capable seems a fatal policy.*

Nor is it an objection, I think, that such an interpretation gives to the words of the statute a varying meaning from time to time. Such words as these do not embalm the precise morals of an age or place; while they presuppose that some things will always be shocking to the public taste, the vague subject-matter is left to the gradual development of general notions about what is decent. A jury is especially the organ with which to feel the content comprised within such words at any given time, but to do so they must be free to follow the colloquial connotations which they have drawn up instinctively from life and common speech. [Emphasis supplied.]

Twenty years elapsed, almost to the day, before Judge Hand's brilliant and incisive criticism of the *Hicklin* rule was to find impressive support. Then, on December 6, 1933, in the United States District Court for the Southern District of New York, came the famous opinion of Judge John Woolsey in the case of *One Book Called "Ulysses"*.[252] This was a customs proceeding, brought against Joyce's book itself, in an effort to prevent its importation into the United States as an obscene work. Judge Woolsey dealt not merely with the test of the "average man" but also with other criteria to be reviewed in the next few pages. But the *Ulysses* case is a great case and it ought not to be dissected for purposes of legal illustration. The one key question went to the novel as a whole: was it obscene? And Judge Woolsey dealt with the question wholly.

"In spite of its unusual frankness," said the court, "I do not detect anywhere *the leer of the sensualist*. I hold, therefore, that it is not pornographic." (Emphasis supplied.)

What was the novelist's purpose? Joyce had attempted "with astonishing success" to depict the stream of consciousness in which his Dublin characters were floating that day in early June of 1904.

He had made a sincere and honest effort "to show exactly how the minds of his characters operate."

It is because Joyce has been loyal to his technique and has not funked its necessary implications, but has honestly attempted to tell fully what his characters think about, that he has been the subject of so many attacks and that his purpose has been so often misunderstood and misrepresented. For his attempt sincerely and honestly to realize his objective has required him incidentally to use certain words which are generally considered dirty words and has led at times to what many think is a too poignant preoccupation with sex in the thoughts of his characters.

The words which are criticized as dirty are old Saxon words known to almost all men and, I venture, to many women, and are such words as would be naturally and habitually used, I believe, by the types of folk whose life, physical and mental, Joyce is seeking to describe. In respect of the recurrent emergency of the theme of sex in the minds of his characters, it must always be remembered that his locale was Celtic and his season spring. . . .

Judge Woolsey then looked with more particularity at these "dirty words." Yes, there were plenty of dirty words, "but I have not found anything that I consider to be dirt for dirt's sake." Each word, he felt, "contributes like a bit of mosaic to the detail of the picture which Joyce is seeking to construct for his readers."

But the court suggested that it may not be enough to conclude that a book is not written with pornographic intent, that it nowhere exhibits "the leer of the sensualist," and that dirt is not employed for dirt's sake. Apart from these considerations, was *Ulysses* legally obscene? Did the novel tend to stir sex impulses or to lead to sexually impure and lustful thoughts? He said this:

Whether a particular book would tend to incite such impulses and thoughts must be tested by the court's opinion as to its effect on a person with average sex instincts—what the French would call *l'homme moyen sensuel*—who plays, in this branch of legal inquiry, the same role of hypothetical reagent as does the "reasonable man" in the law of torts and "the man learned in the art" on questions of invention in patent law.

Judge Woolsey asked two acquaintances, whose sex instincts he reckoned were average, to read *Ulysses*. They were not unduly aroused.

> I was interested to find that both agreed with my opinion: that reading *Ulysses* in its entirety, *as a book must be read on such a test as this,* did not tend to excite sexual impulses or lustful thoughts, but that its net effect on them was only that of a somewhat tragic and very powerful commentary on the inner lives of men and women.
>
> It is only with the normal person that the law is concerned. [Emphasis supplied.]

The Joyce novel is a "strong draught," Judge Woolsey agreed, to ask some sensitive, though normal, persons to take; but in his opinion the book, while it might have a somewhat emetic effect on the reader, does not tend to be an aphrodisiac. *"Ulysses* may, therefore, be admitted into the United States."

But the book's odyssey was far from over. The government appealed Judge Woolsey's ruling, and the following August the case reached the Second Circuit Court of Appeals.[253] In a split decision Judge Augustus Hand and Judge Learned Hand voted to sustain the lower court; Judge Manton warmly dissented.

The cousins Hand were not quite so enthusiastic about *Ulysses* as their literary brother in the court below. Page after page of the book, they said, "is, or seems to be, incomprehensible." They were not at all certain the novel "will permanently stand among the great works of literature." That it contained numerous long passages that were obscene "cannot be gainsaid."

Yet on every key point of law laid down by Judge Woolsey the circuit court affirmed his view. True enough, the motive or intent of the author "is not the test of whether a book is obscene," but literary criteria cannot be discarded entirely. The circuit court found that *Ulysses* "has become a sort of contemporary classic"; that it is "a sincere portrayal with skillful artistry"; that it seems to be "sincere, truthful, and . . . executed with real art"; and that it shows "excellent craftsmanship of a sort."

What of dirt for dirt's sake? The court found that the admittedly obscene passages had been introduced "to give meaning to the whole, rather than to promote lust or portray filth for its own sake." The net effect even of portions most open to attack, such as the closing monologue of Molly Bloom, "is pitiful and tragic, rather than lustful." The book *as a whole,* the court emphasized, is not pornographic:

The erotic passages are submerged in the book as a whole and have little resultant effect. If these are to make the book subject to confiscation, by the same test *Venus and Adonis, Hamlet, Romeo and Juliet,* and the story told in the Eighth Book of the *Odyssey* by the bard Demodocus of how Ares and Aphrodite were entrapped in a net spread by the outraged Haephaestus amid the laughter of the immortal gods, as well as many other classics, would have to be suppressed. Indeed, it may be questioned whether the obscene passages in *Romeo and Juliet* were as necessary to the development of the play as those in the monologue of Mrs. Bloom are to the depiction of the latter's tortured soul.

The final test of individual passages, said the court, is whether erotic material is introduced "to promote lust," and one must inquire into "the dominant note of the publication." The question in each case "is whether a publication taken as a whole has a libidinous effect."

The government had objected strongly, in its appeal from Judge Woolsey's ruling, to this idea of considering a publication "as a whole" and appraising its "dominant note." After all, the *Bennett* case had appeared to establish a solid rule that the obscenity of a book could be judged by offending passages taken from context.

To this argument the Judges Hand replied, in effect, that the time had come to abandon the old rules. Little by little the nineteenth-century yardsticks had been neglected. To insist upon measuring an entire book by isolated passages "would exclude much of the great works of literature and involve an impracticality that cannot be imputed to Congress." They were ready to let the yardstick go.

More than this. In appraising the "dominant effect" of a book, they suggested that trial courts might consider "persuasive evidence" along two lines: (1) the relevancy of the objectionable parts to the theme, and (2) the established reputation of the work in the estimation of approved critics, if the book is modern, and the verdict of the past, if it is ancient.

They concluded with this paragraph:

It may be that *Ulysses* will not last as a substantial contribution to literature, and it is certainly easy to believe that, in spite of the opinion of Joyce's laudators, the immortals will still reign, but the same thing may be said of current works of art and music and of many serious efforts of the mind. Art certainly cannot advance under compulsion to traditional forms, and nothing in such a field is more stifling to progress than limitation of the right to experiment with a new technique. . . . We think that *Ulysses* is a book of originality and sincerity of treatment and that it has not the effect of promoting lust. Accordingly, it does not fall within the statute, even though it justly may offend many.

Judge Manton disagreed with his colleagues on every point. On the question of the "dominant effect," he felt that "the decision to be made is dependent entirely upon the reading matter found on the objectionable pages of the book," and he proceeded to enumerate the pages: 173, 213, 214, 359, and so on.

"Who can doubt the obscenity of this book after a reading of the pages referred to, which are too indecent to add as a footnote to this opinion? Its characterization as obscene should be quite unanimous by all who read it."

And what of Judge Woolsey's test of the book's effect on the normal man, of average sex instincts? Judge Manton thought the rule of *Hicklin* and of *Bennett* still an excellent rule; the test was a book's tendency "to deprave and corrupt the morals of those whose minds are open to such influences, and into whose hands a publication of this sort may fall."

And what of the argument that various obscene passages truly described characters in the novel? "A book that is obscene is not rendered less so by the statement of truthful fact."

His colleagues had urged eloquently that *Ulysses* was a book of great literary merit. "No matter what may be said on the side of letters," responded Judge Manton, "the effect on the community can and must be the sole determining factor."

If we disregard the protection of the morals of the susceptible, are we to consider merely the benefits and pleasures derived from letters by those who pose as the more highly developed and intelligent? To do so would show an utter disregard for the standards of decency of the community as a whole and an utter disregard for the effect of a book upon the average less sophisticated member of society, not to mention the adolescent. The court cannot indulge any instinct it may have to foster letters. The statute is designed to protect society at large, of that there can be no dispute; notwithstanding the deprivation of benefits to a few, a work must be condemned if it has a depraving influence.

The *Ulysses* case has been reviewed at length because the views of the four judges touch directly upon almost every major point in the law of obscenity. Whenever a publication having the slightest literary merit is brought before a court, the rule of *Ulysses* offers a highly persuasive voice in favor of holding the publication not obscene. And in the bleak winter of 1933, the case shed a brilliant light.

The rules of *Ulysses* also are important in weighing trash, as the Second Circuit Court was to point out at a later time, in the case of Esar Levine.[237] He had been convicted in a New York district court under postal laws, for mailing a circular advertising, among other things, *Secret Museum of Anthropology, Crossways of Sex,* and *Black Lust*. The first of these had at most an "extremely tenuous" pretension to being a serious work of anthropology; the second was a questionable treatise on sexual pathology by an anonymous author (Augustus Hand thought this booklet so plainly obscene that Levine's conviction should have been left to stand regardless of errors); the third was a patently erotic piece of fiction "that would arouse libidinous feelings in almost any reader."

In brief, a properly instructed jury might well have ruled all three of the books obscene, and the circuit court was ready to agree that testimony could be considered to show that the circulars had been addressed to juveniles. But the jury had not been properly instructed. The trial court had told the jurors to convict if the books contained a single passage that would incite lustful thoughts in the minds of those "into whose hands they might come." This was a repetition of the old *Hicklin-Bennett* rule, and Judge Learned Hand, speaking this time for a unanimous court, wanted to make it clear that in his circuit this rule was no longer to be followed:

> This earlier doctrine necessarily presupposed that the evil against which the statute is directed so much outweighs all interests of art, letters or science, that they must yield to the mere possibility that some prurient person may get a sensual gratification from reading or seeing what to most people is innocent and may be delightful or enlightening. No civilized community not fanatically puritanical would tolerate such an imposition, and we do not believe that the courts that have declared it, would ever have applied it consistently. As so often happens, the problem is to find a passable compromise between opposing interests, whose relative importance, like that of all social or personal values, is incommensurable.

But how is a jury, weighing a charge of obscenity, to find its way to such a passable compromise? Judge Learned Hand said this— and it is vital to any understanding of a reasonable development of the law in this field—that there can be no hard and fast rules, no absolute standard independent of a book's effect on its readers:

> Obscenity is a function of many variables, and the verdict of the jury is not the conclusion of a syllogism of which they are to find only the minor premise, but really a small bit of legislation *ad hoc,* like the standard of care. . . .
>
> The standard must be the likelihood that the work will so much arouse the salacity of the reader to whom it is sent as to outweigh any literary, scientific or other merits it may have in that reader's hands; of this the jury is the arbiter.

The *Ulysses* and *Levine* decisions marked a great turning point in the law of obscenity censorship. Little by little the old obeisance to the rule of the "most susceptible persons" began to fall into neglect. In 1945 the Supreme Judicial Court of Massachusetts agreed that Lillian Smith's *Strange Fruit* should not be condemned because it might have an unfortunate effect upon a few susceptible readers.[47] The fundamental right of the public to read, said the court, is not to be trimmed down to the point where a few prurient persons can find nothing upon which their hypersensitive imaginations may dwell. That same year the United States Court of Appeals in Washington summarily upset the Post Office Department's effort to prevent the mailing of a pamphlet on "Preparing for Marriage."[273] What counts, said the court, is "the effect of a publication on the ordinary reader." In May of 1947 a New York magistrate's court refused to convict the publishers of Calder Willingham's *End as a Man* for selling what was charged to be an obscene work.[144] The story, laid in a Southern military academy, contained language that was unquestionably foul, but "the use of foul language will not of itself bring a novel or play within the condemnation of the statute." Rather, said the court, the test of obscenity must depend "upon the effect of the whole book on reasonably normal readers both young and old."

In October of that year, District Judge Thomas F. Meaney of Newark delivered himself of some quotable comments on this point in weighing a charge brought against William Goldstein for mailing a pamphlet, "The Ideal Intercourse."[221] Plainly enough, the idea of prohibiting the mailing of anything remotely acceptable was not a pleasant thought for Judge Meaney. He thought the old rule of the susceptible person "might lead to appalling absurdities," in view of the wide variety of apparently innocent items that will excite desire in the easily aroused. "Is that which is erotic to the neurotic to be forbidden to the sound and sane mind?" asked the court. "Are we to substitute the mental pabulum of the adolescent for the properly nourishing fare of the adult?" Plainly, some more elastic standard was required "than the narrow, prejudicial and prejudiced delimitations which would concern themselves with protection of immature minds and guardianship of a salacious few."

But with all that off his chest, Judge Meaney turned to the Goldstein pamphlet and found it wanting. Though the pamphlet purported to be purely education, it was filled with a "lush, phony heartiness," with a "sly, mock concern," and it went considerably beyond the bounds of decency in serving its asserted purpose.

While the statute does not intend that we shall reduce our treatment of sex in writing or literature to the standard of a child's library, it certainly does not intend that, under the guise of publishing an educational treatise, the purveyor of obscene and licentious accounts of ordinary sexual relations is to find exculpation. The unwillingness of courts to be unduly censorious is not to be used as a go-sign for snide trafficking in salacity.

Almost ten years later, in February of 1957, the Supreme Court itself signaled the end of *Hicklin's* reliance upon the susceptible man.[31] Here Justice Frankfurter, speaking for a unanimous court, reversed the conviction of a Detroit bookseller, Alfred E. Butler, who had been found guilty, under the Michigan penal code, of selling to an adult a book "manifestly tending to the corruption of the morals of youth."

The book put on trial was John Griffin's *The Devil Rides Outside,* the story of a young man's brief sojourn as a guest in a French monastery. He has gone there to study medieval music; he also studies, among other things, his own weaknesses of the flesh. It is a beautifully written novel and surely ranks among the most moral books of this generation; its whole theme is the young man's struggle against the sin of lust. Nevertheless the book impressed the judge of the recorder's court of Detroit as an obscene work. Even viewing the book as a whole, said the trial judge primly, the objectionable language "was not necessary to the proper development of the theme of the book nor of the conflict expressed therein."

This prudish literary criticism was more than Justice Frankfurter could stomach. In an unusually brief and pointed opinion (Mr. Justice Frankfurter often is pointed but he seldom is brief), the court found it clear on the record that Butler had been convicted for making available to the general public a book potentially deleterious only to youth. The state of Michigan's view was that by quarantining the general reading public against books "not too rugged for grown men and women," in order to shield juvenile innocence, it was exercising its power to promote the general welfare.

"Surely," said Frankfurter, "this is to burn the house to roast the pig."

Indirectly the court suggested that it would have no objection to statutes specifically designed to protect children against obscene matter, but the broad sweep of the Michigan law went far beyond protection against such an evil. The effect of the law "is to reduce the adult population of Michigan to reading only what is fit for children. It thereby arbitrarily curtails one of those liberties now enshrined in the Due Process clause of the Fourteenth Amendment, that history has attested as the indispensable conditions for the maintenance and progress of a free society."

The effect of the *Butler* decision was to make a fresh, clean division in state and local laws aimed at checking obscenity. Here the court set up a double standard under which local governing bodies must proceed hereafter: one law covering the sale of material to adults, another covering the sale of material to children. As an alternative, if there is to be one statute only, the offense imputed to an adult may not be measured by the effect of the allegedly obscene material upon children.

The following June, in *Roth,* this general proposition was spelled out explicitly, and since then, in Virginia[72] and elsewhere, the rule of the average person has been widely adopted. It is not a rule, however, that courts will be able to follow without some common-sense application. This is true for two reasons, among others. First, obscene materials do not ordinarily fall, all unbidden, into the hands of average persons; such materials ordinarily fall into the hands of those unaverage persons who have gone searching for them, and the damage to society must be measured indirectly in the danger to normal families created by the whetted salacity of the dung-seekers. Second, appalling quantities of obscene material, notably the bondage photographs, carry sexual appeal only to sexual deviates; the average person is merely baffled by them. Yet psychiatrists seem to agree uniformly that this sado-masochistic and fetishistic material "would, upon being viewed by those persons subject to certain sexual deviations, tend to cause erotic and lustful sexual stimulation."[54.1, 91.1] At least one expert witness, Alan Canty, head of the psychopathic clinic of the Detroit recorder's court, has concluded that such perverted material is strongly exciting *to the perverted,* whose sexual appetite, thus inflamed, may be vented in the rape and strangulation of the first little girl that passes by.

It should be emphasized, also, that neither in *Butler* nor in *Roth* did the Supreme Court frown upon statutes that treat offenses involving sales to juveniles in a separate classification. As far back as 1944 the court had made the distinction clear: "The state's authority over children's activities is broader than over like actions of adults. . . . A democratic society rests, for its continuance, upon the healthy, well-rounded growth of young people into full maturity as citizens, with all that implies. It may secure this against impeding restraints and dangers within a broad range of selection. . . . It is too late now to doubt that legislation appropriately designed to reach such evils is within the state's police power."[154]

The flaw that states and localities must guard against lies in attempting to bring charges on the basis of sales to adults of works thought to be obscene by juvenile standards. Trial courts and legislative bodies must keep the offenses separate: the average adult, the average juvenile.

So the test of obscenity, to continue, is whether to the average person,

applying contemporary community standards . . .

The second of the five points of the *Roth* rule requires little exposition. All that any jurors can apply, at any time, are "contemporary community standards." The requirement was stated early in the game, in the case of Moses Harmon, the Kansas Lucifer, when the jury was told to test the obscenity of his newspaper "according to the judgment of the aggregate sense of the community."[225]

To be sure, contemporary community standards may not be susceptible to precise delimitation, though there is some suggestion that the present Supreme Court will sanction expert testimony on the point.[175] This "inexactness of the law" was discussed by Judge Robert F. Wagner in 1924, when the Supreme Court of New York County was urged to consider that *Casanova's Homecoming* had been welcomed in foreign countries and embraced by literary critics.[142] This was of no consequence: "Acceptance in other places than our own of a publication is of no importance to us, unless the moral standard of these other countries is a replica of our own." Judge Wagner thought the opinions of critics "valueless . . . and inadmissible at a trial." The trouble with critics, said the court, is that they look with a single eye at purity of construction and vividness of phrase, and concern themselves with construction rather than motive, with means rather than the result.

> We therefore cannot accept a book's adoption by another land or the approval of critics as conclusive of nonobscenity under the statute, for we may assert with pride—thought not boastfully—that we are essentially an idealistic and spiritual nation and exact a higher standard than some others.

Experts often can be divided in appraising a community's contemporary standards. This became evident in Chicago in 1935, when Mayor Edward J. Kelly banned performances of the play *Tobacco Road*. In the ensuing litigation one camp of expert witnesses, including the mayor, a former governor, a circuit judge, and members of the bar, felt that the play offered more obscenity than Chicagoans wished to tolerate. Another group of eminent witnesses, including ministers, a professor of literature, and members of civic dramatic organizations, saw no objection to the play and indeed thought it inspiring. The first group, said the Seventh Circuit Court of Appeals, "sees obscenity unexcused by any motive and unredeemed by good intent."[35] The second "sees revolting realism wholly excused, by the further and nobler intent of inspiring desire to remedy evil conditions." In any event, said the court, Mayor Kelly was not being merely arbitrary and capricious in his assessment of community standards, and his ban was upheld.

That same year a magistrate's court in New York ably summarized these considerations of contemporary public morals.[136] At stake was the prosecution of one Herbert Miller, at the instance of the New York Society for Suppression of Vice, for selling a copy of Flaubert's *November*. Commented the magistrate:

> The criterion of decency is fixed by time, place, geography and all the elements that make for a constantly changing world. A practice regarded as decent in one period may be indecent in another. The practice of "bundling" approved in Puritan days would be frowned upon today. . . . Twenty-five years ago women

were arrested and convicted for appearing on the beach in sleeveless bathing suits, or without stockings.

The language of the law under which they were convicted is identical with the language of the statute today. The ordinance required the wearing of bathing suits that would not "indecently" expose the body. While the language of the ordinance has remained unchanged, the public point of view has undergone distinct change.

In 1906 the play *Sappho* was suppressed because the leading lady was carried up a flight of stairs in the arms of a man. In 1907, Mary Garden was prevented from appearing in the opera *Salome*. I could multiply such examples endlessly. Whether we like it or not, the fact is that the public concept of decency has changed. What was regarded as indecent in the days of the Floradora Sextette, is decent in the days of the Fan and Bubble Dances.

It is not my function as a judge to express agreement or disagreement with the present accepted standards.

To change standards of morals is the task of school and church; the task of the judge is to record the tides of public opinion, not to emulate King Canute in an effort to turn back the tide. My duty is to act as observer and recorder, not as regulator.

The only question before him, said the magistrate, was this: is Flaubert's *November* obscene in the Fourth District of the Borough of Manhattan, in May of 1935? His answer was no.

The acquittal of Flaubert was followed a few months later by a not guilty verdict for André Gide.[133] John S. Sumner, secretary of the New York Society for the Suppression of Vice, perceiving in Gide's autobiography some vice worth suppressing, brought charges against the Gotham Book Mart for selling an obscene book. The case came on for trial before Magistrate Nathan D. Perlman, one of the group of magistrates who kept their heads in this period while Mr. Sumner was losing his, and Judge Perlman threw the case out. Echoing the theme of his brother magistrates, Judge Perlman remarked that standards of morality change from one generation to another: "The heroine of the American novel is no longer the girl making cookies in the kitchen." The court found nothing in Gide's personal revelations that might be obscene by New York's standards.

This was the same view taken in Massachusetts some years later, in the *Strange Fruit* case.[47] The effect of a book, said the court, must be judged "in the light of customs and habits of thought of the time and place of the alleged offense."

So, too, a federal court refused to sustain the Post Office's ban on Paul Popenoe's marriage pamphlet, prepared for the American Institute of Family Relations in 1945.[273] Postmaster General Frank C. Walker thought the leaflet obscene, and in one era this view might have been justified. But "there are no absolute and enduring standards of what is obscene; the border line between obscenity and decency changes with the times, with public taste in literature and with public attitudes on sex instruction."

Probably the most significant case in this area of the law was the long and drawn-out case of Murray Winters, a New York bookdealer convicted in 1941 of selling obscene magazines in violation of the state law. The magazine was *Headquarters Detective*. At the time the law forbade the sale of any magazine "principally made up of criminal news, police reports, or accounts of criminal deeds, or pictures, or stories of deeds of bloodshed, lust or crime."

Winters' case reached the Court of Appeals of New York in the summer of 1945. The court gazed distastefully upon the exhibits in the case; the magazines dealt with fiendish and gruesome crimes, and it was not suggested that any of the contributors was distinguished by his place in the literary world or by the quality of his style. The court felt that obscenity "is a question of the times which must be determined as a matter of fact," and in the court's view, the times regarded *Headquarters Detective* as obscene.

It was March of 1948 before the Supreme Court of the United States, after twice hearing reargument, at last handed down an opinion in the *Winters* case.[275] By a 6-3 vote, with Frankfurter, Jackson, and Burton passionately dissenting, the court majority reversed the conviction and held the New York statute invalid by reason of vagueness. The majority went to some pains to recognize the states' police power to minimize incentives to crime, "particularly in the field of sanguinary or salacious publications with their stimulation of juvenile delinquency." The court also asserted flatly that magazines are "subject to control if they are lewd, indecent, obscene or profane." In this case, however, the majority felt that the detective magazines under review—"though we can see nothing of any possible value to society in these magazines"—were as much entitled to the protection of free speech as the best of literature.

The appellate courts of New York had construed the state law to prohibit the publication of crime stories "so massed as to become vehicles for inciting violent and depraved crimes." In this sense the magazines were indeed obscene: they "plainly carried an appeal to that portion of the public who (as many recent records remind us) are disposed to take to vice for its own sake." And the New York Court of Appeals had said this:

> In the nature of things there can be no more precise test of written indecency and obscenity *than the continuing and changeable experience of the community* as to what types of books are likely to bring about the corruption of public morals or other analagous injury to the public order. Consequently, a question as to whether a particular publication is indecent or obscene in that sense *is a question of the times which must be determined as a matter of fact,* unless the appearances are thought to be necessarily harmless from the standpoint of public order or morality. [Emphasis supplied.]

Nevertheless Justice Stanley Reed and his five brothers found New York's law "too uncertain and indefinite" to justify Winters' conviction. To uphold his conviction, said the majority, would be to make it utterly impossible for authors and publishers of detective stories to know where a standard of guilt might be drawn.

Frankfurter, joined by Jackson and Burton, assailed the majority's decision bitterly. In their view, Reed and the others had managed to strike down similar statutes from Connecticut, Illinois, Iowa, Kansas, Kentucky, Maine, Maryland, Massachusetts, Michigan, Minnesota, Missouri, Montana, Nebraska, North Dakota, Ohio, Oregon, Pennsylvania, Washington, and Wisconsin. The New York law under which Winters was convicted had been in effect for more than sixty years.

"This body of laws," said the dissenters, "represents but one of the many attempts by legislatures to solve what is perhaps the most persistent, intractable, elusive, and demanding of all problems of society—the problem of crime, and more particularly, of its prevention." In striking down New York's law (and, by inference, the laws of nineteen other states) on the grounds of "indefiniteness," the majority had itself applied an indefinite criterion. There was nothing so reckless in the New York law, said the dissenters, as to justify the majority in holding it void. After all, said Frankfurter, it would be a bold man indeed "who is confident that he knows what causes crime."

Those whose lives are devoted to an understanding of the problem are certain only that they are uncertain regarding the role of the various alleged "causes" of crime. Bibliographies of criminology reveal a depressing volume of writings on theories of causation. . . . Is it to be seriously questioned, however, that the state of New York, or the Congress of the United States, may make incitement to crime itself an offense? He too would indeed be a bold man who denied that incitement may be caused by the written word no less than by the spoken. If "the Fourteenth Amendment does not enact Mr. Herbert Spencer's Social Statics" [quoting Holmes in the *Lochner* case, 198 U. S. 45], neither does it enact the psychological dogmas of the Spencerian era. The painful experience which resulted from confusing economic dogmas with constitutional edicts ought not to be repeated by finding constitutional barriers to a state's policy regarding crime, because it may run counter to our inexpert psychological assumptions or offend our presuppositions regarding incitements to crime in relation to the curtailment of utterance.

Frankfurter also leaped upon the majority's description of the detective magazines as having "nothing of any possible value to society." Such a description, he snorted, "merely denies them goodness. It disregards their mischief."

The essence of the Court's decision is that it gives publications which have "nothing of any possible value to society" constitutional protection but denies to the states the power to prevent the grave evils to which, in their rational judgment, such publications

THE ROTH-ALBERTS CASE 135

give rise. The legislatures of New York and the other states were concerned with these evils and not with neutral abstractions of harmlessness.

This long dissent by Frankfurter in the *Winters* case should be read and studied by any person who seeks to understand the law of obscenity. His is one of the great liberal minds on the court, yet the tides of his liberalism are profoundly affected—most of the time—by the conservative pull of the Constitution. This tug and haul of the Republic's basic law constantly remind him that the states have the power to legislate broadly under their inherent police power, subject only to the clear prohibitions of the Constitution itself. And such state laws are valid, he insisted, even though they may be wrongly applied now and then.[16]

One significant point that grew out of the *Winters* case is that obscenity, as a matter of law, must relate to the sexually obscene. Violence alone is not enough, nor crime, nor even, in itself, profane language. The "contemporary community standard" that figures in obscenity prosecutions is the community's standard of sexual mores. The point was made in California in 1954, when District Judge Ernest A. Tolin refused to sanction an "unlawful" order sought by Postmaster Otto Olesen against a movie-of-the-month club. The question was whether eleven girlie movies were nonmailably obscene. Judge Tolin felt a determination of the question required him to estimate some national standard of decency and modesty, no easy task "for supermen, let alone postmen and judges." But after allowing for a wide variety of tastes from coast to coast, he concluded the films were not obscene. They portrayed young women dancing, in various bumps and grinds that Postmaster Olesen regarded as sexually suggestive, but the court found this no worse than "the great bulk of modern dancing." The girls wore "something considerably less than usual street dress," but their costumes were not materially less than modern beach wear. The court added this:

While probably some individuals might derive some sexual provocation from a viewing of the films, these same people would find equal or more stimulation from a perusal of the underwear advertisements in the daily papers, or in viewing the ballet or modern stage presentations, or in reading any one of many classics, or in viewing public parades or the holiday assemblages of persons at public beaches. These films are not unlike parts of major film productions of today shown, without challenge, at all theaters. The continued multimillion dollar gross from these major studio presentations *indicates their community acceptance*. To say the films have no reference to sex, would be naïvete in the ultimate. However, all references to sex are not unmailable. It is those references which violate and offend the common sense of decency and modesty of the community and which are calculated to promote the general corruption of morals, that are unmailable. [Emphasis supplied.]

The Supreme Court was to emphasize this very point in its *Roth* decision, and it is one that local law-enforcement officers and citizens' groups should keep firmly in mind: *sex and obscenity are not synonymous*. It is almost equally important to keep in mind that nudism and obscenity are not synonymous either. In each case one of the key considerations is the extent to which a community will tolerate some form of sexual discussion or some degree of undress.

This was made clear in one of the landmark decisions in the obscenity field, the decision of the U.S. Court of Appeals for the District of Columbia in *Parmelee* v. *United States* in 1940.[117] Maurice Parmelee had imported from England six books, collectively entitled *Nudism in Modern Life*. It was conceded that the text of the books contained no obscene material; however, each book contained three or four small unretouched photographs of nude men and women. The trial judge held the photographs obscene, and ordered the books confiscated.

Parmelee appealed. The higher court split as sharply as the Second Circuit Court had split on *Ulysses*. Associate Justice Wilbur K. Miller and Chief Justice Fred M. Groner thought the books not obscene, and ordered the lower decision reversed and the proceeding dismissed. Associate Justice Vinson thought the books plainly offensive to community standards and dissented from his colleagues. Both the majority and the minority made some excellent points, and together they compiled an impressive annotation on the law of obscenity.

Two key points were advanced by Justice Miller in the majority opinion: first, that the word "obscene" is not susceptible to exact definition, and more particularly, that it cannot be assumed that nudity is obscene in itself and under all circumstances; second, that times change, and what is legally obscene at one time, in one community, may not be legally obscene sometime later and somewhere else.

"It is customary to see, now, in the daily newspapers and in the magazines, pictures of modeled male and female underwear which might have been shocking to readers of an earlier era," said the court. Nudity in art is not obscene; nude photographs and illustrations in medical treatises, once frowned upon, now are everywhere permitted.

It is apparent that civilization has advanced far enough, at last, to permit picturization of the human body for scientific and educational purposes. That fact is decisive of the present case. The picturization here challenged has been used in the libeled book to accompany an honest, sincere, scientific and educational study and exposition of a sociological phenomenon and is, in our opinion, clearly permitted by present-day concepts of propriety.

Associate Justice Vinson, dissenting, complained that his colleagues had "evidently concluded that the country-wide sense of decency has altered in the past few years to the extent that in the present day only a Rip Van Winkle could regard the book in question as obscene." He disagreed. In his view the law on obscenity—whether or not one followed *Hicklin-Bennett* or *Ulysses*—was clear: obscenity must be judged by the effect of a book upon a reasonable man, applying contemporary community standards. And he made the point, which carries substantial weight, that higher courts should exercise the greatest care in substituting the personal opinions of appellate judges for the verdict of trial judges or jurors in lower courts.

"Accepting the premise that 'time marches on,'" said Justice Vinson, "I am nevertheless unable to agree that we have here and now 'progressed' to the point where a publication of this character is, beyond the possibility of reasonable difference of opinion, acceptable to the community. This publication, it must be repeated, is to be judged in the light of the present-day standard, not that of the world of tomorrow."

One may agree with everything Vinson had to say in those dissenting comments and yet make the point that he failed to comprehend one of the most essential factors in any fair judicial appraisal of obscenity. The nudity in the Parmelee book was merely incidental to the sociological and anthropological theme of the book. And this is the third of the five factors the *Roth* decision nailed into the law in 1957. The test, to continue, is whether to the average person, applying contemporary community standards,

the dominant theme of the material . . .

An excellent example of the difficulties that lie in weighing isolated offensive material on the one hand and the dominant theme of the material on the other may be found in a series of cases involving prosecution of nudist magazines. Sometimes the decisions have gone one way, sometimes the other. Thus a nudist magazine may be obscene in Arkansas,[79] New York,[127,184,67] and North Dakota,[230] but not obscene in Ohio,[178] and not obscene where it counts most of all, in the view of the Supreme Court of the United States.[186]

Some of these questions were discussed by the Supreme Court of New York County in 1952, in denying an injunction sought by the Sunshine Book Company against New York's License Commissioner Edward T. McCaffrey.[184] It appeared that Mr. McCaffrey had sent a notice to newsdealers, advising them their licenses would be revoked if they continued to sell *Sunshine and Health, Sunbathing for Health,* and other nudist magazines. The publishers, complaining of prior restraint, sought a court order to suppress the McCaffrey attack.

The court did not agree with the plaintiff publishers that such prior restraint was unlawful. A community is not helpless, said Justice Thomas L. J. Corcoran, to prevent the open and continuous sale of obscene publications. In this case the nudist magazines featured innocuous articles combined with provocative photographs—front views "cleverly colored to picture clearly the female breasts and pubic hair." This sort of thing was "obscene and indecent in the state of New York in the year 1952," and that was all that mattered:

The statute prohibits obscenity and indecency as we understand those terms in this state today. It is true that in determining what is obscene, "the law will not hold the crowd to the morality of saints and seers" (Cardozo, *Paradoxes of Legal Science,* p. 37). But neither will it accept the judgment of sensualists and libertines. Nor is a criterion of proper conduct to be established by the antics of faddists. The test of decency is the fair judgment of reasonable adults in the community.

The court went on to say some cold and realistic things about the nudist magazines. These publications profess to be no more than journals of the nudist cult, dedicated to health, to sunbathing, and to innocent reflection upon the form divine. Nonsense, said the New York court:

> *Where the dominant purpose of nudity is to promote lust, it is obscene and indecent.* The distribution and sale of the magazines in this case is a most objectionable example. The dominant purpose of the photographs in these magazines is to attract the attention of the public by an appeal to their sexual impulses. The sale of these magazines is not limited to any mailing list of members or subscribers. They are sold and distributed indiscriminately to all who wish to purchase the same. . . . They will have a libidinous effect upon most ordinary, normal, healthy individuals. Their effect upon the abnormal individual may be more disastrous. Their sale and distribution is bound to add to the already burdensome problem of juvenile delinquency and sex crimes. . . . [Emphasis supplied.]

Three years later Judge Samuel E. Driver of Spokane applied substantially the same criteria in the West.[230] Customs authorities had seized a large number of paperbound books and magazines coming from abroad—4,200 copies of the nudists' *International Journal,* 2,000 copies of *Sunshine and Health,* 1,800 copies of *Helios,* 500 volumes of *Tidlosa,* and others.

The importers staunchly insisted that they perceived nothing obscene in nudist magazines, and put both a mother and a grandmother on the witness stand to say they saw nothing obscene in them either.

"But nudism is a deviation from the norm at the present time in the United States," said Judge Driver, and "its practitioners are very much in the minority and cannot be said to represent the common viewpoint in this country." The average American, for whom the statute is designed, finds "a brazen display of the adult male and female genitalia indecent and shocking."

Because of the dominant emphasis placed in these photographs on "normally private areas," Judge Driver held the publications obscene under the customs law. He commented that the magazines were not imported solely for the benefit of members of the nudist cult, but rather were to be sold to the public generally. "In this connection," he added drily, "it is interesting to note that of the twenty-seven publications introduced in evidence, twenty have on the front cover prominently displayed nude pictures of well-developed, shapely young women. One would be naïve, indeed, not to appreciate the commercial value of displaying such front-cover material on the newsstands."

But the nudist magazines fared much better at about this same time in Washington, D. C., where Postmaster General Summerfield engaged in five years of siege operations to keep them from the mails. Early in 1954 Summerfield sought to prohibit the delivery of mail to the Sunshine Book Company under Section 259a of the postal laws. The company's publications were typical nudist magazines, though at the time some of the photographs depicted the sexual parts of their subjects. (Today pubic parts are retouched in most American nudist publications offered for general sale). The P.M.G. felt the photographs obscene, but Judge Henry A. Schweinhaut disagreed and granted the publishers a permanent injunction.

Summerfield appealed and found a somewhat more favorable forum in the Circuit Court of Appeals for the District of Columbia.[183] This court upheld the basic constitutionality of the 259a procedure, and Judge John A. Danaher had no doubt that the photographs were obscene. Nonetheless the court concluded that the effect of the "unlawful" order—and this was an important point—was to suppress *future* editions of a magazine on a finding that *past* issues were obscene. This was prior censorship, and the court did not intend to permit it.

Undaunted, General Summerfield returned to the wars with an order under Section 1461, the basic nonmailability statute, refusing to accept for mailing, specifically, the February, 1955, issue of *Sunshine and Health* and the January-February issue of *Sun* magazine.

In the department's view these issues were "obscene and indecent when judged by the ordinary community standards of the vast majority of citizens of this country." Judge James R. Kirkland, making a desperate effort to bring system to a field of law that cannot be systematized, accepted the department's contention. The court ruled that silhouettes and drawings of nude persons were not obscene; photographs retouched to eliminate pubic areas were not obscene; photographs taken from a considerable distance, even if they showed pubic areas, were not obscene; posterior views of male and female were not ordinarily obscene; side views, not revealing genitalia, ditto; pictures of children under the age of seven, though such pictures might reveal diminutive and undeveloped genitalia, also not obscene. Wielding this clumsy yardstick, Judge Kirkland measured the magazines in question; he concluded that many of the pictures were indeed obscene, lewd, and lascivious when judged by contemporary community standards, and he had no trouble in finding that the dominant theme of the issues was an obscene treatment of sexual interest.

By the time Judge Kirkland's ruling reached the circuit court, the *Roth* case had been decided, and the circuit court applied the new language. A majority affirmed: the magazines "deal with sex in a manner appealing to prurient interest." Three members dissented, and their objections evidently were well founded. They felt that in the absence of a judicial proceeding, in which a judge or jury had passed upon the specific questions of obscenity in each particular case, the postmaster general had no authority to bar any publication from the mails as a consequence of purely departmental proceedings. Moreover, in view of the innocuous text of the magazines, they doubted that the publications *as a whole* were obscene in any event. The Supreme Court of the United States refused to discuss the case. In a characteristically terse *per curiam* order it reversed the lower courts in January of 1958 and ordered the magazines admitted to the mails. General Summerfield withdrew.

Just as nudity is not to be equated with obscenity, so discussion of sex must not be equated with obscenity. In every case a publication must be examined in terms of its dominant characteristics. This was emphasized by the United States Court of Appeals for the District of Columbia in 1945, in upholding an injunction obtained by the American Institute of Family Relations against Postmaster General Walker.[273] The P.M.G. had attempted to bar from the mails a pamphlet by Paul Popenoe, "Preparing for Marriage," but a trial court granted the requested injunction against him, and the appellate court affirmed. Associate Justice Henry White Edgerton, abandoning the precepts of *Hicklin,* held that "the effect of a publication on the ordinary reader is what counts," and moreover, "the dominant effect of an entire publication determines its character." The pamphlet constituted a serious, decent treatise on family relations, and though isolated phrases, by reason merely of their subject matter, "may stimulate the senses of some persons," this was no reason to bar the pamphlet from the mails.

In passing, it may be noted that the court objected especially to the procedure the Post Office Department had followed. Walker had taken the view that he had power "to exclude from the mails, without a hearing, any publication which in his judgment was obscene." Such a procedure, by which a postmaster general may cause "irreparable injury to a publisher without the minimum safeguard of an opportunity to present his case," is a denial of due process. Said the court:

> To deprive a publisher of the use of the mails is like preventing a seller of goods from using the principal highway which connects him with his market. In making a determination whether any publication is obscene, the postmaster general necessarily passes on a question involving the fundamental liberty of a citizen. This is a judicial and not an executive function. It must be exercised according to the ideas of due process implicit in the Fifth Amendment. . . . There are no absolute and enduring standards of what is obscene. The border line between obscenity and decency changes with the times, with public taste in literature and with public attitudes on sex instruction. The determination of whether a publica-

tion violates such changing standards is certainly one which should not be undertaken without a hearing.

In thus granting judicial approval to "Preparing for Marriage," the court in Washington was echoing some observations made in 1934 by the Supreme Court of New York in construing the sort of questions that must be asked of a work about sex. Is the dominant theme of a book or pamphlet likely "to lower the standards of right and wrong as to the sexual relation"? Is the theme one of "sexual impurity"? Is the result "the exciting of lecherous thoughts and desire"? A work that deals with sex, and does none of these things, is not obscene. On the other hand, the court thought, "filth, however it may be bedizened or its grossness concealed, must remain plain filth in all ages."[120]

But is this so? The *Roth* opinion denies it. Filth is or is not filth according to community standards at any given time. The point may be made by recalling the judgment rendered against Dial Press by a magistrate's court on Staten Island, in banning *The First Lady Chatterley*. In the view of Magistrate Charles Keutgen: "The author's central theme and the dominant effect of the whole book is that it is dangerous to the physical and mental health of a young woman to remain continent . . . and that the most important thing in her life, more important than any rule of law or morals, is the gratification of her sexual desire."[124] The book was "clearly obscene"; in other words, filth. This was in 1944. Fifteen years later, in the eyes of another New York judge, Lawrence's Lady Constance was no filthier than the Bobbsey twins.[77]

As New York's Justice Louis I. Kaplan once commented, in upholding a conviction for sale of an obscene magazine: "Obscenity is an indefinable something in the minds of some and not in the minds of others, and it is different depending upon the individual's taste, occasion, background, and time. It is not the same today as it was yesterday or will be tomorrow." This is a far wiser rule than the rule of "filth once, filth always." In the case before Judge Kaplan, the dominant theme of a stag magazine, judged by 1958 community standards, was of "sex, indelicately treated and unrestrainedly emphasized," and this dominant theme was "of such a character and so pervades the publication as to give the whole a sensual and licentious quality calculated to produce the harm the statute was intended to prevent."[140] The conviction was upheld; but just a few weeks later, in Kings County Court an issue of *Gent* magazine, by precisely the same standards, was found not obscene.[122] The magazine's dominant theme was sex, but it was sex with "reasonable accuracy and balance."

This brief discussion of the "dominant theme" factor may be concluded with a reference to the *Tropics* case, one of the more significant obscenity prosecutions of its day.

In 1948 Henry Miller republished in Paris his two autobiographical works of the 1930's, *Tropic of Cancer* and *Tropic of Capricorn*. Two years later Ernest J. Besig, director of the American Civil Liberties Union in San Francisco, attempted to import the two books into the United States. The books were libeled by the government in August of 1950, under Section 1305 of the United States Code, and Besig sued for the books' release.

He hit an unsympathetic judge in Louis E. Goodman, who read the books, and denounced them in stinging terms:

> In my opinion the dominant effect of the two respondent books is obscene. Both books are replete with long passages that are filthy and revolting and that tend to excite lustful thoughts and desires. While the books also have passages, and indeed chapters, that may be said to have literary merit, the obscene portions have no literary value; they are directly, completely and wholly filthy and obscene and have no reasonable relation to any literary concept inherent in the books' theme.
>
> I should like very much to observe Mr. Besig reading the innumerable filthy passages in the books to young people of his acquaintance. If he is the high-minded person that I have believed him to be, I would expect all thoughts of "free speech" and "civil liberties" to then and there disappear into complete desuetude. . . . "Civil liberties" and "freedom of speech" are certainly not synonymous with license and obscenity.

Judge Goodman made these comments in denying Besig's motion to take the depositions of nineteen literary critics, at home and abroad, in support of Miller's reputation as a serious writer, and in defense of the *Tropics* as works of literature.[262] A year later the case came on for actual trial before Judge Goodman, in the absence of a jury. By that time Besig had obtained, and offered in evidence, eighteen reviews of Miller's work and seventeen statements from critics describing the books in terms of literary merit. Judge Goodman was not at all impressed.[263]

The claimant here, as well as some of the critics and reviewers who speak in his behalf, have presented a species of "confession and avoidance" defense of Henry Miller. The many long filthy descriptions of sexual experiences, practices and organs are of themselves admitted to be lewd. They are sought to be justified by the claim that the books as a whole have an artistic pattern, into which the obscene and scatological portions fit as part of a whole literary mosaic. But I must conclude that this is mere sophistry. The filthy scatological portions are written in a bluntly different and distinct style from the pretentious metaphysical reflective manner of writing otherwise. Thus the conclusion is justified that either the alleged literary ability of the author deserted him or that he had his eye on "the box office."

It may be that the modern trend toward frankness in sexual matters has influenced the viewpoint of claimant and the critics who espouse the cause of Miller. Certainly the theater, the moving pictures, other similar media and Mr. Kinsey may have affected our attitude as to such matters. It is sufficient to say, however, that the many obscene passages in the books have such an evil stench that to include them here in footnotes would make this opinion pornographic. For example, there are several passages where the female sexual organ and its function are described and referred to in such detailed and vulgar language as to create nausea in the reader. If this be importable literature, then the dignity of the human person and the stability of the family unit, which are the cornerstones of society, are lost to us.

Besig appealed Judge Goodman's decision to the Ninth Circuit Court of Appeals, but he fared no better there.[17] On October 23, 1953, the appellate court unanimously affirmed the government's position. In an opinion by Circuit Judge Albert Lee Stephens, the court picked up where Judge Goodman had left off:

> The vehicle of description is the unprintable word of the debased and morally bankrupt. Practically everything that the world loosely regards as sin is detailed in the vivid, lurid, salacious language of smut, prostitution, and dirt. And all of it is related without the slightest expressed idea of its abandon. Consistent with the general tenor of the books, even human excrement is dwelt upon in the dirtiest words available. The author conducts the reader through sex orgies and perversions of the sex organs, and always in the debased language of the bawdy house. Nothing has the grace of purity or goodness. . . .

In brief, "dirt appears as the primary purpose rather than the relation of a fact or adequate description of the incident." And in reaching that conclusion, the court had accepted the contention of the defense that Miller's books should be considered in their entirety and not on the basis of isolated passages. This was the point the *Roth* case also was to accept, as the second of its clean breaks with *Hicklin*. The first break was in replacing the "susceptible" person with the "average" person; now the court was to reject the old rule by which one touch of obscenity could contaminate an entire book. The *Roth* test, continuing, is whether to the average person, applying contemporary community standards, the dominant theme of the material

taken as a whole . . .

In the early years of obscenity prosecutions, following adoption of the Comstock Act, courts held almost without exception that books or magazines need not be viewed as a whole; the custom was to mark offending passages in red, and either to read these parts to a jury or to pass the exhibits to jurors for their silent perusal. The rule was applied to newspapers[224] and magazines[46] just as it was applied to books; one ad, or one article, was sufficient to convict. (To a degree the rule obtains to this day, and it probably would accord with *Roth* when applied as the rule was applied by the

Superior Court of Pennsylvania in upholding a conviction based upon the sale of *Tipster* magazine. The court said it had no fault to find with the statement that in determining whether a work is obscene "it must be construed as a whole and that regard shall be had for its place in the arts." In this case, however, the filthy items and articles within the magazine bore no relation to other items and articles; they stood alone and were to be judged in their separate totalities. So judged they were plainly obscene. A New Hampshire court, in 1958, threw out an issue of *Manhunt* magazine when a single color drawing, unintentionally flawed in retouching or engraving, apparently depicted a man with an erect organ; in this case the lone drawing constituted the "material to be taken as a whole.")

The more significant decisions in this area of obscenity law always have involved books. The question of whether a book must be considered as a whole was considered in 1906 by Judge Willis Van Devanter, as a circuit judge prior to his elevation to the Supreme Court. A Minneapolis printer, Burton, had entered into a contract with a local doctor, Malchow, for publishing and writing a book of sex advice. Their principal defense, when they were cited under postal laws, was that only a part of their work, at best, was obscene. Judge Van Devanter was ready to concede that brief extracts would not suffice for conviction in such a case, but here, even with much of the book eliminated from consideration, enough remained to send Burton and Malchow before the jury.[30] Van Devanter, who hated smut, re-emphasized his point a few weeks later in affirming the conviction of a Trinidad, Colorado, newspaper editor for publishing two obscene articles in a labor weekly: "It is not essential to the commission of the offense proscribed by the statute that the entire contents of the newspaper, or other parcel, deposited in the mail, be objectionable in character."[53]

Van Devanter's uncompromising views were not universally shared. Two years later the Seventh Circuit Court had occasion to review the conviction of one Konda, who had mailed out a sixty-nine-page pamphlet identified as "A Victim of Circumstances, or, Memoirs of a Carnolian Priest."[93] Nothing at all was complained of in more than half the sixty-nine pages; from the other pages "excerpts were taken here and there." The Seventh Circuit did not approve:

Now these excerpts may have correctly disclosed the scope and tone of the pamphlet. On the other hand, when they were thus taken from their settings and deprived of the support of their full context, it may be that they did not fairly represent the character of the work. For instance, the results of an investigation into the conduct of some of our penal and charitable institutions possibly might be set forth in a way capable of arousing libidinous passions; or the same results might be framed in an attack upon wrongs and an appeal for correction, so that they would stir up, not lecherous thoughts, but only reformative instincts. So in this case . . . it was wrong to base the decision on the untested assumption that the excerpts truly gauged the scope and character of the pamphlet.

By the early twenties, however, some rebel voices were being heard. The Court of Appeals of New York struck a blow for reason in 1922, when it affirmed an award of damages to Raymond D. Halsey in a suit for damages against Sumner and the New York Society for the Suppression of Vice.[81] Sumner had arrested the bookdealer for selling a copy of Gautier's *Mademoiselle de Maupin,* a book published originally in 1835. The case came on for trial and a jury promptly set Halsey free. The outraged bookdealer turned upon Sumner and sued him, with evident success, for malicious prosecution.

The Court of Appeals divided sharply in reviewing the suit. Five members of the court, speaking through Judge William S. Andrews, held that Gautier's work was so plainly *not* obscene that there was not even probable cause for Sumner to have sought Halsey's arrest in the first place. The majority conceded freely that many paragraphs, taken by themselves, were vulgar and indecent; but looking thirty-five years into the future, the New York court of 1922 had this to say:

No work may be judged from a selection of such paragraphs alone. Printed by themselves they might, as a matter of law, come within the prohibition of the statute. So might a similar selection from Aristophanes, or Chaucer, or Boccaccio, or even from the Bible. The book, however, must be considered broadly, as a whole. . . .

And viewed in this way the book plainly did not impress the majority as obscene; in any event its obscenity was not so immediately apparent that Halsey's guilt was obvious. What counted was the jury's opinion—the opinion of men "drawn from those of varied experiences, engaged in various occupations, in close touch with the currents of public feeling, fitted to say whether the defendant had reasonable cause to believe that a book such as this was obscene or indecent."

In a dissenting opinion Judge Frederick Crane said tartly that *he* thought Sumner had abundant probable cause to have Halsey arrested. The book in his eyes was plainly obscene: "If the things said by Gautier in this book . . . were stated openly and frankly in the language of the street, there would be no doubt in the minds of anybody that the work would be lewd, vicious, and indecent. . . . Gautier may have a reputation as a writer, but his reputation does not create a license for the American market. The fact that the disgusting details are served up in a polished style, with exquisite settings and perfumed words, makes it all the more dangerous and insidious, and none the less obscene and lascivious."

Unhappily Judge Crane's views prevailed in this period more often than the views of his colleagues prevailed. In various censorship proceedings, works of Sinclair Lewis, James Branch Cabell, Upton Sinclair, Scott Fitzgerald, Ernest Hemingway, and Erich Remarque fell under censorial ban. Sam Roth himself, it may be recalled, suffered his first jail sentence at this time for selling *Ulysses* in Philadelphia. These assaults upon works of literary merit reached a climax in Massachusetts in May of 1930, when the State Supreme Judicial Court upheld the conviction of bookseller Donald Friede for offering Theodore Dreiser's *An American Tragedy* to his customers. Dreiser had encountered censorship trouble earlier for *The Genius* and *Sister Carrie,* but at least the censors had descended rapidly upon those earlier works. *An American Tragedy,* based upon the 1908 case of Chester Gillette and Grace Brown (the story is vividly told in *People* v. *Gillette,* 191 N. Y. 107), had appeared in 1925 as a two-volume work. It is generally forgotten now that H. L. Mencken, who was Dreiser's most loyal supporter in fighting for his freedom of expression, ripped into *An American Tragedy* as a "shapeless and

forbidding monster—a heaping cartload of raw materials for a
novel, with rubbish of all sorts intermixed—a vast, sloppy, chaotic
thing of 385,000 words—at least 250,000 of them unnecessary."
But if Mencken thought large parts of this tome dreadful bilge, he
was ready to do battle to defend Dreiser's right to publish a million
words if he chose, and the words Mencken regarded as unnecessary
were by no means the same words viewed as unnecessary by censors.
On the obscenity of these few passages Friede went to trial, with his
attorneys insisting lustily that the whole work—the whole two volumes—had to be read as a whole.

In affirming Friede's conviction the Massachusetts court gave its
approval to the "certain passages" rule.[103] The prosecution, during
trial of the case, had followed the prim and self-defeating example
of Don Juan's tutors, who, it will be remembered, had carefully excised the dirty passages from his schoolbooks and assembled them
in an appendix.

> . . . there we have them all "at one fell swoop,"
>   Instead of being scattered through the pages;
> They stand forth marshalled in a handsome troop,
>   To meet the ingenuous youth of future ages. . . .

Just so, Dreiser's stuffy references to the illicit love of Clyde and
Roberta were read *seriatim* to the jury; this and no more. Were these
passages, wrenched from context, sufficient to make the whole work
obscene? Were these passages, standing alone, likely to cause serious
corruption of the morals of youth? The Massachusetts court answered
yes.

"Even assuming great literary excellence, artistic worth and an
impelling moral lesson in the story," the court asserted, "there is
nothing essential to the history of the life of its principal character
that would be lost if these passages were omitted. . . . The seller
of a book which contains passages offensive to the statute has no
right to assume that children to whom the book might come would
not read the obnoxious passages or that if they should read them
would continue to read on until the evil effects of the obscene passages were weakened or dissipated with the tragic denouement of
a tale."

As it turned out, the court's opinion served a good purpose. For the first time, a large number of book lovers began to question seriously whether a responsible book, by a responsible author, should be banned because of isolated passages of "impure language." Arthur Garfield Hays, speaking for the defense, had argued strenuously that the level of reading matter permissible for adults ought not to be fixed by what might tend "to corrupt the morals of youth." Mencken ridiculed the opinion boisterously, and pressure mounted for a more sensible approach to the whole problem of censorship law. The following year Massachusetts abandoned the statute under which Friede had been convicted and adopted in its place a law requiring that books be considered as a whole. In 1945 the Massachusetts law was further revised to make separate offenses of sales to adults and sales to juveniles.

Back in New York, the uproar over the *An American Tragedy* decision bolstered city magistrates in a series of decisions limiting obscenity convictions to plain obscenity only. The acquittal of Flaubert, mentioned earlier, was soon followed by Magistrate Perlman's not-guilty verdict for André Gide.[133] Here the court solemnly spoofed the Vice Society's mathematical approach. It was not charged that the whole book was obscene, but only that seventy-six pages, or approximately one fifth, of the book were obscene. Indeed, marked paragraphs appeared on only twenty-two of these seventy-six pages, which would indicate (though the court did not actually compute it) an obscenity quotient of 5.789 per cent.

But the old rule of convicting on isolated passages no longer was to be observed, said Judge Perlman: "The determination of the issue may not be found in the slide rule. This is the tool of the engineer. Books are not so dissected. A book does not lend itself to either mathematical or comparative analysis." And he was not inclined to establish any "judge-made list of what people should or should not read."

Book lists, if they are to be prepared, I leave to other and more competent persons. Books, like friends, must be chosen by the readers themselves. We must pick and choose our friends in the book world just as we do in the real world, not looking for perfection in books any more than we do in people. The material must be coextensive with reality, and comprise the ugly as well as the beautiful. It is no part of the duty of courts to exercise a censorship over literary productions or to regulate manners or morals.

Nevertheless, Judge Perlman agreed, there are many books that "intentionally exploit smut," and these the law prohibits. In his view the author's intention was the main consideration: would a reasonable, cautious, and prudent man, considering the book as a whole and not merely in isolated passages, conclude that the book had been published "for no useful purpose, but simply from a desire to cater to the lowest and most sensual part of human nature"? If so, the book fell within the law's proscription.

What of Gide's autobiography? Judge Perlman turned to the critics, whose opinions on the book were divided, though their opinions on Gide were unanimous. He noted that Gide had a distinguished reputation. The court formed its own opinion that the section singled out by the Society for the Suppression of Vice, dealing with the author's homosexuality, contained paragraphs that taken by themselves "are undoubtedly vulgar and indecent." Considered in the context of a "penitent" work, they were vital to the book as a whole. Without them "we would have a distorted and untruthful picture of our subject." The book, he concluded, is not obscene.

On the same basis, however, the Supreme Judicial Court of Massachusetts convicted a seller of Strange Fruit. It was not the court's function to assume a liberal or a conservative attitude; it was the court's duty to set aside personal opinions, to avoid judicial legislation, and simply to enforce the public policy of Massachusetts. The public policy of Massachusetts now demanded that Lillian Smith's novel be considered as a whole and not on the basis of isolated passages; the problem was not to be solved by counting pages, but rather by considering the impressions likely to be created. The court counted impressions, found them all bad, and affirmed a trial court judgment.[47] Yet the same court shortly afterward let Forever Amber go free.[10]

Two years after the Strange Fruit decision in Massachusetts, the developing doctrine that an obscene publication must be considered as a whole gained support from an influential court when the Los Angeles Superior Court reversed the conviction of Harry Wepplo for selling a copy of Edmund Wilson's *Memoirs of Hecate County*.[147] The case actually turned on the state's failure to establish *scienter*— that is, that the bookseller knowingly sold an obscene book—but the Los Angeles court's solid acceptance of the *Isenstadt* (*Strange Fruit*) decision became a significant factor on the West Coast.

> In *Isenstadt,* the Massachusetts court had said that a book is not to be condemned merely because it may contain somewhere between its covers some expressions which, taken by themselves alone, might be obnoxious to the statute. But this does not mean that every page of the book must be of the character described in the statute before the statute can apply to the book. It could never have been intended that obscene matter should escape proscription simply by joining itself to some innocent matter. A reasonable construction can be attained only by saying that the book is within the statute if it contains prohibited matter in such quantity or nature as to flavor the whole and impart to the whole any of the qualities mentioned in the statute, so that the book as a whole can fairly be described by any of the adjectives or descriptive expressions contained in the statute.[47]

So far as the California court was concerned, Wilson's graphic account of the golden-haired princess so flavored the *Memoirs* as to make the whole book obscene. It made no difference what the critics said: "If the book sold by the defendant was in fact, obscene, judged by its contents, it would not become any less so because other book-dealers were selling it, or the public library had copies of it, or literary critics praise it as a work of literary merit, or because other books equally bad were being openly sold."

The doctrine that books must be considered in their entirety gained additional support from a widely quoted decision of the magistrate's court of mid-Manhattan in 1947 dismissing an obscenity charge against Vanguard Press based upon Charles O. Gorham's novel *The Gilded Hearse*.[148] The book told the story of one day in 1938 in the life of a young publicity director for a large book publishing house;

during the course of a bleak twenty-four hours, both husband and wife fall into acts of sexual infidelity. Unquestionably, said the court:

> the characters generally are a shoddy lot. How persons so emotionally immature, intellectually limited and morally bankrupt could achieve positions of responsibility in any field, particularly in book publishing, is difficult to comprehend. Their language is coarse and vulgar. They make occasional references to sexual contacts that are sophomoric and nasty. These references are, however, wholly incidental and are not descriptive. They are minor phrases and sentences serving in the aid of characterization.

Viewing the book as a whole, and weighing such factors as "the theme of the book, the degree of sincerity of purpose evident in it, its literary worth, the channels used in its distribution, contemporary attitudes toward the literary treatment of sexual behavior, and the types of readers (particularly with respect to age and intellectual development) reasonably to be expected to secure it for perusal," Magistrate Strong concluded that the book would not have any sexually demoralizing effect upon its readers. The adulterous acts of intercourse "contain little anatomical detail and refer only to momentary physical pleasure," and in both cases the acts are followed immediately by scenes of remorse, shame, and guilt. Nowhere does the book "invite to vice or voluptuousness."

The court was not especially impressed, in passing, with the proffered testimony of literary critics and voluntary letters in support of the book. Opinions of professional critics are "proper aids to the court in weighing the author's sincerity of purpose and the literary worth of his efforts," but such expressions of opinion can be of aid "only to the extent that [the court] determines it may rely upon them as disinterested and well founded."

Ten years later came the *Roth* decision, nailing the rule down that books must be considered as a whole; and since then, as in the case of John O'Hara's *Ten North Frederick,* assailed in Albany,[119] courts repeatedly have ruled that novels or other books cannot be considered on the basis of isolated passages. They must be read in full. And even as suspected books are read in full, one question must be kept constantly in mind: what is the purpose, the intention, of the book? For the fifth and final criteria of the *Roth* definition is the heart of the whole thing. The test is complete when a book is judged by whether (1) the average person, (2) applying contemporary community standards, finds that (3) the dominant theme of the material (4) when taken as a whole

appeals to prurient interest.

In the end, this is all that matters, and almost from the beginning of obscenity law in this country many judges have recognized the fact. "The law is founded on reason and common sense," said the Kansas district judge in the *Lucifer* case in 1889. "The statute was enacted to prevent the mails from being used to disseminate . . . those things *calculated and intended* to create and cater to a morbid appetite for obscenity and lewdness."[224] (Emphasis supplied.) And anticipating Justice Brennan almost seventy years later, the Kansas court asserted its determination to foster the widest latitude of discussion of all subjects of interest to the people: "Any thought which may contain the germ of an idea calculated to benefit any human being, when couched in decent language, ought to be disseminated among the people." Nevertheless, said the court, there is such a thing as obscenity, and it can be determined in any particular article *"by the place, manner, and object of its publication."* (Emphasis supplied.)

It is imperative, in any prosecution under an obscenity law, that consideration be given to these factors. Some effort must be made to get at the intention of the publisher, the author, or the distributor. Ordinarily this will be found no more difficult to establish than the intent of any other defendant in any other field of law. Some years ago, it is true, courts thought this question immaterial. In a famous case in 1909 a Federal judge convicted a newspaper writer in Deadwood, South Dakota, Freeman T. Knowles, for publishing a compassionate editorial pleading for some sympathy toward an unwed mother who had died as a consequence of an abortion. Knowles urged that his article contained a sincere discussion of an important social question and that he was actuated only by the highest motives. Said the court: "Such matters are immaterial in determining the issue here involved. His motive may have been never so pure; if the paper he mailed was obscene, he is guilty."[92]

The Supreme Judicial Court of Massachusetts, about the same time, felt this question of an author's intention was at least a jury question.[42] Joseph Buckley had been convicted for selling copies of a book, *Three Weeks*. He contended earnestly that there was not a dirty line in the book, and that while the book dealt with sex it was not intended to arouse depraved or immoral reactions. The court felt this was something for a jury to decide. An artist, engaged in painting a nude model, may not have the slightest impure thought, "but it by no means follows that if he should open wide the doors of his studio and fill it with people from the crowded streets, they would be moved by the same lofty and pure feelings." Just so with this book. Some readers might view it as a psychic study of a wanton woman, couched by the author in attractive literary style, "but such an author cannot expect that the reading public as a whole will so read her production." An author who had "disclosed so much of the way to the adulterous bed and who has kept the curtains raised in the way that the author of this book has kept them, can find no fault if the jury say that not the spiritual but the animal, not the pure but the impure, is what the general reader will find as *the most conspicuous thought suggested to him as he reads*." (Emphasis supplied.)

If this appeal—this "most conspicuous thought"—involves no deliberate cultivation of a prurient interest in sex, no obscenity is present. For this reason, books of sex education, responsibly prepared and responsibly advertised, ought not to be attacked as obscene though some persons may view them as immodest and even as distasteful. On this line of reasoning a Chicago company, specializing in mail-order remedies for venereal disease, back in 1907 won the right to mail its circulars. A federal circuit court agreed that the company's pamphlets made "repulsive reading," but their purpose was not "to pander to lascivious curiosity," and the questioned booklets were not mailed broadside but only upon specific request.[83] Similarly, in 1926 the Supreme Court of the United States reversed the conviction of a Texan, John Carlton Dysart, who had mailed circulars advertising a home for unwed mothers; the high court found nothing in the circulars calculated to corrupt anyone's mind.[57]

Three famous cases on this point arose in 1930 and 1931. The first of them centered upon Mary V. Dennett, a mother of two children who wished to teach her sons something about sex. Finding no instruction books that seemed to her sufficiently honest and detailed, she herself wrote a pamphlet, "Sex Side of Life." It proved a lively best seller, at twenty-five cents a copy. The YMCA, the YWCA, the Union Theological Seminaries, state public health departments, and hundreds of welfare and religious organizations ordered copies in quantity. No one seemed to see anything wrong in it until a copy came through the mails to a woman in Grottoes, Virginia. Then Mrs. Dennett was arrested and indicted for mailing an obscene publication; on conviction she was fined $300.

Judge Augustus N. Hand, speaking for the Second Circuit Court, ordered her conviction reversed. His opinion is a landmark in that area of the field covering medical or quasi-medical instruction in sex practices.[217] What was the nature of this pamphlet? Was it willfully lewd and lascivious? Was it intended to arouse sensual desires? The court said:

> It may be assumed that any article dealing with the sex side of life and explaining the functions of sex organs is capable in some circumstances of arousing lust. The sex impulses are present in every one, and without doubt cause much of the weal and woe of human kind. But it can hardly be said that, because of the risk of arousing sex impulses, there should be no instruction of the young in sex matters, and that the risk of imparting instruction outweighs the disadvantages of leaving them to grope about in mystery and morbid curiosity and of requiring them to secure such information, as they may be able to obtain, from ill-informed and often foul-minded companions, rather than from intelligent and high-minded sources. . . .
>
> The statute we have to construe was never thought to bar from the mails everything which *might* stimulate sex impulses. If so, much chaste poetry and fiction, as well as many useful medical works, would be under the ban. Like everything else, this law must be construed reasonably, with a view to the general objects aimed at. While there can be no doubt about its constitutionality, it must

not be assumed to have been designed to interfere with serious instruction regarding sex matters unless the terms in which the information is conveyed are clearly indecent.

The circuit court found nothing clearly indecent in Mrs. Dennett's pamphlet—indeed nothing indecent at all. Her booklet, written with sincerity of feeling and with an idealization of the marriage relation, tended to rationalize and dignify such emotions and not to arouse lust. And the court ruled in plain terms that "an accurate exposition of the relevant facts of the sex side of life in decent language and in manifestly serious and disinterested spirit cannot ordinarily be regarded as obscene."

Judge Hand's opinion in the Dennett case, involving postal laws, was buttressed the following year in the Southern District of New York, where Judge Woolsey dismissed the government's attempt, under customs laws, to ban the importation from England of Dr. Marie C. Stopes' *Married Love*.[254]

This was the Customs Bureau's second crack at the book. Nine years earlier a district judge in Philadelphia had rejected a seizure effort, but he had filed no opinion, and presumably fresh complaints had been leveled at the book. The proceeding was brought under Title 19, Section 1305, which prohibits any person from importing "any obscene book, pamphlet, paper, writing, advertisement, circular, print, picture, drawing or other representation, figure . . . or any article whatever for the prevention of conception. . . ."

As it happened, the copy of the book submitted to Judge Woolsey had been stripped of all references to contraception, so that the latter clause had no relevance. Judge Woolsey thought the clause probably would not have been relevant anyhow. He liked the book, and found nothing obscene in it. Marie Stopes' book does for adults, he said, what Mrs. Dennett's book does for adolescents. He continued:

I cannot imagine a normal mind to which this book would seem to be obscene or immoral within the proper definition of these words or whose sex impulses would be stirred by reading it.

Whether or not the book is scientific in some of its theses is unimportant. It is informative and instructive, and I think that any married folk who read it cannot fail to be benefited by its counsels of perfection and its frank discussion of the frequent difficulties which necessarily arise in the more intimate aspects of married life, for as Professor William G. Sumner used aptly to say in his lectures on the Science of Society at Yale, marriage, in its essence, is a status of antagonistic co-operation. In such a status, necessarily, centripetal and centrifugal forces are continuously at work, and the measure of its success depends on the extent to which the centripetal forces are predominant.

The book before me here has as its whole thesis the strengthening of the centripetal forces in marriage, and instead of being inhospitably received, it should, I think, be welcomed within our borders.

Judge Woolsey found another occasion to endorse Dr. Stopes' writings just three months later,[251] when the persistent customs authorities sought to ban importation of her book *Contraception*. Again, as he had done in the case of *Married Love,* Judge Woolsey firmly upheld the constitutionality of Section 1305 itself, but he pointed out that the plain language of the statute did not prohibit the importation of *books* about the prevention of conception, but only of "any *article* for the prevention of conception." The only grounds on which the book might be confiscated, he said, were those of obscenity, and the book was not obscene.

Contraception is written primarily for the medical profession. It is stated, in an introduction written by an eminent English doctor, to be the first book dealing fully with its subject matter— the theory, history, and practice of birth control. It is a scientific book written with obvious seriousness and with great decency, and it gives information to the medical profession regarding the operation of birth control clinics and the instruction necessary to be given at such clinics to the women who resort thereto. It tells of the devices used, now and in the past, to prevent conception, and expresses opinions as to those which are preferable from the point of view of efficiency and of the health of the user.

Such a book, although it may run counter to the views of many persons who disagree entirely with the theory underlying birth control, certainly does not fall within the test of obscenity or immorality laid down by me (in the case of *Married Love*), for the reading of it would not stir the sex impulses of any person with a normal mind.

"It would not stir the sex impulses. . . ." That is the test. The Bronx County Court of Special Sessions followed this reasoning in 1938, in dismissing a charge of obscenity against *Life* magazine for its photographic series on "The Birth of a Baby." The court concluded that *"because of the manner in which it was presented,"* the photographs could have no tendency to corrupt morals or to lower the standards of right and wrong.[134] Here the pictures were offered with evident honesty and sincerity, under the auspices of a responsible medical group; there was nothing furtive or salacious in the presentation.

By way of contrast, one may consider the case of Ben and Ann Rebhuhn, which reached the courts at about the same time.[158] They too were engaged in sex education—one of the books that figured in their trial was *Sex Life in England,* another dealt with the sex life of aborigines; and the courts were prepared to concede that most of their works were perhaps not in themselves obscene. But the defendants had made no effort to sell the books as serious works to a serious audience; they had mailed out thousands of circulars at random:

> They had indiscriminately flooded the mails with advertisements, plainly designed merely to catch the prurient, though under the guise of distributing works of scientific or literary merit. . . . The circulars were no more than appeals to the salaciously disposed, and no sensible jury could have failed to pierce the fragile screen set up to cover that purpose. . . . It needed less than the time they [the jurors] actually took for reasonably sagacious men and women to see exactly what the defendants had been doing, and how transparent was the pretense that they were not simply pandering to the lascivious cravings of their customers.[256]

Frequently, of course, it is a fine line that divides a work of honest sociological or literary value from a work produced primarily for its appeal to prurient interest. Thus the appellate division of New York's

Supreme Court divided in 1920 in a prosecution against Harper & Brothers for a book, *Madeleine,* the autobiography of an anonymous prostitute.[121] One member of the court thought the book "simply an effort to exploit prurient curiosity." The majority found nothing in the book that tended "to excite lustful or lecherous desire," though the majority could find no useful purpose in the work's publication.

Literary values are easier to detect, especially when they are old, leather-bound literary values. A mellowing process occurs, as in wine or cheese. Fifty-odd years ago the Supreme Court of New York made this clear by acquitting Voltaire of a charge of obscenity.[78] The court remarked that the last time the *Philosophical Dictionary* was judicially condemned "was in France in 1766, when, together with a youth who was suspected of an act of malicious mischief and in whose possession a copy of the book was found, it was publicly burned in the streets of Paris." As for a second work complained of, *The Maid of Orleans,* it had a history less tragic, "although sufficiently exciting to have given even the careless Voltaire many moments of anxiety for his own safety on account of it." But in New York of the early twentieth century, these works of Voltaire had no prurient appeal and they were not to be condemned on the basis of a few isolated passages.

It is a sudden jump from Voltaire to *Frankie and Johnny,* but some of the same legal principles were in the mind of the Court of Appeals of New York in 1932 in refusing to ban the play's performance in New York.[146] The play was undeniably coarse, vulgar, profane, cheap, tawdry, indecent, roughhewn, uncultured, and shocking to modesty. For all of that,

> It cannot be said to suggest, except to a prurient imagination, unchaste or lustful ideas. It does not counsel or invite vice or voluptuousness. It does not deride virtue. Unless we say that it is obscene to use the language of the street rather than that of the scholar, the play is not obscene under the penal law, although it might be so styled by the censorious.

A majority of the court emphasized that it was not intended to sanction indecency on the stage, or to let down the bars against immoral shows, or to hold that the depiction of scenes of bawdry on the stage is to be tolerated: "We hold merely that the fact that Frankie and Johnny and their companions were not nice people does not in itself make the play obscene."

Authors and playwrights are expected to deal now and then with people who are "not nice people." A magistrate's court in Manhattan said as much in an historic case in 1933, in refusing to convict Viking Press for publishing Erskine Caldwell's *God's Little Acre*.[145]

In defense of the book Viking Press rounded up an impressive display of favorable reviews and commendatory letters. The roll call is worth listing; more than a quarter of a century ago the fight for a serious author's freedom enlisted these warriors: Franklin Pierce Adams, William Soskin, Horace Gregory, James T. Farrell, Louis Kronenberger, Gilbert Seldes, Jonathan Daniels, Joseph Henry Jackson, Lewis Gannett, John Mason Brown, Sidonie M. Gruenberg, Solomon Lowenstein, Marc Connelly, Horace M. Kallen, Carl Van Doren, Herbert Bayard Swope, J. Donald Adams, Raymond Weaver, Malcolm Cowley, Henry S. Canby, Nathan Ottinger, Elmer Rice, John Cowper Powys, and Sinclair Lewis.

John S. Sumner, on behalf of the Vice Society, objected furiously to testimony from these writers and critics. The law was not meant for literati, he said. But Judge Benjamin Greenspan commented drily that he did not believe "so large and representative a group of people would rally to the support of a book which they did not genuinely believe to be of importance and literary merit." And looking squarely at Mr. Sumner, Judge Greenspan remarked that he felt these critics were better qualified "to judge the value of a literary production than one who is more apt to search for obscene passages in a book than to regard the book as a whole." Caldwell's novel, said the court, was undoubtedly an effort to paint a realistic picture:

Such pictures necessarily contain certain details. Because these details relate to what is popularly called the sex side of life, portrayed with brutal frankness, the court may not say that the picture should not have been created at all. The language, too, is undoubtedly coarse, and vulgar. The court may not require the author to put refined language into the mouths of primitive people.

Judge Greenspan said the novel, viewed as a whole, was clearly not a work of pornography; whether it was a work of literature was not his concern. But in any event:

> This is not a book where vice and lewdness are treated as virtues or which would tend to incite lustful desires in the normal mind. There is no way of anticipating its effect upon a disordered or diseased mind, and if the courts were to exclude books from sale merely because they might incite lust in disordered minds, our entire literature would very likely be reduced to a relatively small number of uninteresting and barren books. . . . Those who see the ugliness and not the beauty in a piece of work are unable to see the forest for the trees. I personally feel that the very suppression of books arouses curiosity and leads readers to endeavor to find licentiousness where none was intended. In this book, I believe the author has chosen to write what he believes to be the truth about a certain group in American life. To my way of thinking, truth should always be accepted as a justification for literature.

Some years later, when Kathleen Winsor's *Forever Amber* came under attack in Massachusetts, some of the same defenses were relied upon successfully. The defense was able to show a reputable publisher (Macmillan) behind the book; expert witnesses were permitted to testify that the book did not tend to arouse sexual impulses; an exhibit was offered of 170 newspaper and magazine reviews of the book; most significantly, the defense was able to persuade the Supreme Judicial Court of Massachusetts that the novel was a reasonably accurate account of Restoration England.[10] (We may pass over in silence the necessary postscript that this same court, a year later, found *God's Little Acre* obscene in Massachusetts, sixteen years after it had been found not obscene in Manhattan.[11] Judges are human. One year after that, the same court acquitted James M. Cain's *Serenade*.[12])

What counts, to return to the main theme, is a given publication's appeal to prurient interest. Smutty magazines, jammed with pictures of nude and seminude women in provocative poses, come into any court with unclean hands.[195] A magazine's pretensions to literary merit must be weighed "by the use of ordinary common sense and reason, taking in account the circumstances in which the matter is employed."[48] And the circumstances are just as important in the case of a book that otherwise might avoid prosecution, as the New York Supreme Court pointed out in 1930 in upholding the conviction of a book store clerk for selling a copy of Schnitzler's *Reigen*[139] (which also encountered censorship difficulties as the French film *La Ronde*). The book, a series of episodic dialogues, begins with an affair between a prostitute and a soldier, moves along to an affair between the soldier and a parlor maid, progresses with an affair between the parlor maid and a young man, and continues around the ring until a nobleman finds himself back with the prostitute. The book might have survived court assault; two members of the New York court thought it a work of literary merit. But the circumstances of publication proved fatal, for the book carried a titillating notice: "This book is intended for private circulation only." The introduction began by praising Schnitzler's "exquisite handling of the licentious," and applauded the Viennese writer for his keen studies "in the etiquette of the liaison and all its nuances." The introduction concluded with some cracks at puritans and censors. In the eyes of the court majority all this made it evident that the book was intended to appeal to salacious curiosity—and that intention made the book obscene.

Just as the endorsement of critics is not necessarily sufficient in itself to prove that a book is not intended to appeal to prurient interest, so other isolated factors may not in themselves upset a prosecution. A vigorous argument was raised in New York in 1946, on behalf of a worthless book known as *Call House Madam*, that the book had been freely available in many reputable bookstores for the preceding four years. City Magistrate Morris Ploscowe could not have cared less. The book impressed him as "essentially a tawdry job of ghost writing, and in spite of its desire to shock the reader, quite dull." It was immaterial that the book dealt with the lives of prostitutes; this was true of *Nana,* and of *Frankie and Johnny,* and of *Madeleine,* and that fact alone would not have warranted a conclusion that the book was obscene. Said the court:

What, in my opinion, brings *Call House Madam* within the purview of the statute is the method of presentation and the multiplicity of indecent passages. These objectionable portions of the book are not isolated phenomena, unavoidable in dealing with the subject of prostitution or running a house of prostitution. They set the tone and the standard for the book. They are frequently irrelevant to the story which is being told, and seem to be inserted merely for the purpose of stimulating the prurient instincts of the reader. . . .[135]

The following year, it may be noted in passing, the Ninth Circuit Court of Appeals on the West Coast agreed fully with Magistrate Ploscowe's appraisal: the court sternly affirmed the conviction of one Marcel Rodd on a charge of shipping a hundred copies of this doubtful work by express from Brooklyn to San Diego.[163]

This same court in 1949 also upheld the conviction of Irving Burstein, on a charge of mailing a filthy book, *Confessions of a Prostitute.* The case has significance in the context under review. Burstein was an old hand at mail-order sales. What he had done, as his trial disclosed, was to take an otherwise reputable book, *Sterile Sun,* which had been published by Macaulay in a limited edition for physicians, psychiatrists, and social workers, and to copy excerpts from it substantially verbatim. Freshly printed, and freshly titled, the book became the subject of a circular mailed by Burstein to a likely mailing list:

Dear Friend:

If you are a mature and broadminded adult and can take it, and if you are one of the many people who enjoy reading really spicy books not obtainable elsewhere, I have a 20,000-word book which I'm sure will open your eyes and make you sit up. It is called Confessions of a Prostitute, *and is a privately printed edition. . . .*

I'll quote a line or two to give you a small idea of what to expect in this startling daring volume—"He went crazy when he saw my legs. He said they were perfect, he kept kissing them and running his hands over them. . . ." You must understand that I cannot say too much as this letter may fall into the wrong hands, so these are just a few of the milder lines. The entire book runs in the same vein, and will give you thrill after thrill—if you care for this type of reading.

Some suckers responded, but postal inspectors also responded, and Burstein was arrested and indicted in New York. After a coast-to-coast chase, which saw him also indicted in California, Burstein was sent to prison for mailing obscene matter. The point worth noting is the circuit court's implied ruling that a book may not be obscene for a selective and limited audience of serious scholars but may well be obscene when it is sold by reason of a prurient appeal to an audience interested in salacity only.[27]

Toward the end of his comments in the *Roth* case, at the circuit court level, Circuit Judge Jerome Frank had confessed his own inability to perceive such a distinction. In his view books, pictures, and paintings either were or were not obscene—the artist, the writer, the audience, the passing of years, the circumstances, the community standards notwithstanding.[257]

This point, of course, has been argued many times. It arose in New Jersey in 1951, when Carl Weitershausen, of Newark, was convicted under state law for possessing (for sale) twenty or thirty thousand photographs alleged to be obscene. At his trial the defendant vainly attempted to offer in evidence an issue of *Life* magazine containing a large reproduction of Goya's "Maja Nude" and Rembrandt's "The Painter's Study." His point was that his humble photographs were no more obscene than *Life's* highbrow nudes.

New Jersey's Superior Court refused to accept this contention.[181] *Life's* reproductions of Goya and Rembrandt "were in no wise comparable to the pictures being sold at defendant's store." True enough, the court agreed, pictures of nude women are not of themselves obscene or indecent; the question "may well depend on the character of the pictures, the pose portrayed, the expression shown, the number and sequence of a group of such pictures, or the sensually suggestive character of the pictures."

In its instructions to the jury the trial court had suggested as a proper test of the obscenity of Weitershausen's pictures "whether their motive as portrayed by them is morally pure or impure, whether they are naturally calculated to excite in a spectator morally impure imaginations and whether the other incidents and qualities however attractive are merely secondary to this as their primary or main representation."

The Superior Court found no fault with that definition, and went a little further on its own with a comment that the pictures here involved (strip sequences of women in progressive stages of undress) "were not being distributed for any socially defensible purpose."

Strip-tease photographs also figured in 1951 in the conviction of one Frank Gonzales and others in a New York magistrate's court.[132] Judge Ploscowe conceded the defendant's argument that a reproduction of a Goya nude "may titillate, fascinate and stimulate." So might a painting of Rubens. Even "September Morn" might arouse some viewers. But in this case:

> No argument can be made in the cases before us that the pictures are works of art. They are not even good photography. When one sees men pawing over such pictures in stores in the Times Square area, as this Court has done, it is obvious that their appeal is frankly sexual. . . . The pictures which are the basis of the present prosecutions are intended to "excite lustful and lecherous thoughts and to stir sexual impulses." If they did not do this, they would not be sought after and bought. If they did not stir sexual impulses, there would be no reason for the strip tease, or the pictures which portray models holding out their breasts in provocative fashion, or the pictures which make such a prominent display of the female buttocks and the anal region.

The cases that have been quoted are typical of scores of such cases that gradually shaped and developed the law of obscenity to the point reached by the Supreme Court in its *Roth* decision. Read in the light of the court's five-point definition, they provide a pattern of some meaning. Citizens of the United States are not to be restricted in their reading to pap suited only for children, morons, or sex deviates; a much higher level of sophistication is to be tolerated in the interests of the average man. In every prosecution under a federal, state, or local obscenity statute contemporary standards must be applied, because community mores are not static and that which was obscene ten or fifteen years earlier may no longer be obscene today. The dominant theme of the material counts heavily, and the material must be considered as a whole; no longer may convictions rest upon isolated passages taken out of context. Most important of all, the question must be kept constantly in mind: does this publication appeal to prurient interest? To get at that question, courts may consider a wide variety of circumstances—the reputation of the author, the reputation of the publisher, the manner of advertising, the testimony of literary critics, the conduct of the defendant, the evidence of community acceptance of the work, the audience for whom a work is manifestly intended—and though no one of these factors in itself may be sufficient to prove or to disprove a prurient intention, collectively they have great meaning.

One other point may be emphasized briefly. This was the court's firm assertion that "all ideas having even the slightest redeeming social importance—unorthodox ideas, controversial ideas, even ideas hateful to the prevailing climate of opinion—have the full protection of the guaranties [of free press], unless excludable because they encroach upon the limited area of more important interest." This paragraph was relied upon by a municipal court in San Francisco in 1957 in dismissing an obscenity charge based upon two books of beatnik poetry; in the view of Judge Clayton W. Horn the poems, though sometimes couched in coarse and vulgar language, were not entirely lacking in social importance.[138] It seems likely that this defense will prove of increasing importance in coming years.

The law of obscenity can never be an easy law for police to enforce or courts to interpret. "The line dividing the salacious or pornographic from literature or science is not straight and unwavering," as Chief Justice Warren commented in his concurring opinion in *Roth*. Yet it may be asked if the same thing cannot be said of many other fields of the law. The law books that deal with due process and the law review articles that grapple with reasonable doubt are as long as any essays on the nature of obscenity. All that a community can do, and all that courts can do, is to inquire in each particular case if defendants have done what Samuel Roth and David Alberts did: "They were plainly engaged," said Chief Justice Warren, "in the commercial exploitation of the morbid and shameful craving for materials with prurient effect." That is the social evil to be combatted. And Warren added: "I believe that the state and federal governments can constitutionally punish such conduct."

2. THE CENSORSHIP OF MOTION PICTURES

In any account of obscenity censorship in the United States, a look at the censorship of motion pictures necessarily can amount to little more than a passing glance. At any given time only a few states and cities have engaged in prior-restraint censorship, and more often than not critical cases of local censorship have not involved obscenity; they have involved something else—violence, or race relations, or Communist propaganda, or the love life of Ingrid Bergman. As this is written, in the spring of 1960, motion-picture censorship by prior restraint is almost a thing of the past; it clings to life on the thread of a single sentence in a Supreme Court opinion; it is not long for this world.

Nevertheless, the rise of motion pictures from the tenements of the Constitution, where they dwelled for a generation in second-class status, tells us a good deal of the nature of censorship and of the changes that time can work in vital areas of the law. The Supreme Court of the United States has come almost full circle here. But oddly enough, just as the industry is about to win freedom from censorship by prior restraint it appears to be taking on new risks of censorship by subsequent punishment. The industry is about to learn, as other media of expression have learned before it, that with freedom comes a form of responsibility. This is a coming of age; but the motion picture industry reaches a metaphorical twenty-one handicapped by a childhood of repressions, inhibitions, strict masters, and a thousand admonitions to be seen and not heard. A new world of adult entertainment lies ahead, and through the deceptive swamps of community attitudes and contemporary standards, the industry will have to thread an uncertain path. In one sense this may not prove a new or difficult experience: the industry has had to thread an uncertain path all along.

The movies flickered into existence early in this century at a time when the moral standards of the late Queen Victoria still weighed heavily on the entertainment world. In New York the proprietors of a playhouse had attempted to offer a strip-tease pantomime that seems tame enough today—a bride's modest preparations for her wedding night. The courts of New York denounced it as an "outrage upon public decency" and sternly prohibited its performance.[124.1] The zealous Mr. Comstock, peering at stereopticons and measuring the skirts of Follies girls, had no intention of permitting a new trap for the young in the form of devilish motion pictures. In Delaware a heavy license fee upon motion pictures won approval on the grounds that a movie was merely another form of a circus.[179.1] In New York movies did not enjoy even this theatrical recognition: they were lumped, for licensing purposes, with "public cartmen, truckmen, hackmen, cabmen, expressmen, drivers, junk dealers, dealers in second-hand articles, hawkers, peddlers, vendors, ticket speculators, coal scalpers, common shows, shooting galleries, bowling alleys, billiard tables, dirt carts, exterior hoists and stands with stoop lines, and stands under the stairs of the elevated stations."[120.1] In Minnesota the town of Deer River (pop. 1,000) gazed with disapproval upon the enterprise of a motion picture exhibitor, and raised his merchant's license from $20 to $200. The Supreme Court of Minnesota found no fault with this: motion pictures were to be classed "among those pursuits which are liable to degenerate and menace the good order and morals of the people." The court was certain that "in and about the entrance of the show place in this small village is undoubtedly the rendezvous of the young and thoughtless as well as the vicious."[84.1]

The industry's early problems of licensing were merged almost from the beginning with problems of prior-restraint censorship. As early as 1907 Chicago enacted an ordinance vesting censorship powers in the chief of police, with right of appeal to the mayor. In a test case involving the chief's ban of *The James Boys* and *Night Riders* the exhibitors protested, with some temerity, that the ordinance violated their rights of free speech.

The Supreme Court of Illinois rejected every contention.[18] The purpose of the ordinance, said the court, was to secure decency and morality in the moving-picture business, "and that purpose falls within the police power." Large numbers of children attended these inexpensive movies; the matter was not analogous to the legitimate theater, which could be attended only by a relative few, and these few normally would be adults. The word "obscene" might be difficult to define by a universal standard, for there were "the shameless and unclean, to whom nothing is defilement," and there were others, professing to be students of the arts, who "would not regard anything as indelicate or indecent which had artistic merit." But the average person of healthy and wholesome mind "knows well enough what the words 'immoral' and 'obscene' mean and can intelligently apply the test to any picture presented to him."

In the case of these early movies the court thought it plain that any films based upon the James boys and night riders could represent "nothing but malicious mischief, arson, and murder," which necessarily would have an evil effect on youthful spectators. The police chief was upheld, the law approved, and the films banned.

The power of the states to censor motion pictures sustained its heaviest assault in 1915, when the Supreme Court of the United States upheld suits brought by the Mutual Film Corporation against censors in Ohio and in Kansas. The complaining film company made three arguments—that the state laws, both enacted in 1913, constituted an unlawful delegation of legislative authority; that they transgressed upon the power vested in Congress to regulate interstate commerce; and that they violated constitutional guaranties of free speech.

Speaking for a unanimous high court, Associate Justice Joseph McKenna found no merit in any of these contentions.[109,110] He had first to explain what a motion picture was. The film, he said, consists of "a series of instantaneous photographs or positive prints of action upon the stage or in the open. By being projected upon a screen with great rapidity there appears to the eye an illusion of motion. They depict dramatizations of standard novels, exhibiting many subjects of scientific interest, the properties of matter, the growth of the various forms of animal and plant life, and explorations and travels. . . ."

But the court was not greatly impressed with this novel invention all the same. The movies might be all right; then again, they might not. In any event the state laws seemed to Justice McKenna adequately equipped with safeguards against capricious action. "We can immediately put to one side the contention that [the laws] impose a burden on interstate commerce." Questions of press freedom, however, gave the court a little more trouble.

"Are moving pictures within the principle, as it is contended they are? They, indeed, may be mediums of thought, but so are many things. So is the theater, the circus, and all other shows and spectacles, and their performances may thus be brought by the like reasoning under the same immunity from repression or supervision as the public press—made the same agencies of civil liberty."

After some thought the court concluded that the exhibition of motion pictures "is a business pure and simple, originated and conducted for profit, like other spectacles, not to be regarded . . . as part of the press of the country or as organs of public opinion. [Movies] are mere representations of events, of ideas and sentiments published and known, vivid, useful and entertaining no doubt, but capable of evil, having power for it, the greater because of their attractiveness and manner of exhibition."

The Supreme Court noted that the state censors were required to pass all films that were moral, educational, amusing, or harmless, and that this commandment left the motion-picture industry free for whatever campaigns it might wish to wage in the public interest. But the power of the censors to prevent the propagation of evil had to be maintained. Movies might not always be wholesome:

Their power of amusement and, it may be, education, the audiences they assemble, not of women alone nor of men alone, but together, not of adults only, but of children, make them the more insidious in corruption by a pretense of worthy purpose or if they should degenerate from worthy purpose. They take their attraction from the general interest, eager and wholesome it may be, in their subjects, but a prurient interest may be excited and appealed to. Besides, there are some things which should not have pictorial representation in public places and to all audiences.

This was the *Mutual Film* rule. It firmly supported what the Minnesota court had said in the *Deep River* case, that "the exhibition of motion pictures is not to be regarded as part of the public press,"[84.1] and it had the effect of fixing the constitutional questions absolutely. While the *Mutual* cases were pending in Ohio and in Kansas, a companion suit in Pittsburgh assailed the constitutionality of Pennsylvania's censorship act of 1911. The Supreme Court of Pennsylvania wrote a brief *per curiam* opinion finding such censorship fully within a state's police power.[25] In Texas an ordinance of the City of Houston, creating a board of seven discreet persons to pass upon entertainments that might be obscene, indecent, immoral, or calculated to encourage racial or sectional prejudices, also was upheld.[277] In Washington the state Supreme Court indirectly approved prior censorship of movies, in an opinion upholding the conviction of a Seattle exhibitor for showing a film in which violence was depicted "in a gruesome manner."[173] In Kansas the state Supreme Court fought off repeated assaults on the state censorship law.[107,197] In Connecticut the Fox Film Corporation raised a vigorous complaint that the state's 1925 act, imposing a tax upon motion pictures, constituted an undue burden upon interstate commerce; a three-judge federal court emphatically disagreed: it upheld the tax not only on Connecticut's taxing power but on the state's police power, too. "The motion-picture industry," said the court, "is of recent origin, and its capacity for good, as well as for evil, is immense. It is an instrument of education and the public welfare demands that it shall be kept clean and its influence tend to promote what is good and not what is evil."[63]

The producers of newsreels were no more successful than the producers of other motion pictures. In 1922 Pathé News earnestly sought an exemption from New York's censorship law, but the state Supreme Court was unmoved by pleas in behalf of a free press.[118] A motion picture, said the court, is "clearly distinguishable" from a newspaper:

It is a spectacle or show, rather than a medium of opinion, and the latter quality is a mere incident to the former quality. It creates and purveys a mental atmosphere which is absorbed by the viewer without conscious mental effort. It requires neither literacy nor interpreter to understand it. . . . Its value as an educator for good is equaled only by its danger as an instructor in evil.

Fox Movietone also failed in its efforts to overcome censorship by pleading free speech when the first talking films came in. A test case in Pennsylvania brought an unyielding ruling that so far as the law was concerned, films that talked were in a class with films that kept quiet.[64] Vitagraph Films, which relied upon an apparatus similar to the ordinary phonograph, in order to synchronize speech with the movement of the actors' lips, fared no better: Vitagraph was ordered to file its records with the censors.[271] In the whole period only two cases come to mind in which the industry won even a single round. In Ohio the state Supreme Court refused to approve a censors' ban upon films of the Dempsey-Tunney fight;[177] and in New Jersey the state Court of Chancery refused to sanction a ban imposed on *The Naked Truth* by the Newark Commissioner of Public Safety.[151] Otherwise, state and local censors swept the field.

Interestingly, few of the early cases of motion-picture censorship turned upon charges of obscenity. One notable case, in Illinois, dealt with a Fox film, *The Deadwood Coach*. The state appellate court was not amused:[62]

The picture portrays, first, a killing, then a fight with Indians and a stagecoach holdup, and an attempt to kill; then the shooting up of some kind of eating house, and a diving from a window; then a holdup of the Deadwood coach and its destruction; then a killing of the guard, the driver being beaten and tied to a tree; then an arrest; then a breaking of the jail by the rougher elements of the town; then a release of a prisoner, and a so-called desperate fight to hold up the stage, then an attempt to escape, and, finally, a man plunges 1,000 feet to his death on the rocks.

In brief, the movie represented no more than a placid half-hour on today's television, but in 1925, in Chicago, this was more than public morals could tolerate. The producers contended warmly that their film was not immoral or indecent, did not incite to riot, portrayed no lynchings, and did not hold Negroes up to ridicule. What, then, was the matter with it? It just had too much shooting, said the court:

> The statistics of indiscriminate shootings, as we all know, are appalling. Obviously, it is the duty of appropriate officers and those of the courts, under the law, to prevent, and not to further, what may be called a "shooting" film. Such pictures should not be shown unless plainly harmless. Where "gun-play," or the shooting of human beings, is the essence of the play and does not pertain to the necessities of war, nor to the preservation of law and order, is for personal spite or revenge, and involves the taking the law into one's own hands, and thus becomes a murder, the picture may be said to be immoral; it inculcates murder.

The Illinois judges unanimously reaffirmed their earlier rulings in support of the constitutionality of motion-picture censorship, and the Deadwood coach did not go through.

A few years later, in 1930, the identical points were again upheld by the Illinois Supreme Court in an opinion dealing with the film *Alibi*.[198] The United Artists Corporation raised grave questions of constitutionality, but once again the court refused to accede: "The power of a city to provide for a board of censors and to require a permit before any moving picture can be exhibited in a municipality cannot be doubted." Respect for law, added the court, "is the basis of our civilization," and when a picture comes along such as *Alibi*, which "could not fail to have a tendency to cheapen the value of human life and cause an increasing disrespect for the law and its officers," the city had full power to prevent the film's display.

Not only films of violence, but also films of sex education have encountered difficulties with state censors. One of the first of these was a film depicting the life of Margaret Sanger, which ran into trouble both in New York and in Illinois during World War I.

In New York the censors banned the movie on the grounds that dissemination of contraceptive knowledge "offends in the extreme against the public welfare." Any film that taught people to prevent conception was *per se* immoral and opposed to public welfare; such films were mere propaganda to limit the production of children, to raise class issues, and to lead all persons, and especially the young and unmarried, into lives of immorality. The appellate court judges unanimously concurred with these objections; they were not concerned with constitutional questions—they were concerned only with determining whether the commissioner of licenses had acted arbitrarily. They concluded that his action was entirely justified.[106]

Illinois judges came to the same conclusion a few months later. In Chicago the superintendent of police had banned the Sanger film for exhibition there. He thought the film immoral, and the appellate court agreed.[141]

In New York a shocked Supreme Court would not even look at a film, *The Naked Truth,* dealing with venereal disease, even though it had been shown across the river in New Jersey. In the view of a New York court, such a film was "not to be exhibited at all."[152] Another film, advocating sterilization in the interest of *Tomorrow's Children,* was banned as immoral.[65] *The Birth of a Baby* impressed New York judges as possibly of scientific value to a restricted audience, "but it becomes indecent when presented in places of amusement."[7] In Lynchburg, Virginia, the film created such scandal that the city manager and city council sought to prevent its exhibition though the state censors had licensed it.[101]

Another film of sex education, *Mom and Dad,* skated along a border line of public censorship over a period of ten years. In Newark the commissioner of public safety threatened to revoke the license of the Broad Street Theater if the film were exhibited there, and it took a ruling of the state Superior Court to call him off.[87] In the Midwest federal judges took a less tolerant view; they upheld an order of the sheriff of St. Louis County prohibiting the display of the film at a drive-in movie.[80] The judges were not exactly certain what was meant by "obscene, indecent and immoral," but they were certain this picture was nothing to be shown indiscriminately "to all classes, ages and conditions." Five years later, however, a New York Supreme Court found the film not indecent, and reversed the state censors' ban.[33]

Censorship for outright immorality dates back at least to 1916, when Pennsylvania censors rejected a film, *The Brand.*[66,73] The state Supreme Court saw nothing arbitrary in the decision. On the contrary the court went out of its way to commend the censors for thus having promoted "the moral and virtuous" and condemned "the immoral and vicious." The picture, laid in Alaska, dealt with a woman who leaves her husband, an older man, in order to live in adultery with an earlier lover. In the end her husband catches up with the seducer and brands him with a knife. Because the state's regulations then prohibited any scenes "showing men and women living together without marriage," the film was banned.

This was entirely agreeable to the state Supreme Court. Not to prohibit the film, said the court, would be "to reduce to a negative quantity the healthful moral influence exerted upon community life by faithful observance of the recognized moral standards." The court suggested that any film which failed to pay "the highest deference and respect to the sanctity and purity of the home and family relation between husband and wife" would fail to qualify for exhibition in Pennsylvania.

New York judges took somewhat the same view a few years later, in upholding a ban upon Hedy Lamarr's *Ecstasy*. This was the first full-length film, intended for general exhibition, to offer any total nudity—even from a discreet and foggy distance. Miss Lamarr's famous sprint along the beach, coupled with another scene in which the camera dwelled upon her face during a purported act of love, resulted in prolonged litigation before the film even could be admitted into the United States from Europe. Then New York censors promptly banned it, and the state Supreme Court affirmed its decree: "The picture unduly emphasizes the carnal side of the sex relationship," said the court, and the fact that the objectionable scenes were short and to a degree obscure was irrelevant.[59]

Two years later the same court relied upon its ruling in the *Ecstasy* case to uphold a ban on *Remous* (Whirlpool) because of its illicit theme: a young woman, whose husband is made impotent by an automobile accident, drifts into an adulterous affair; with her husband's suicide she bitterly repents—but her repentance was not enough for an unforgiving court:[104] "The picture purports to portray the nervous, emotional, and mental state of the wife arising because of the impotence of the husband, and the consequent unbalanced moral character and indiscretions of the wife. Such is not fit subject for screen display."

By 1947 the New York Supreme Court showed signs of tending toward a more sophisticated view. The court agreed to uphold some deletions ordered in *Amok,* a film dealing with the abortion of a young woman whose husband is about to return after a year's absence, but the court was not especially happy about the situation: "A standard in matters of this kind is flexible. Stories of clandestine affection and even illicit intercourse are circulated and filmed, and after we pass the stage of believing in the stork, it is generally understood that conception might follow illicit intercourse and if the wronged husband was beyond the seven seas, abortion would be necessary to prevent disclosure through the birth of a child. It is understandable, though, that some reviewing bodies would think this film offended; thus there doubtless is some evidence to sustain the finding."[54]

If the censorship of motion pictures had been confined entirely to the banning of films as indecent or immoral, or even as excessively violent, the practice might have survived as a legitimate exercise of the states' police power. But very early in the game local authorities began banning films because of the ideas contained in them, and in the end this was to bring down the whole structure of prior-restraint censorship.

The Birth of a Nation was one such film. Half a century had passed since Appomattox when the film was produced, but passions in the North had not subsided. The film, which dealt heavily with excesses of the Reconstruction in South Carolina, was banned in Chicago, St. Louis, Pittsburgh, and Denver, and provisionally banned in Atlantic City, Boston, and St. Paul. In Minneapolis the mayor's flat refusal to permit the film to be shown led to a decision by Minnesota's highest court upholding the mayor's authority.[13] While some residents of the city were in favor of letting the film be shown, many others felt the movie would engender race hatred, revive old animosities, and lead to breaches of the peace. Substantially the same arguments were made a couple of years later in Cleveland when the mayor and the city council sought to suppress the film. The producing corporation sought an injunction against them. A former officer in the Union cavalry, occupying the bench of the Court of Common Pleas in Cuyahoga County in 1917, reluctantly concluded that the local officials had exceeded their authority.[58]

The 1920's saw films banned as "pro-labor" in Ohio and Pennsylvania, as an aftermath of coal strikes. During the 1930's censors in Pennsylvania and in New England attempted to ban pro-Loyalist films that infuriated adherents of General Franco. Films on Communist themes ran into repeated objections from state and local boards. Ohio turned down the Soviet movie *Of Greater Promise* because it tended "to encourage social and racial equality, thereby stirring up racial hatred." The Supreme Court of Rhode Island in 1939 refused to interfere with the ban imposed by Providence censors on *Professor Mamlock,* a film they regarded as purest Communist propaganda.[190] The exhibitor argued vigorously that motion pictures had become a positive medium for the expression of ideas and as such were entitled to be seen as a matter of right under the Constitution. The Rhode Island court felt otherwise; motion pictures, the court said, were no more than mere shows and exhibitions, to be considered "along with rope or wire dancing, wrestling, boxing and sparring matches, and also roller skating and dancing in rinks and public halls, as subject to regulation and even prohibition under the police power of the state."

In Michigan, however, when various religious, civic, and patriotic organizations compelled the banning of *The Youth of Maxim,* as Soviet propaganda "likely to instill class hatred and hatred of the social order of the United States," the state Supreme Court observed coldly that it knew of no law vesting in the police commissioner of Detroit any duty "of preserving the international relations between the United States of America and the Union of Soviet Socialist Republics."[172] The exhibitor, said the court, "has a constitutional property right to show a film which is not indecent or immoral."

That was in 1936. It represented possibly the first time an appellate court had given so much as a friendly nod to the industry's assertions of "constitutional rights," but for a period of more than ten years the comment languished in a splendid judicial isolation. Then, on May 3, 1948, in one of those grandly casual remarks that spring so frequently from the brow of Zeus, the Supreme Court scrapped the *Mutual* precedent as if McKenna's opinion of 1915 were last month on the calendar. The Justice Department had brought a massive antitrust proceeding against Paramount Pictures and others, with a view toward cutting exhibitors loose from producers. The defendants contended, among other things, that producers had rights of free speech that were beyond infringement by antitrust laws. Mr. Justice Douglas, though he thought the argument irrelevant, accepted the basic hypothesis with a why-of-course comment that left the industry's attorneys giddy: "We have no doubt that moving pictures, like newspapers and radio, are included in the press whose freedom is guaranteed by the First Amendment."[255]

"Have no doubt!" For the preceding thirty-three years the highest state and federal courts had relied, without significant exception, upon the Supreme Court's unanimous opinion of 1915 in which the supreme law of the land had been found in precisely the opposite position; then the court had viewed the motion-picture industry as "a business pure and simple, originated and conducted for profit, like other spectacles, not to be regarded . . . as part of the press of the country." But Mr. Justice Douglas, who is inclined to view *stare decisis* as Emerson viewed consistency, brushed aside *Mutual* without a backward glance.

Lower courts and local censors, not knowing exactly what to do about Douglas's shattering remark, did nothing about it. The Supreme Court of Georgia wrote an opinion, upholding a ban on *Valley of the Nude,* in which the court relied upon the same criteria it had used all along.[74] In Tennessee United Artists sought to create a test case by challenging a ban imposed by Memphis censors upon the Hal Roach film *Curley.* The local board had advised the United Artists Corporation, at its St. Louis office, that it could not approve "your *Curley* picture with the little Negroes, as the South does not permit Negroes in white schools nor recognize social equality between the races even in children." The Tennessee Supreme Court uncomfortably ducked all constitutional questions by deciding the cause under the law governing foreign corporations.[196]

Questions of race relations also figured in a key case in Atlanta at the same time. There Mrs. Christine Smith Gilliam, the Atlanta censor, had frowned upon *Lost Boundaries* as a film likely to have an adverse effect upon the peace, morals, and good order of the city. The exhibitor took the case to federal court, where Judge M. Neil Andrews reluctantly decided in the censor's favor. He felt himself still bound by *Mutual,* despite Douglas's statement in the *Paramount* case, but he commented coldly upon Atlanta's attempt "at a degree of thought control." He thought it high time that ordinances imposing any sort of gag rules should be put away "in the attic which contains the ghosts of those who arrayed in the robe of Bigotry, armed with the spear of Intolerance, and mounted on the steed of Hatred, have through all the ages sought to patrol the highways of the mind." And for his own part he doubted exceedingly that the Atlanta censor any longer had the power, in the light of the dicta in *Paramount,* "to determine what is good and what is bad for the community . . . without any standard other than the censor's personal opinion."[156] Judge Andrews' uncertainties were not shared by his superiors on the Fifth United States Circuit Court of Appeals.[157] They were positive the states and localities still had power to censor motion pictures, and they could not imagine that the Supreme Court of the United States would overrule "or in any manner depart from" its unanimous decision in the old *Mutual Film* case. They confidently expected, contrary to the plaintiff's prophecy, to see the *Mutual* ruling "fully reaffirmed." In any event, said the circuit judges, it was not their duty to attempt to outguess the United States Supreme Court, to consult crystal-ball gazers, or to base a decision on mere speculation. Their duty was to apply established judicial principles, including the principle of *stare decisis,* to the question at hand. On that basis they were ready to stand by the *Mutual* case. Said the court:

We particularly disagree with, and dissent from, the view . . . that moving pictures have now emerged from the business of amusement into instruments for the propagation of ideas and, therefore, like newspapers [with] freedom of speech, must be regarded as within the protection of the Fourteenth Amendment; that censorship of moving pictures by states or local communities is contrary to the new enlightenment and the trend of the new national opinion; and that the *Mutual Film* decision, standing in the way, is now antiquated and tottering to its fall, and should be decently and finally interred.

The decision has been on the books for years, not only unchanged but uncriticized. When written it was based on the settled views in, and the decisions of many of the state courts. Since its writing, it has been quoted from and followed without varying in decisions without number. In such circumstances, something more compelling than the mere desire of a large and powerful industry to be free of local restraints should be presented to induce a court to overrule and set it aside. For, no matter how much may be said in favor of judicious judicial flexibility of interpretation, it is still the law of state and federal courts that long standing decisions of the Supreme Court should not be set aside on the mere personal opinions of later judges, especially when such decisions have been in part induced, and for more than a generation have been in turn followed, by the decisions of the state courts of last resort of comparable standing and dignity.

On October 16, 1950, the Supreme Court of the United States denied a writ of *certiorari* in the *Lost Boundaries* case, but barely a month later the machinery was put into motion, far away in New York City, that was to prove the Fifth Circuit judges poor prophets indeed.

On November 30, 1950, the Motion Picture Division of New York's Department of Education granted a license for the exhibition of *The Miracle,* and two weeks later, on December 12, the film had its first viewing in Manhattan at the Paris Theater. The story by now is well known: a simple-minded woman, charged with tending a herd of goats, one day is approached by a bearded stranger. In her madness she conceives him to be St. Joseph, come to take her to heaven. The stranger plies her with wine and when she is in a state of religious ecstasy, ravishes her. A bit later, when the woman discovers she is with child, townspeople abuse her cruelly. In the end, she finds her way to a mountain church, bears her baby, and regains her sanity.

It is difficult to understand, a decade later, how this film could have aroused the great protest that it evoked at the time—denunciation by Cardinal Spellman, fierce protests in the Catholic press, equally passionate rejoinders from Protestants (and from some Catholics), parades of pickets and counter pickets—but in any event heavy pressure was exerted upon the regents of the University of the State of New York, who serve in New York as an appellate motion-picture review board, to revoke the license. Following a hearing, the regents concluded that the film was "sacrilegious," and on February 16, 1951, rescinded and canceled the November order of approval. Joseph Burstyn, Inc., American distributors of the film, brought suit to set aside the regents' decision and to restore the original order, but in the fall of 1951 the New York Court of Appeals in a 5-2 decision sustained the regents' decision.[28]

Speaking for the majority, Judge Charles W. Froessel went back to *Mutual* to comment that movies were "primarily entertainment, rather than the expression of ideas, and are engaged in for profit." The majority felt that a public showing of an obscene, indecent, immoral or sacrilegious film "may do incalculable harm." The state had a valid right, under its police power, to legislate in this field.

The term "sacrilegious" gave the court no trouble: the word was synonymous with "profane," which in its application to motion-picture censorship had been upheld by the Supreme Court earlier in the *Chaplinsky* case.[34] And this film, *The Miracle,* was plainly sacrilegious: it not only encroached upon the sacred relationship of Jesus, Mary, and Joseph, but utterly destroyed it by associating it with "drunkenness, seduction, mockery and lewdness, and, in the language of the script itself, with 'passionate attachment . . . sexual passions' and 'gratification' as a way of love." For the state to legislate as to religion was not to confuse church and state; the rule of-separation is simply this, "that no religion, as that word is understood by the ordinary, reasonable person, shall be treated with contempt, mockery, scorn and ridicule to the extent it has been here, by those engaged in selling entertainment by way of motion pictures." To forbid the exhibition of this movie was not to impose upon any First Amendment right; if one point of law had been well settled, it was that freedom of speech is not absolute but may be limited when an appropriate occasion arises. Neither did the ban infringe upon the American exhibitor's right to free exercise of religion: "The offering of public gratuitous insult to recognized religious beliefs by means of commercial motion pictures is not only offensive to decency and morals, but constitutes in itself an infringement of the freedom of others to worship as they choose."

In a long dissenting opinion, Judge Stanley H. Fuld noted that the film had been written by a Roman Catholic, Roberto Rossellini, produced and directed by Roman Catholics, filmed in Catholic Italy, and first exhibited in Rome where religious censorship exists. The Vatican's own newspaper had found no impropriety in its being viewed by Catholics. New York film critics had acclaimed it as the best foreign language film of 1950. To deny the picture an opportunity to be shown in New York seemed to Judge Fuld "censorship in its baldest form." He felt the statute offended both the First and Fourteenth Amendments of the Constitution, "since it imposes a prior restraint— and at that, a prior restraint of broad and undefined limits—on freedom of discussion of religious matters." No censor, he thought, could define "sacrilegious" except in terms of his own philosophy, training and education; a determination of sacrilege necessarily must rest "in the undiscoverable recesses of the official's mind." And no official, high or petty, he told his colleagues of the majority, "can prescribe what shall be orthodox in politics, nationalism, religions, or other matters of opinion."

Distributors of *The Miracle* refused to give up. Burstyn appealed once more, this time to the Supreme Court of the United States, and there, on May 26, 1952, the walls of motion-picture censorship, cracked by Douglas in 1948, began to tumble down.[29] In a unanimous decision the court set the industry essentially free from the fetters of prior restraint: not altogether free, as the court was careful to point out. ("It does not follow that the Constitution requires absolute freedom to exhibit every motion picture of every kind at all times and all places.") But within wide limits the court held that "expression by means of motion pictures is included within the free speech and free press guarantees of the First and Fourteenth Amendments."

"It cannot be doubted," said the court, "that motion pictures are a significant medium for the communication of ideas. They may affect public attitudes and behavior in a variety of ways, ranging from direct espousal of a political or social doctrine to the subtle shaping of thought which characterizes all artistic expression. The importance of motion pictures as an organ of public opinion is not lessened by the fact that they are designed to entertain as well as to inform."

Turning from this new broad principle to a specific application of it, the court held that no state might prohibit the exhibition of motion pictures on an objection of "sacrilege."

This is far from the kind of narrow exception to freedom of expression which a state may carve out to satisfy the adverse demands of other interests of society. In seeking to apply the broad and all-inclusive definition of "sacrilege" given by the New York court, the censor is set adrift upon a boundless sea amid myriad conflicting currents of religious views, with no charts but those provided by the most vocal and powerful orthodoxies. New York cannot vest such unlimited restraining control over motion pictures in a censor. . . . The state has no legitimate interest in protecting any or all religions from views distasteful to them which is sufficient to justify prior restraints upon the expression of those views. It is not the business of government in our nation to suppress real or imagined attacks upon a particular religious doctrine, whether they appear in publications, speeches, or motion pictures.

Echoing the language of the majority, Justice Frankfurter, in a long concurring opinion, said he could not possibly define "sacrilegious," nor was an impressive array of dictionaries any help to him. To permit any censor, no matter how conscientious he might strive to be, to pass upon movies that might seem sacrilegious to any one of New York's three hundred known religious sects was more than he was willing to allow. Such permission, he thought, would be

bound to have stultifying consequences on the creative process of literature and art—for the films are derived largely from literature. History does not encourage reliance on the wisdom and moderation of the censor as a safeguard in the exercise of such drastic power over the minds of men.

While the case of *The Miracle* was pending in New York and before the Supreme Court's decision of May 26, 1952, the Court of Criminal Appeals of Texas sought to hold the line for state censorship of the movies.[68] A case had come up from Marshall, where the town, after hastily creating a board of censors, had denied a license to exhibit the film *Pinky*. The exhibitor, W. L. Gelling, seized upon this denial for a frontal assault upon motion-picture censorship as a whole. He appealed all the way up the line, but in January of 1952 the Texas court ringingly upheld the Marshall ordinance and delivered itself of a lecture on states' rights:

"The Supreme Court of the United States may extend the Fourteenth Amendment to include motion pictures, and thus nationalize the industry and remove it from state and municipal control, but we are not expecting this until it has done so, and certainly will not yield that important function on behalf of the state and the municipality until we are forced to do so."

The Texas court was not ready to concede that the motion-picture industry had emerged from the business of amusement "and become propagators of ideas entitling it to freedom of speech." The court said this, and it merits a thoughtful moment:

> The desire of a great industry to reap greater fruits from its operations should not be indulged at the expense of Christian character, upon which America must rely for its future existence. Every boy and every girl reaching manhood or womanhood is, to an extent, the product of the community from which he comes. If the citizens of that community are divested of all power to surround them with wholesome entertainment and character building education, then their product will go forth weak indeed. If the community surrenders its power voluntarily, if the state does, then we may expect our federal government to move into fields with which it should not be encumbered and in which it cannot best serve. . . . We cherish the history of a federal government which has been based on a Constitution as solid as the rocks and whose constancy is not shifted by the changing winds.

These solemn reminders were lost upon the Supreme Court of the United States. Gelling appealed the Texas decision, and in June of 1952, the high court resolutely followed the direction it had set in May with the *Burstyn* (*Miracle*) decree. The Texas decision was reversed; and Mr. Justice Frankfurter, concurring, spelled out a valid reason: the Marshall ordinance, permitting town censors to ban a film whenever they were "of the opinion" that the picture was "of such character as to be prejudicial to the best interests of the people of said city," was too indefinite to meet constitutional tests. Mr. Justice Douglas, also concurring, went further: "The evil of prior restraint," he commented, "is present here in flagrant form. If a board of censors can tell the American people what it is in their best interests to see or to read or to hear, then thought is regimented, authority substituted for liberty, and the great purpose of the First Amendment to keep uncontrolled the freedom of expression is defeated."

The censoring states and localities were not willing to let go easily. In *Burstyn*, a unanimous court had outlawed censorship based upon grounds of sacrilege. In *Gelling* the court had thrown out an indefinite ordinance based upon the "best interests" of a community. What remained? In Ohio the state Supreme Court overturned the state censors' ban on *Native Son*, as a film calculated to "contribute to racial misunderstanding," but upheld a ban upon *M* as a picture "filled with brutal crime." In doing so the Ohio court remarked that it did believe *Burstyn* had destroyed state censorship altogether.[187]

> There still remains a limited field in which decency and morals may be protected from the impact of an offending motion-picture film by prior restraint under proper criteria. There can be no inherent right of publicity which tends to destroy the very social fabric of the community, and consequently in such instances there is no right of free speech or free press to be infringed. In these times of alarming rise in juvenile delinquency and of increasing criminality in this country, attributed by social agencies, at least in part, to the character of the exhibitions put on in the show houses of the country, criminal prosecution after the fact is a weak and ineffective remedy to meet the problem at hand.

A month later a sorely divided Court of Appeals of New York took the same view. New York's censors had rejected the film *La Ronde* as immoral and denied it a license for exhibition. A divided New York Supreme Court had somewhat reluctantly upheld the regents' decision.[38] A majority of the New York Supreme Court judges felt that the Supreme Court of the United States had not intended to prohibit to the states a power to ban films on the ground of immorality.

Judge Sydney F. Foster, dissenting, was ready to throw overboard New York's entire motion-picture censorship law. In his view the high court's decision in *Burstyn* meant that motion pictures were entitled to full protection against prior restraints upon their freedom of expression. "Either motion pictures may be censored or they cannot be; I can see no practical middle ground."

> That is not to say, of course, that punishment may not follow after the event if a law against obscenity or immorality has been violated. This is the traditional constitutional view as to speech and press. The individual is free to say or write what he thinks, but he must accept the responsibility therefor and may be punished if he offends the law.

So far as *La Ronde* was concerned, Judge Foster thought it "certainly not obscene," and he doubted it was immoral either. True, he said,

> It deals with illicit love, usually regarded as immoral. But so is murder. The theme alone does not furnish a valid ground for previous restraint. As to its presentation's corrupting the morals of the public, this issue is highly debatable. The record indicates a vast body of informed opinion to the contrary.

Distributors of the film, the Commercial Pictures Corporation, carried their fight for a license on to the Court of Appeals of New York. There the judges gazed unhappily at the one key question remaining for decision: in the light of the *Burstyn* decision did the New York censors any longer have power to reject a film for immorality?

A majority of the court, speaking through Judge Froessel, emphatically said yes.[39] This film "from beginning to end deals with promiscuity, adultery, fornication and seduction. . . ." Said Judge Charles S. Desmond, concurring: "The film depicts a series of illicit sexual adventures, nothing more; its only discoverable theme is this: that everyone is sexually promiscuous, and that life is just a 'round' of sexual promiscuity."

No guaranties of press freedom, thought the majority, prevent New York from banning such a film. Said Judge Froessel:

> Of course it is true that the state may not impose upon its inhabitants the moral code of saints, but, if it is to survive, it must be free to take such reasonable and appropriate measures as may be necessary to preserve the institution of marriage and the home, and the

health and welfare of its inhabitants. History bears witness to the fate of peoples who have become indifferent to the vice of indiscriminate sexual immorality—a most serious threat to the family, the home and the state. An attempt to combat such threat is embodied in the sections of the education law here challenged. It should not be thwarted by any doctrinaire approach to the problems of free speech raised thereby.

A majority of the New York court raised three objections—that "immoral" was too vague a term to stand up under familiar legal tests; that since the *Burstyn* case, prior censorship of motion pictures no longer could be sanctioned; and that *La Ronde* wasn't immoral anyhow. Judge Marvin R. Dye, dissenting, concluded on this thoughtful note:

As has been said in a great variety of ways, we deem the evil complained of here far less dangerous to the community than the danger flowing from the suppression of clear constitutional protection. In our zeal to regulate by requiring licenses in advance, we are prone to forget the struggle behind our free institutions. We must keep in mind on all occasions that beneficent aims however laudable and well directed can never serve in lieu of constitutional powers. . . .

It is no answer to say that the exhibition of motion pictures has a potential for evil which cannot be successfully dealt with except by censorship in advance. Such a conclusion overlooks the very significant circumstance that other media of expression are not so censored, for they may not be, but are nonetheless successfully controlled by our penal laws.

The producers appealed both the Ohio decision on *M* and the New York decision on *La Ronde* to the Supreme Court of the United States, and on January 18, 1954, in brief *per curiam* orders, the high court reversed both state rulings.[40,188] Justice Douglas, joined by Justice Black, added a concurring *coup de grace,* with a comment that prior censorship of newspapers certainly could not be sustained, nor could the publishers of books be compelled by any law to submit their manuscripts to a censor before publication.

Nor is it conceivable to me that producers of plays for the legitimate theater or for television could be required to submit their manuscripts to censors on pain of penalty for producing them without approval. . . . The same result in the case of motion pictures necessarily follows. . . .

Motion pictures are of course a different medium of expression from the public speech, the radio, the stage, the novel, or the magazine. But the First Amendment draws no distinction between the various methods of communicating ideas. . . . Which medium will give the most excitement and have the most enduring effect will vary with the theme and the actors. It is not for the censor to determine in any case. The First and the Fourteenth Amendments say that Congress and the states shall make "no law" which abridges freedom of speech or of the press. In order to sanction a system of censorship I would have to say that "no law" does not mean what it says, that "no law" is qualified to mean "some laws." I cannot take that step.

In this nation every writer, actor, or producer, no matter what medium of expression he may use, should be freed from the censor.

The Supreme Court of Illinois was not convinced. Four months later, when Chicago censors rejected *The Miracle* as immoral, the court's Chief Justice Walter V. Schaefer noted that the film had been banned in New York merely as sacrilegious. True enough, since then the court had upset state orders against *M* and *La Ronde* as immoral, but "we do not regard those decisions as invalidating all film censorship." In Judge Schaefer's view, a state still had power to prevent the showing of films that were plainly "obscene"—that is to say, films whose dominant purpose had a probable and substantial tendency to arouse sexual desires on the part of a normal, average person.[5] The state Supreme Court remanded the case for a trial court to reconsider; and on reconsideration a Chicago circuit judge found *The Miracle* not obscene. Another appeal followed, and this time the Appellate Court of Illinois let *The Miracle* pass, with a comment that "it is not at all probable that *The Miracle* would arouse sexual desires in the 'average, normal' individual contemplated by Judge Schaefer; indeed, it appears unlikely that even the salaciously inclined individual would be so affected by a film whose central character is clothed only in rags and whose personality is devoid of any charm; there is no gloss of glamour anywhere in the film."[6]

Nor were Kansas judges convinced. When *The Moon Is Blue* came along and state censors rejected it ("sex theme throughout . . . too frank bedroom dialogue . . . obscene, indecent and immoral") the Kansas Supreme Court carefully reread the *Burstyn* decision and noted the loophole left for state censorship "under a clearly drawn statute designed and applied to prevent the showing of obscene films." The Kansas judges regarded the Kansas statute as clearly drawn, and they viewed the film as clearly obscene.[86] The Supreme Court of the United States disagreed. With a laconic *per curiam* order the high court reversed on October 25, 1955, citing *Burstyn* and no more. There was nothing to suggest whether the Supreme Court thought all prior censorship was invalid, or thought the Kansas law was invalid, or thought the Kansas law in itself was valid but was wrongly applied to this particular film. The court, as Mr. Justice Frankfurter himself has complained,[175] is not always the most helpful body on earth.

In Ohio appellate judges gave up the fight. When RKO Pictures launched a frontal assault upon the state's censorship law, Judge Ralph C. Bartlett of the Court of Common Pleas in Franklin County resisted stoutly.[162] He was confident that "the sovereign State of Ohio has [not] been relegated to the helpless state of being limited in its authority solely to the remedy of criminal prosecution after the fact for any abuse of the privilege of free speech and free publication." He rebelled from the thought "that the sovereign State of Ohio should ever be denied the right to protect the decency and morals of its people from the impact of any offending motion-picture film, regardless of the gross immorality depicted and its effect on the public welfare." The state Supreme Court, with a sigh, could not agree. Late in 1954 the court concluded that Ohio's entire program of motion-picture censorship was dead.[162]

Fifteen months later, in March of 1956, a majority of the Pennsylvania Supreme Court also threw in the sponge.[79.1] The Pennsylvania law at that time permitted state censors to ban films that were "sacrilegious, obscene, indecent, or immoral, or such as tend in the judgment of the board, to debase or corrupt morals." Censorship on grounds of sacrilege had vanished with *Burstyn*. Censorship on grounds of indecency and immorality had vanished with *M* and *La Ronde*. The authority to reject films that might tend to corrupt morals had vanished with *Gelling*. That left only the grounds of "obscenity," and perhaps not even this. A majority of the court tossed out the whole of the Pennsylvania law. Judge John C. Bell, Jr., sadly remarked in a concurring opinion that the statute "had protected the interests of the highly moral and deeply religious people of Pennsylvania for over forty years." He himself believed the censorship law wise, necessary and valid. But he bowed to the Supreme Court, and surrendered.

Judge Michael A. Musmanno dissented at the top of his lungs. The particular film before the court was "a monstrosity of a motion picture entitled, *She Should'a Said No!*" The picture dealt with the narcotics traffic, especially among juveniles; state censors had not acted arbitrarily in banning the picture: at a lower court proceeding they carefully had adduced competent evidence of the damaging effects of such a film on youthful viewers. He felt certain that Pennsylvania had not been stripped of power to prevent the exhibition of "the vilest motion picture devised," and he complained bitterly that the action of his colleagues in voiding the statute was "gratuitous and uncalled for." He went on to sum up the whole case in behalf of *prior-restraint* censorship of motion pictures, as distinguished from the theory of *subsequent punishment*. Hear him out:

How will the punishment of the exhibitor heal the lacerating wounds made in the delicate sensations of children and sensitive adults who witness a picture of lewdness, depravity and immorality? Damage is done at the very first exhibition of the film. There are theaters in Pittsburgh and Philadelphia which accommodate 4,000 patrons for one show. If a picture should last but one day, many thousands nevertheless have seen it by the time it is withdrawn from circulation. That is why reason dictates that control over immoral films must be found in prevention and not in subsequent punishment.

It is no answer to a demand for motion-picture censorship to say that if the people do not like a film they can stay away. How are people to know if a certain production is immoral and indecent? And why should anyone be required to be offended in a theater with scenes that sting decent eyes and with language that shocks respectable ears? If one is to learn of impurities in water only after he has drunk it, the municipal authorities have done very little to protect the citizens who make up and maintain the municipality.

There is a very fallacious notion afloat on the waves of idle thought that in a free society, the least control makes for the biggest happiness. The slightest reflection will demonstrate that there would be considerable misery, not to say plagues and pestilences, if government did not hold an analytical and punitive eye on producers of medicines, drugs, foods and beverages, and did not supervise the tillers in the fields of sanitation, hygiene and therapeutics. A good citizen not only does not object but is happy for the fact that someone far more skilled than he determines whether the can of peaches he opens or the box of pills he obtains at the drugstore is free of poisonous and deleterious ingredients. A worthy member of society, who is just as much concerned about mental purity as he is over bodily cleanliness, is grateful that the government which protects him from contact with physical contagion will also save him from association with moral trash and garbage. No one can sensibly object to the regulation by municipal authorities over the use of public highways, parks, streams, tunnels and buildings. The streets of a city cannot be used for immoral purposes. Why should the avenues of the mind and the soul be polluted with the parading of indecencies and obscenities which can and do sometimes appear in films? . . .

Our Pennsylvania Board of Censors views over a thousand pictures a year. In 1953, it passed on 1,144 subjects. It rejected ten pictures outrightly and in 34 others eliminated 84 scenes. Who can say that he has lost any of his freedom because he was not given the opportunity to see the ten bad pictures and the 84 outlawed scenes? The virtue in rejection does not lie alone in the discarding of what is improper but in the maintenance of a standard of decency and morality which assured each year the manufacture of less and less undesirable films. But with the elimination of censorship, the light in the lamps of standardized corruptness dims, and as a consequence, there will not be lacking producers who will be guided only by the beacon of profit which can hardly be depended upon to keep the course of the ship of production traveling within pure waters.

Judge Musmanno's dissenting opinion in Pennsylvania was very nearly the dying gasp on behalf of prior-restraint censorship. In March of 1956 a federal district judge in Chicago upheld the action of local censors in banning *The Game of Love* as an obscene movie; the decision seems not to have been appealed.[192] Otherwise almost every subsequent attempt to defend state censorship has fallen under judicial assault. In July of 1957 a divided New York Court of Appeals reversed the state regents' ban on *Garden of Eden,* a film produced in a Florida nudist colony, as not sufficiently obscene to meet new standards; Judge Marvin R. Dye took the occasion to recommend that New York's censorship law be tossed out completely—"it has ceased to serve any practical or useful purpose."[60] In Massachusetts the Supreme Judicial Court refused to tolerate the censorship of movies to be shown on Sunday: "It is unthinkable that there is a power, absent as to secular days, to require the submission to advance scrutiny by governmental authority of newspapers to be published on Sunday, or sermons to be preached on Sunday, or public addresses to be made on Sunday." Motion pictures, said the Massachusetts court, were now entitled to the same protection under rules of free speech.[22] Shortly thereafter a United States district court voided a section of Chicago's municipal ordinance by which exhibition of *Desire Under the Elms* had limited to patrons over twenty-one. Such a law was "a patent invasion of the right to freedom of speech guaranteed by the First Amendment."[115] And in Maryland state censors were told by the state Court of Appeals that they could not reject films on nudity alone. The court assumed, "possibly naïvely," that a power still remained with the states to enforce some form of prior-restraint censorship, but obscenity would have to be judged by the basic rules of *Roth,* in terms of an entire picture's appeal to the prurient interest of the average moviegoer.[102]

On June 29, 1959, the Supreme Court of the United States dropped another blockbuster. It was a unanimous sort of six-way blockbuster.[90.1] New York censors had banned *Lady Chatterley's Lover* (and the state Court of Appeals had upheld them) as an immoral movie, in that its theme presented adultery "as a desirable, acceptable and proper pattern of behavior." Neither the censors nor the New York courts had found the film obscene. Rather, they had followed the New York law which required the denial of a license to any motion picture which approvingly portrayed an adulterous relationship, without reference to the manner of its portrayal. Said Associate Justice Potter Stewart, speaking for the court:

> What New York has done, therefore, is to prevent the exhibition of a motion picture because that picture advocates an idea—that adultery under certain circumstances may be proper behavior. Yet the First Amendment's basic guarantee is of freedom to advocate ideas. The state, quite simply, has thus struck at the very heart of constitutionally protected liberty.

> It is contended that the state's action was justified because the motion picture attractively portrays a relationship which is contrary to the moral standards, the religious precepts, and the legal code of its citizenry. This argument misconceives what it is that the Constitution protects. Its guarantee is not confined to the expression of ideas that are conventional or shared by the majority. It protects advocacy of the opinion that adultery may sometimes be proper, no less than advocacy of socialism or the single tax. And in the realm of ideas it protects expression which is eloquent no less than that which is unconvincing.

In a concluding paragraph the court's opinion once again left unanswered the ultimate question the tribunal had avoided in the *Burstyn* case seven years earlier; the court found no occasion to consider the exhibitor's contention "that the state is entirely without power to require films of any kind to be licensed prior to their exhibition." Neither did the court choose to say whether the controls which a state may impose upon motion pictures "are precisely coextensive with those allowable to newspapers,[111] books,[90] or individual speech." The court thought it sufficient simply to reaffirm "that motion pictures are within the First and Fourteenth Amendment's basic protection."

Mr. Justice Frankfurter filed a concurring opinion. He thought

Lady Chatterley's Lover a dull film and was amazed that New York should have banned it in the first place. Beyond this, however, he felt compelled to hold that New York was out of bounds in enforcing a statute which prohibited the public showing of any film that deals with adultery "except by way of sermonizing condemnation." But he felt his brothers had gone too far in voiding the New York law altogether. Statutes in this field, he emphasized, are not easy to write. A difficult problem lies in "the formulation of constitutionally allowable safeguards which society may take against evil without impinging upon the necessary dependence of a free society upon the fullest scope of free expression." For his own part he did not construe *Burstyn, Gelling,* and other cases as prohibiting all state censorship of movies. On the contrary he thought these decisions

> left no doubt that a motion-picture licensing law is not inherently outside the scope of the regulatory powers of a state under the Fourteenth Amendment.

And in a passing comment, Mr. Justice Frankfurter went out of his way to remark that, "I hardly conceive it possible that the Court would strike down as unconstitutional the federal statute against mailing lewd, obscene, and lascivious matter, which has been the law of the land for nearly a hundred years."

Associate Justice Tom Clark filed a concurring opinion, in which he criticized the New York law, in its application to *Lady Chatterley's Lover,* as granting the censors a sort of roving commission in which their individual impressions would become a yardstick for public regulation. He feared, however, that the broad language of the court's opinion would serve only to create more confusion in the field of state censorship. He added a significant comment: "I see no grounds for confusion, however, were a statute to ban 'pornographic' films, or those that 'portray acts of sexual immorality, perversion, or lewdness.'"

A third concurring opinion came from Mr. Justice Harlan, who emphasized his feeling that the New York statute was not necessarily unconstitutional; it merely was applied unconstitutionally to *Lady Chatterley's Lover.* A fourth concurring opinion came from Mr. Justice Douglas, who reiterated his view that all forms of prior-restraint censorship are unconstitutional. Mr. Justice Black brought up the rear with a fifth concurring opinion, in which he derided his brothers as "about the most inappropriate Supreme Board of Censors that could be found."

From this litter of judicial expressions we may fairly conclude that Douglas, Black, and almost certainly Chief Justice Warren oppose any sort of prior-restraint censorship of motion pictures. In 1953, when Justice Brennan was on the Supreme Court of New Jersey, he commented in a Newark case, upholding the denial of a license to a burlesque house, that "only in exceptional cases" can prior restraint be justified, but "by universal agreement, one such exception is speech which is outrightly lewd and indecent."[2] (The opinion he wrote on that occasion was reaffirmed in New Jersey in 1956 in another decision upholding the Newark ordinance as wholly within a community's right to prevent moral contamination.[1]) From this we may deduce that Brennan and Clark stand about together, in sanctioning of prior restraint only of manifestly pornographic films. Harlan and Frankfurter are far more tolerant of state efforts to enforce a prior-restraint censorship. The views of Stewart and Whittaker are not clear.

Meanwhile, federal judges appear to be proceeding on the assumption that prior-restraint censorship still is valid in the field of obscenity if it is valid nowhere else. This was the conclusion of Chief Judge William J. Campbell of the United States District Court in Chicago in April, 1960, when he upheld Chicago's ban upon *The Lovers*.[278] He found it "implicit that motion picture censorship is possible," and he found, too, that "there is a *need* for censorship which extends beyond the sanction of subsequent punishment." In passing, it may be noted that exhibition of *The Lovers* led to jail sentences for two Ohio theater operators; Chief Judge Campbell saw the film as "completely centered around and dominated by sexual play and gratification."

As this is written only four states—Kansas, Maryland, New York, and Virginia—persist in statewide censorship by prior licensing. A few cities also have such laws, though the ordinances are erratically enforced. One of these years, it may be confidently predicted, the motion-picture industry will pick out some wholly innocent and innocuous film, a comedy or a musical or a routine horse opera, or perhaps an "idea" film, and demand the yes-or-no answer the

Supreme Court has been avoiding so successfully. When that day arrives the remaining ordinances will be done for. The motion-picture industry, for good or ill, will find itself at last in a class with newspapers, books, and magazines, blessed with freedom to publish but responsible for the abuse of that freedom. That is the way the laws of obscenity censorship should operate; in a free country, indeed, they cannot operate in any other way.

Such a ruling may be forthcoming early in the 1960's. While this manuscript was in preparation, a Chicago exhibitor brought a direct challenge to the whole concept of censorship by prior restraint under a municipal ordinance. His flat contention is that Chicago's requirement that all motion pictures be submitted for censorship prior to their exhibition violates the First and Fourteenth Amendments to the Constitution. In March, the Supreme Court of the United States granted *certiorari* in the case, and agreed to consider the question during its 1960–61 term.

PART III

THE CONFLICT

The real problem is the formulation of constitutionally allowable safeguards which society may take against evil without impinging upon the necessary dependence of a free society upon the fullest scope of free expression.

JUSTICE FELIX FRANKFURTER
concurring in Kingsley International Pictures Corporation
v. Regents of the University of the State of New York, 360 U.S. 684
(1959)

1. THE CENSOR AT WORK

In January of 1960, while this book was in preparation, the United States Information Agency sent out a pleasant little press release. The gist of it was that one thousand paperback bookshelves were about to be sent overseas to the agency's 160 libraries abroad. Each shelf was to include twenty inexpensive classics of American literature, "among them Hawthorne's *The House of Seven Gables,* Twain's *Huckleberry Finn,* and Whitman's *Leaves of Grass."*

What a gentle irony was here! Each of the three classic American authors at one time or another was censored for the obscenity of his writing. A century ago Hawthorne saw his *Scarlet Letter* banned all the way to Russia; as recently as 1925 Hollywood censors insisted that poor Hester be married on the screen. Twain's *Huckleberry Finn* was banned in Concord, New Hampshire, and his scatological essay, "1601," remains to this day a work of suppressed erotica. "If there is a decent word in it," Twain once remarked, "it is because I overlooked it." Whitman published *Leaves of Grass* in 1855, lost his job in the Department of the Interior ten years later because of it, and fought off the censors the last thirty years of his life. Today the three of them rank among the finest exemplars of American writing the USIA could select to represent the United States abroad. Mr. Clemens would have been pleased.

A fourth member of the USIA's classic team was Benjamin Franklin, a bawdy essayist in his own right, who left to posterity an epigram on two certainties of mortal life. He might have added a third: censorship. It has been always with us. In one sense it is a manifestation of a community's understandable desire to protect itself from shock and indecency; in another view it is no more than a manifestation of that itch to do good that has had mankind scratching since Socrates took the hemlock and Plato denounced Homer as unfit for the youth of Athens.

To glance down a list of authors whose work has been condemned as obscene—and many editors have compiled such lists—is to be impressed, at first glance, with the apparent follies of all censorship, at all times, in all places. Shaw's aphorism often seems to find justification here: "Censorship ends in logical completeness when nobody is allowed to read any books except the books nobody can read." The roll call of the beautiful and the banned is long; it is eloquent, but it may be misleading also. It is perhaps unfair to view censorship, historically, with a sort of 20/20 hindsight; and it may be equally unfair to damn all activities of today's decent literature committees because of the follies and excesses of some of them. Those caveats aside, even the briefest backward look at censorship provides a sobering experience.

Plutarch two thousand years ago thought some of the comedies of Aristophanes obscene; and so, for that matter, did the United States Bureau of Customs in 1958. Ovid is long dead; his comments upon the arts of love may be acceptable now in Latin; they are still obscene in English. The late D. J. Juvenal is today barely within the accepted pale; he was once beyond it. The *Golden Ass* of Apuleius was banned in Cleveland as recently as 1953, and for a silly reason: the title might give offense. Rabelais to this day is banned in South Africa, and with him, Tennessee Williams, Nicholas Monsarrat, Phyllis Bottome, and James T. Farrell. Boccaccio, after six centuries, is just emerging from the academic strait jacket in which Mr. Comstock left him; published in Italian and bound in morocco, the *Decameron* seemed to the Great Reformer suitable for cloistered scholars, but not suitable, otherwise, for anyone else.

Byron was damned for *Don Juan* and *Cain* (Lord Eldon thought the latter blasphemous). Shelley suffered for *Queen Mab*. Swinburne's poems were too rich for the Victorian morals of 1866. Charlotte Brontë saw *Jane Eyre* condemned as "too immoral to be ranked with decent literature." Elizabeth Barrett Browning's *Aurora Leigh* was first seen as no more than the "hysterical indecencies of an erotic mind." To the censors of another day *Adam Bede* was the "vile outpouring of a lewd woman's mind." In the London of 1907

Edward Garnett's *The Breaking Point* fell to a censor's ruling that "the tragic emotions of an unwed girl about to become a mother" were too immoral for public consumption. Long before the statistical tables of Dr. Kinsey reached the best-seller lists, a bookdealer who sold Havelock Ellis's *Studies in the Psychology of Sex* went to trial on a charge of "intending to vitiate and corrupt the morals of liege subjects of our said Lady the Queen, and to raise and create in them lustful desires, and to bring said liege subjects into a state of wickedness, lewdness, and debauchery."

And what of our own more enlightened times? Joyce had one thousand copies of *The Dubliners* printed, and saved back one for himself; the other nine hundred and ninety-nine went into the flames. Anatole France, Sigmund Freud, Montaigne, Voltaire, Tolstoi, Ibsen, Zola—they knew suppression. Defoe saw *Moll Flanders* banned, and Sterne saw *Tristam Shandy* condemned.

Comstock died in 1915, but the chase went on. Two writers in the *Boston Law Review,* Sidney S. Grant and S. E. Angoff, once compiled a small index of books subjected to Boston banning, during that long night of intellectual and alcoholic prohibition. There was Dreiser, of course, for *Sister Carrie, The Genius,* and *An American Tragedy;* and St. John Ervine's *The Wayward Man* and *The Irishman;* Sherwood Anderson's *Dark Laughter;* Arthur Train's *High Winds;* Conrad Aiken's *Blue Voyage;* Bertrand Russell's *What I Believe;* Upton Sinclair's *Oil* (a book clerk went to jail for six months for selling this one). The same period saw Branch Cabell in trouble with *Jurgen,* F. Scott Fitzgerald in court for *The Beautiful and Damned,* and Faulkner fighting for the right to sell *Mosquitoes* and *Sanctuary.* Leon Feuchtwanger was damned for *Power,* and John Dos Passos for *1919* and *Manhattan Transfer,* and Ben Hecht for *Count Bruga* and *Gargoyles,* and Sinclair Lewis for *Elmer Gantry,* and Judge Ben Lindsey for *The Revolt of Modern Youth.* James A. DeLacey, manager of the Dunster House Bookshop in Cambridge, went to jail for a month and suffered a fine of $500 for selling Lawrence's *Lady Chatterley's Lover.*

Nor does the melancholy roll call of the 1920's stop with Judge Woolsey's great break-through of 1933 in the *Ulysses* case.[252] Gautier had been dead for fifty years when John Sumner denounced him in

Manhattan. Gide and Flaubert, in our own generation, have been thought too obscene to be read. James T. Farrell's *Studs Lonigan* trilogy figured in *Commonwealth* v. *Gordon*. John O'Hara's *Ten North Frederick* may have won the National Book Award but it was too obscene for Cleveland, Detroit, and Albany. In Wheeling, West Virginia, J. D. Salinger's tender *Catcher in the Rye* was not tender; it was dirty. Rhode Island created a board of censors, in part because of Henry James's *The Turn of the Screw*. John Griffin's intensely moral *The Devil Rides Outside* led to the famous case of *Butler* v. *Michigan*. Saul Bellow's *The Adventures of Augie March* could not be tolerated in McMechen, West Virginia. Leon Uris, John Steinbeck, Erskine Caldwell, Lillian Smith, Edmund Wilson, Arthur Schnitzler, Erich Maria Remarque, Vivian Connell, Conan Doyle—the list seems never to end.

And if obscenity censorship is to be understood at all it must be understood that the roll call never will end. In his excellent book, *Obscenity and the Law,* Norman St. John-Stevas recalled the comment of Critic James Douglas in the *Sunday Express,* when *Ulysses* first appeared in 1924:

> I have read it and I say deliberately that it is the most infamously obscene book in ancient or in modern literature. The obscenity of Rabelais is innocent compared with its leprous and scabrous horrors. All the secret sewers of vice are canalized in its flood of unimaginable thoughts, images and pornographic words. And its unclean lunacies are larded with appalling and revolting blasphemies directed against the Christian religions and against the holy name of Christ—blasphemies hitherto associated with the most degraded orgies of Satanism and the Black Mass.

It is an instructive experience to go back and read the critical reviews of *Lady Chatterley's Lover* when the novel first appeared in 1928. Today the work bears the imprimatur of an Archibald Mac-Leish and the *nihil obstat* of a learned district judge; it was not always so. Some of the most respected critics of Lawrence's day, reflecting the shocked opinions of the "very best people," regarded the amours of Lady Constance as dirt for dirt's sake. Filth. Obscenity. Thirty years before General Summerfield came on the scene they asked his fine rhetorical question, "If this is not dirt, pray, what is?"

Enough. The point perhaps is made. Censorship has moved from the pagan to the baroque to the Christian to the puritanic, and from heresy to treason to obscenity. In every age the censors have ranked among the most upstanding citizens of their day, and some of the books they have condemned have become the great classics of our own. No sarcasm is intended here. The point will be lost if sarcasm, contempt, or ridicule is read into this chronology. Obscenity censorship is a function of the times in which it is imposed; it is a manifestation of customs, of mores, and can be judged fairly only in a context of time and place. That which was obscene yesterday may not be obscene today; and that which is universally condemned as obscene today—even the hardest of hard-core pornography—may not be obscene a generation hence. Viewed in this light, acts of censorship that may seem at first absurd are seen more clearly as no more than curious. When Whitman's *Leaves of Grass* offended public decency a traveler counted a month lost in going from coast to coast; we fly this distance in six hours now and complain of the time lost in reaching the airports. Tomorrow the flight will take two hours, and the day after, thirty minutes. But the travel conditions of 1865 are viewed not with contempt, as we seem to view a ban on *Leaves of Grass,* but with the understanding eye of history. Why should it be otherwise with obscenity censorship? Our jurors today are no less intelligent, and no more foolish, than the jurors of Mr. Comstock's day.

2. THE CASE AGAINST CENSORSHIP

There always have been censors, and thankfully, there always have been men to fight against censors. It never has been a wholly one-sided affair. Milton fought the licensors of Charles I, and Ingersoll fought Comstock, and Mencken fought Chase, and Morris Ernst and Alexander Lindey and a host of good colleagues have fought the past six postmasters general. One ought not to imagine that the excesses of censorship have gone unchallenged. Not recently, at least. Nor has the alignment of forces changed essentially these past three hundred years. The conflict now is the same unchanging conflict it has always been, world without end, *in saecula saeculorum,* the rights of the individual pitted against the power of the state; and where do you draw the line?

The case against obscenity censorship is a strong and appealing case. The principal arguments may be grouped under five general headings.

1. Obscenity censorship is unconstitutional; it violates the great principle of freedom of the press, and it takes from the American people their corollary freedom to read.

It is said at the outset (Justices Black and Douglas have said it repeatedly) that no affirmative authority for obscenity censorship ever was vested in the Congress by the Constitution. Whatever the powers may be that authorize Congress to establish post roads and to regulate commerce among the states, these powers are limited by the plain and unequivocal commandment of the First Amendment: Congress shall make *no law* abridging the freedom of the press. The words "no law" do not mean "some law." They are to be read literally: "no law." And because the prohibitions laid upon Congress by the

First Amendment have been extended to the states by the Fourteenth, the states also are prohibited by the Constitution from exercising any power to abridge the freedom of the press.

Mr. Justice Harlan outlined the case against Federal obscenity censorship with brilliant clarity in his dissenting opinion in the *Roth* case.[166] The Congress, he wrote:

> has no substantive power over sexual morality. Such powers as the federal government has in this field are but incidental to its other powers, here the postal power, and are not of the same nature as those possessed by the states, which bear direct responsibility for the protection of the local moral fabric. . . .
>
> The danger is perhaps not great if the people of one state, through their legislature, decide that *Lady Chatterley's Lover* goes so far beyond the acceptable standards of candor that it will be deemed offensive and nonsellable, for the state next door is still free to make its own choice. At least we do not have one uniform standard. But the dangers to free thought and expression are truly great if the federal government imposes a blanket ban over the Nation on such a book. The prerogative of the states to differ on their ideas of morality will be destroyed, the ability of states to experiment will be stunted. The fact that the people of one state cannot read some of the works of D. H. Lawrence seems to me, if not wise or desirable, at least acceptable. But that no person in the United States should be allowed to do so seems to me to be intolerable, and violative of both the letter and the spirit of the First Amendment.

Mr. Justice Harlan went on to remark that Roth had been convicted under jury instructions defining a book as nonmailably obscene if the book "tends to stir sexual impulses and lead to sexually impure thoughts." The federal government, he said flatly, "has no business, whether under the postal or commerce power, to bar the sale of books because they might lead to any kind of 'thoughts.' "

Justices Douglas and Black dissented in both *Roth* and *Alberts*. Examining press freedom historically, Douglas could find no evidence that literature dealing with sex was to be treated differently by those who drafted the First Amendment. The founding fathers were concerned with freedom of speech totally. They never would have consented to any limitations upon discussion of religion, economics, politics or philosophy in terms of what might offend the common conscience of a community. "How does it become a constitutional standard when literature treating with sex is concerned?"

The only power the federal government and the states might possibly have in this field, said Douglas, is the power to proscribe *conduct* on the grounds of good morals.

> Government should be concerned with antisocial conduct, not with utterances. Thus if the First Amendment guarantee of freedom of speech and press is to mean anything in this field, it must allow protests even against the moral code that the standard of the day sets for the community. In other words, literature should not be suppressed merely because it offends the moral code of the censor.
>
> Freedom of expression can be suppressed if, and to the extent that, it is so closely brigaded with illegal action as to be an inseparable part of it. As a people, we cannot afford to relax that standard. For the test that suppresses a cheap tract today can suppress a literary gem tomorrow. All it need do is incite a lascivious thought or arouse a lustful desire. The list of books that judges or juries can place in that category is endless.
>
> I would give the broad sweep of the First Amendment full support. . . .

In thus denouncing both state and federal obscenity laws Douglas was echoing the views of a Pennsylvania jurist, Judge Curtis Bok, who in 1949 had written an eloquent decision, widely quoted, refusing to convict Philadelphia bookdealers of selling half a dozen books thought to be obscene.[44] To the argument that Congress might not have power to censor at the federal level but that the states had much broader powers at their own level, Judge Bok asserted that "it no longer is possible that free speech be guaranteed federally and denied locally."

> Under modern methods of instantaneous communication, such a discrepancy makes no sense. If a speech is to be free anywhere, it must be free everywhere, and a law that can be used as a spigot

that allows speech to flow freely or to be checked altogether is a general threat to free opinion and enlightened solution. What is said in Pennsylvania may clarify an issue in California, and what is suppressed in California may leave us the worse in Pennsylvania. Unless a restriction on free speech be of national validity, it can no longer have any local validity whatever. Some danger to us all must appear before any of us can be muzzled.

Judge Jerome Frank of New York, an old foe of censorship laws, criticized Roth's conviction on constitutional grounds when the case was before the Court of Appeals for the Second Circuit.[257] He recalled Jefferson's horrified reaction to the suppression of a religious work: "If we are to have a censor, whose imprimatur shall say what books may be sold and what we may buy? Whose foot is to be the measure by which ours are all to be cut or stretched?" Framers of the First Amendment lived at a time when there were no statutes on obscene publications as such; the publication of obscenity was at best a crime under English common law, "and the framers of the Amendment knowingly and deliberately intended to depart from the English common law as to freedom of speech and freedom of the press."

The danger in obscenity laws, Judge Frank warned, is not to be judged on aesthetic grounds alone—that some classic novel might be suppressed, or some work of art destroyed. There are more serious implications here. It is an easy path from mild governmental control of what adults may read about sex to stern governmental control of what adults may read about politics or religion. Milton, Jefferson, Madison, Mill, and Tocqueville, he observed,

have pointed out that any paternalistic guardianship by government of the thoughts of grown-up citizens enervates their spirit, keeps them immature, all too ready to adopt toward government officers the attitude that, in general, "Papa knows best." If the government possesses the power to censor publications which arouse sexual thoughts, regardless of whether those thoughts tend probably to transform themselves into antisocial behavior, why may not the government censor political and religious publications regardless of any causal relation to probable dangerous deeds?

Through any number of cases on free speech the same theme may be traced. If the Constitution permits any limitation on what a citizen sets in type and publishes, the limitation must rest in some emergency situation—in "the probability of serious injury to the state," as Brandeis once defined it,[274.1] or in a "clear and present danger," in Holmes' famed remark.[168] If the supposed damage to society from a particular publication be merely trivial, the constitutional prohibitions come into play; for as Mr. Justice Black remarked in a case involving an obscene phonograph record,[199] statutes that treat a smutty record as a serious danger to society "may readily be converted into instruments for dangerous abridgments of freedom of expression."

The risk of tyranny on the part of government is not the only ill the First Amendment sought to guard against. Laws that limit free expression not only enhance the control of government; by their very existence they also blight the growth of literature. John Stuart Mill, a century ago, asked in his essay on liberty: "Who can compute what the world loses in the multitude of promising intellects combined with timid characters, who dare not follow out any bold, vigorous, independent train of thought, lest it should land them in something which would admit of being considered irreligious or immoral?" The experience of other lands provides an answer for the question Mill raised. In testimony in February, 1960, before a House committee, Dan Lacy, representing the American Book Publishers Council, made a telling point:

The five countries that today probably most consistently and thoroughly, through government and industry means, apply a control over the content of publications in the area of sex are Communist China, Ireland, Russia, South Africa and Spain. It is by no means an accidental coincidence that all of these also practice an extensive political censorship of varying degree; but here I am speaking only of moral censorship and its consequences. Though such a control by no means prevents writings of moral vacuity and disorientation, it is quite successful in eliminating salacious and obscene writing and the overdramatization of sex. It has also, in the process, substantially eliminated from those countries the main body of contemporary world literature. Almost no Western novelists appear in China; few in Russia. Among world renowned authors whose writings have been banned from Ireland are Theodore Dreiser, Sherwood Anderson, James Branch Cabell, Sinclair Lewis, Aldous Huxley, William Faulkner, Lillian Smith, Erich Remarque, John Steinbeck, and James T. Farrell. . . .

The consequences are seen not only in this blocking of the international flow of the masterpieces of contemporary world literature, but also in the drying up of creative writing within those countries. All, with the partial exception of South Africa, are countries of the richest creative tradition; but their literature lives today only in the sort of rebellion against the controlling morality expressed by an O'Casey, a Pasternak, or a Paton.

One final argument against obscenity censorship may be raised on broad questions of constitutionality. While it is true that the language of the First Amendment protects the writer in specific terms, the tradition of free expression embraces the reader implicitly also. The act of communication necessarily requires a hearer as well as a speaker; thus a statute that inhibits the author's freedom to write in the same moment inhibits the people's freedom to read. What good does it do to let the winds of doctrine blow, if no man is free to wet his finger to them?

In May of 1953 a joint conference of the American Library Association and the American Book Publishers Council defended this "freedom to read" in an eloquent statement. Their primary concern at the time was with political censorship—with the suppression of ideas thought to be anti-American or merely controversial—but their declaration applied with equal force to the suppression of works thought to be corruptive of morals:

We are deeply concerned about these attempts at suppression. Most such attempts rest on a denial of the fundamental premise of democracy: that the ordinary citizen, by exercising his critical judgment, will accept the good and reject the bad. The censors, public and private, assume that they should determine what is good and what is bad for their fellow-citizens.

We trust Americans to recognize propaganda, and to reject obscenity. We do not believe they need the help of censors to assist them in this task. We do not believe they are prepared to sacrifice their heritage of a free press in order to be "protected" against what others think may be bad for them. We believe they still favor free enterprise in ideas and expression. . . .

We believe that free communication is essential to the preservation of a free society and a creative culture. We believe that these pressures toward conformity present the danger of limiting the range and variety of inquiry and expression on which our democracy and our culture depend. We believe that every American community must jealously guard the freedom to publish and to circulate, in order to preserve its own freedom to read. . . .

2. Assuming for the sake of argument that statutes attempting to impose obscenity censorship are within the Constitution, such statutes are invalid on other grounds: they are vague, inconsistent, and incapable of being enforced except by arbitrary and capricious administration.

A law may be constitutional in principle and yet be invalid on other grounds. Especially is it true of criminal statutes, which must be narrowly construed, that an offense must be spelled out exactly. No man should be fined or imprisoned for doing "something wrong" unless it is clear what this something wrong is. If a motorist be convicted for traveling seventy miles an hour in a zone plainly marked for fifty, he cannot complain of uncertainty in the law. The man who willfully sets fire to a dwelling house in the nighttime may be found guilty of arson; the elements of the crime are clear and distinct. But what is to be said of a law that makes it a crime to sell a book that appeals "to the prurient interest of the average citizen applying contemporary community standards"?

Such a statute, said Justice Douglas, dissenting in *Roth,* is entirely too loose and too capricious ever to be sustained:

Under that test, juries can censor, suppress, and punish what they don't like, provided the matter relates to "sexual impurity" or has a tendency "to excite lustful thoughts." This is community censorship in one of its worst forms. It creates a regime where in the battle between the literati and the Philistines, the Philistines are certain to win.

The law likes to be orderly, but in its effort to create an objective orderliness in the subjective field of obscenity censorship the law has signally failed. Thus when the film *Disraeli* reached Boston, one line —"Damn your collar"—had to be excised on Sundays; on weekdays Mr. George Arliss could damn as he pleased. In Chicago, until the courts threw the ordinance out, a married serviceman of twenty, the father of a child, was the object of the city's solicitous protection: he could not view *Desire Under the Elms*. Judge Kirkland, in the case of the nudist magazines, attempted to devise some formula in feet and inches from camera to subject.[185] The peak of the 1959 controversy over *Lady Chatterley's Lover* saw a respected churchman tabulating the derivatives of an old Anglo-Saxon word in a span of three pages. Total, seven; verdict, obscene. But suppose it had been six? Or five, or four, or three, or two, or one?

This practical problem of reaching an objective, clear-cut, and easily understandable definition of a crime poses a particular difficulty in obscenity cases for this reason: in most cases of criminal law everyone understands exactly what the criminal act is, and the object is to find out whether the defendant committed it. But in obscenity cases, as Dan Lacy has pointed out, there is usually no doubt that the defendant committed the act. The problem is to find out whether the act itself was a crime. There is nothing inherently criminal in driving a car; there is nothing inherently criminal in selling a book. But a charge of excessive speed is susceptible to some sort of objective proof; a charge of excessive indecency is not. The blips of obscenity cannot be tracked on a radar screen.

The trouble with the majority's opinion in *Roth-Alberts,* said the dissenting Justice Harlan, was the court's presumption that some sort of speech known as "obscene speech" is not the sort of speech the founding fathers had in mind when they commanded the Congress to make no law that abridged free speech. Such a sweeping formula, he said:

appears to me to beg the very question before us. The Court seems to assume that "obscenity" is a peculiar *genus* of "speech and press," which is as distinct, recognizable, and classifiable as poison ivy is among other plants.

But this is not so. It is historically not so, as Judge Sydney Goldman of the Superior Court of New Jersey once pointed out, in refusing to hold Vivian Connell's *The Chinese Room* an obscene book.[14] "Even the most cursory account of literary censorship," he wrote, "will show its contradictions, the absence of valid standards, its lack of inner logic, and outward consistency." To look for a common standard and purpose in censorship, he added, "is to seek the impossible."

Judge Bok made the same point in his *Commonwealth* v. *Gordon.* In the broad fields of sexual morality and written or oral expression, such offenses as open and notorious lewdness, indecent public exposure, sedition, blasphemy, blackmail, libel, false advertising, and the sending of anonymous letters have acquired reasonable definitions. Not so with obscenity: "There is no constant or reliable indication of it to be found in human experience."

One rule of thumb applied by the Post Office in weighing the obscenity of a nude photograph is whether a woman's pubic hair is shown. (D. H. Lawrence once called this a process of splitting pubic hairs.) On this basis the department was made to look absurd. This rule of pubic hair, in itself, will not suffice.

Does a book use profane and vulgar words to describe the excretory acts or the sexual organs? Everyone knows what these words are. Chaucer used them in "The Miller's Tale"; Shakespeare's players spell one of them out in *Twelfth Night*. Obscene words, in themselves, cannot establish obscenity.

Nor can any other objective test establish the fact of obscenity in a criminal prosecution. Judge Frank, in an early case against Samuel Roth, had occasion to ponder a book of dirty stories Roth had sent through the mails. They were precisely the same stories, he noted, that "are freely told at many gatherings of prominent lawyers."[165] He was not able to perceive that the lawyers were corrupted or depraved thereby, and he hardly thought the lawyers a race apart from common men. Judge Frank also had dropped by a public library and checked out a copy of Balzac's *Droll Stories*: "For the life of me," he wrote, "I cannot see, nor understand how anyone else could see, anything in that book less obscene than in *Waggish Tales* which the Postmaster General has suppressed."

But it is not only that the obscenity of a book defies precise measurement. Other elements that contribute to the determination of guilt or innocence are equally indefinable. How does one establish a book's "dominant tone" save by counting the dirty pages—a process forbidden by the requirement that the book be considered as a whole? What is meant by "contemporary community standards"? A typical community will have many standards, some strict, some not so strict. Is it said that one must judge by the standards of the "average person"? Who is the average modern reader, Judge Bok asked in *Commonwealth* v. *Gordon*?

> It is impossible to say just what his reactions to a book actually are. . . . If he reads an obscene book when his sensuality is low, he will yawn over it or find that its suggestibility leads him off on quite different paths. If he reads the mechanics lien act while his sensuality is high, things will stand between him and the page that have no business there. How can anyone say that he will infallibly be affected one way or another by one book or another? The professional answer that is suggested is the one general compromise— that the appetite of sex is old, universal, and unpredictable, and that the best we can do to keep it within reasonable bounds is to be our brother's keeper and censor, because we never know when his sensuality will be high. This does not satisfy me, for in a field where even reasonable precision is utterly impossible, I trust people more than I do the law.

The argument also is made against obscenity prosecutions—Judge Frank has made it most effectively[257]—that they suffer from a strange inconsistency. The Comstock Act in one breath undertakes to punish the mailing of matter that makes sex attractive, alluring, and exciting. In the next breath it undertakes to punish the mailing of matter that makes sex ugly, depraved, and repulsive. No other meaning can be read into the statute's ban on "filthy" material. But if the object of obscenity laws is to prevent the people from embracing the attractions of illicit sex, why should the repulsive items be proscribed? Is it worse to be alluring or worse to be repellant? Or is discussion of sex in any form obscene? The courts have not said so; indeed such a position was emphatically disclaimed in the *Roth* opinion.

> *3. Even if precise, consistent, and comprehensible statutes could be drafted, censorship laws should be rejected as poor public policy; such laws represent an unwarranted and impudent attempt to regulate other people's morals, and without just cause—for no causal relationship ever has been established between obscene literature and delinquency.*

Here we approach the heart of the case against obscenity censorship. The one great, precious factor that distinguishes a free society from a totalitarian society is the absence of unwarranted governmental restraint upon the free man. Within the broadest possible limits the free man may work as he pleases, live as he pleases, come and go as he pleases, think, read, write, vote, and worship as he pleases. His liberties, of course, are not absolute, and these days they seem to be more steadily infringed all the time, but his liberties in theory extend to the point at which Citizen A causes some serious loss, risk, or inconvenience to Citizen B.

This theory underlies the whole structure of our law. The right of a man to be secure in his household is a basic right, but no man, in the heart of a residential neighborhood, may leave filth for rats, or shoot firearms from an upstairs window, or play his radio too loudly after midnight, or raise pigs, or launch into the business of making glue. Considerations of the neighborhood's health, safety, and welfare are superior to his rights as an individual. On this same basis society restricts the dispensation of poison and narcotics, because poison and narcotics demonstrably cause harm. In Virginia, where Jefferson wrote his Statute of Religious Freedom, the state forbids faith healers to handle rattlesnakes in public squares; the bite of a rattler, beyond doubt, may cause death. Speed causes accidents, and watered stocks cause financial loss, and contaminated water supplies may cause epidemics, and the law says to the motorist, the promoter, the farmer, "Thou shalt not." It is the causal factor that counts—the direct and measurable relationship between the action and the antisocial consequence—and the very essence of our law is this abiding principle that man's freedom of action should not be inhibited where such consequence cannot be shown.

The case against obscenity censorship holds that such a causal relationship never has been established so far as pornographic materials are concerned. In the earlier of the two *Roth* cases[165] Judge Frank said:

> I think that no sane man thinks socially dangerous the arousing of normal sexual desires. Consequently, if reading obscene books has merely that consequence, Congress, it would seem, can constitutionally no more suppress such books than it can prevent the mailing of many other objects, such as perfume, for example, which notoriously produce that result. But the constitutional power to suppress obscene publications might well exist if there were ample reason to believe that reading them conduces to socially harmful sexual conduct on the part of normal human beings. However, convincing proof of that fact has never been assembled.

In the second *Roth* case[257] Judge Frank expanded upon this theme. If it could be shown that the reading of obscene material caused antisocial *actions* he could support an obscenity law; but to ban material that might produce merely antisocial *thoughts* seemed to him an abuse of governmental power:

> Suppose it argued that whatever excites sexual longings might *possibly* produce sexual misconduct. That cannot suffice. . . . It may be that among the stimuli to irregular sexual conduct, by normal men and women, may be almost anything—the odor of carnations, the sight of a cane or a candle or a shoe, the touch of silk or a gunnysack. For all anyone now knows, stimuli of that sort may be far more provocative of such misconduct than reading obscene books or seeing obscene pictures.
>
> To date there exist, I think, no thoroughgoing studies by competent persons which justify the conclusion that normal adults' reading or seeing of the "obscene" probably induces antisocial conduct. Such competent studies as have been made do conclude that so complex and numerous are the causes of sexual vice that it is impossible to assert with any assurance that "obscenity" repre-

sents a ponderable causal factor in sexually deviant adult behavior. Although the whole subject of obscenity censorship hinges upon the unproved assumption that "obscene" literature is a significant factor in causing sexual deviation from the community standard, no report can be found of a single effort at genuine research to test this assumption by singling out as a factor for study the effect of sex literature upon sexual behavior. What little competent research has been done points definitely in a direction precisely opposite to that assumption.

Alpert reports that, when, in the 1920's, 409 women college graduates were asked to state in writing what things stimulated them sexually, they answered thus: 218 said "Man"; 95 said books; 40 said drama; 29 said dancing; 18 said pictures; 9 said music. Of those who replied that the source of their sex information came from books, not one specified a "dirty" book as the source. Instead, the books listed were: The Bible, the dictionary, the encyclopedia, novels from Dickens to Henry James, circulars about venereal diseases, medical books, and Motley's *Rise of the Dutch Republic*. Macaulay, replying to advocates of the suppression of obscene books, said: "We find it difficult to believe that in a world so full of temptations as this, any gentleman whose life would have been virtuous if he had not read Aristophanes or Juvenal, will be made vicious by reading them." Echoing Macaulay, "Jimmy" Walker remarked that he had never heard of a woman seduced by a book.

Morris Ernst, in *The Censor Marches On,* makes the point that the American Republic survived for almost a century without a federal obscenity law. Nothing indicates that the nation was headed for perdition in those days, nor is there evidence to suggest that public morality improved after the Comstock Act of 1873. Three quarters of a century have passed in unrelenting war upon obscenity. What has this battle accomplished? Whose morals have been saved? Assuredly the morals of the censors have not been saved, for the censors' morals were never in danger. In *To the Pure* Ernst remarks that no one ever has urged a strict law against obscenity with the statement, "Please pass this statute to protect *me* from this sexually abhorrent material." No, the necessity is always to protect someone else. "We are so fearful for other people's morals," wrote Judge Bok. "They so seldom have the courage of our own convictions." In this connection Ernst recalls the statement of Mary Boyce Temple some years ago at a meeting in Knoxville of the Daughters of the American Revolution. John Coltor and Clemence Randolph's play *Rain* was under discussion. Said this well-intentioned lady:

> We do not fear the effect which such a play would have on us. We of the DAR and the United Daughters of the Confederacy have had the advantages of education and travel and have been prepared for such things. Such a play would not injure us; it would only disgust us. But there are other women who have not had these advantages, and there are the young people who are inexperienced in the problems of life. It is for their benefit and protection that we seek to prevent the showing of such plays in Knoxville. Such a play would not injure me, but I have seen the world. Nobody knows the world better than I. No woman has had greater educational advantages, has been more in social life, or has traveled more than I. I am able to judge of the temptations that come to the young and the inexperienced. It is the duty of us to protect those who have not had our advantages.

In *Commonwealth* v. *Gordon* Judge Bok took a view of free speech, on the battleground of obscenity censorship, that represents the most advanced position any judge has taken. He indicated he would sustain a conviction only where some "clear and present danger" could be proved to result from the reading of an obscene book, and he doubted that such a consequence ever could be shown.

> [A book] cannot be a present danger unless its reader closes it, lays it aside, and transmutes its erotic allurement into overt action. That such action must inevitably follow as a direct consequence of reading the book does not bear analysis, nor is it borne out by general human experience; too much can intervene and too many diversions take place.

Substantially the same position was suggested from the bench of the Supreme Court of the United States, during argument in Doubleday's appeal from a conviction in New York state courts for selling

Edmund Wilson's *Memoirs of Hecate County*.[55.1] This was the curious case that came and went through four courts without leaving a single reported opinion behind. Counsel for the publishing company pitched almost their entire argument upon the issue of "clear and present danger," but no court was willing to grapple with this knotty idea in public. At last the case reached the Supreme Court. Whitney North Seymour, as chief counsel, said this: "The question here is not whether the legislature of New York State believed that morality would be better served by the suppression of a discussion of sexual subjects. The question is rather what, if any, danger has been threatened by the appellant's publication. And if it be assumed that such a danger existed, what was the nature and extent of that danger? Was it sufficiently grave to warrant suppression otherwise prohibited?"

Associate Justice Wiley B. Rutledge interrupted the oral argument to express his wholehearted agreement: "Before we get to the question of clear and present danger, we've got to have something which the state can forbid as dangerous. We are talking in a vacuum until we can establish that there is some occasion for the exercise of the state's power. . . . It is up to the state to demonstrate that there was a danger, and until they demonstrate that, plus the clarity and imminence of the danger, the constitutional prohibition would seem to apply."

In other cases involving free speech, apart from obscene speech, the Supreme Court many times has insisted upon this rule of "clear and present danger." Seymour cited some of them in his brief. In 1940, in *Thornhill* v. *Alabama,* the court had emphasized that the mere likelihood that some substantive evil might result is not sufficient to justify a restriction upon freedom of speech or of the press. An apprehended evil must be "substantial" and "serious." The following year, in *Bridges* v. *California,* the court was still more emphatic:

> What finally emerges from the "clear and present danger" cases is a working principle that the substantive evil must be extremely serious and the degree of imminence extremely high before utterances can be punished.

Three years later, in *Thomas* v. *Collins* (1945), the court again spoke strongly on liberties of speech and press:

. . . any attempt to restrict those liberties must be justified by clear public interest, threatened not doubtfully or remotely, but by clear and present danger. The rational connection between the remedy provided and the evil to be curbed, which in other contexts might support legislation against attack on due-process grounds, will not suffice. These rights rest on firmer foundation. Accordingly, whatever occasion would restrain orderly discussion and persuasion, at appropriate time and place, must have clear support in public danger, actual or impending. Only the gravest abuses, endangering paramount interests, give occasion for permissible limitation.

Was Edmund Wilson's collection of six stories such a grave abuse of press freedom, and such a clear and present danger to the people of New York, that its suppression could be justified under New York law? The state judges thought so: they fined Doubleday $1,000 for publishing the book. Precisely what the Supreme Court of the United States thought will never be known; the court affirmed the conviction, without opinion, by a tie vote of 4-4.

Yet even when all questions of constitutionality and free press have been put to one side the argument of causal relationship remains as a plain statement of public policy, applicable to any field of the law: no man ought to be prohibited from doing any act unless it is plain that his act causes some demonstrable antisocial consequence. In the case of obscene materials, it is contended, such a relationship cannot be shown. There is real danger, Judge Bok agreed, recalling Holmes' old rule, that a theater audience may rush in panic for the doors if a man cry "Fire!" But the public does not read a book, he said, "and simultaneously rush by the hundreds into the streets to engage in orgiastic riots."

4. Obscenity censorship, regardless of its validity as a matter of law, is a futile exercise at best; it does not eliminate obscene materials, but by attempting to suppress them, only makes such material more desirable.

In advancing this argument the foes of censorship appeal to the common experience of mankind. Heard melodies are sweet, but those unheard are sweeter; and whatever you do, said the departing mother to her children, don't put those beans up your nose. So long as obscene books and photographs are viewed as sinful, sinful men will go in search of them. The prohibition laws did not keep man from finding liquor; just so, the obscenity laws do not suppress traffic in obscenity—they merely make it profitable. If the laws were wiped out, Morris Ernst once speculated, the price on dirty postcards might drop from three for a dollar to three for a nickel. At that point no profit would remain. Plainly enough, pornography thrives on the very statutes that are intended to kill it; where such laws are lax, as in France, the people pay scant attention to smut and the racket survives only on export trade. Here at home the Post Office Department's own figures indicate that despite more intensive law enforcement than ever, violations of the obscenity law are mounting at an astonishing rate.

William Sloane, director of Rutgers University Press, has stated this argument succinctly:

I am unimpressed with the record of repressive legislation in this country. The laws against narcotics, for example, are supporting a large criminal class and leading to large-scale corruption of our youth. The laws against off-track betting, at least in the State of New York, are supporting a large criminal class and lead directly to police corruption. No set of laws will prevent the bootlegging of pornography, and it seems to me that the proponents of repressive legislation in this field have got to calculate whether the legislation will do any real good or not. There has been plenty of antipornography legislation in the past and the stuff is still being bootlegged across state lines. In other words, is repressive legislation the way to get at the problem of pornography, if it is a problem at all?

It is an old rule of the police that "you can't flimflam an honest man." The argument is equally valid that filthy pictures can't corrupt the man who is not anxious to be corrupted. Little but prurient curiosity tempts a normal person to thumb through *Sunshine and Health* or *Adam's Bedside Reader*. The fellow who answers an ad for sexy movies is the victim not of accident but of his own design. If he is sufficiently determined to acquire salacious material, never fear, he will find it—and at a high price, with resulting neglect of other more socially useful goods.

5. *If obscene literature does exert a corrupting influence on young people, the best counter-influence lies in education, parental guidance, and in the freedom to learn.*

A great many advocates of censorship laws, when they can be persuaded to look at the problem squarely, are inclined to agree that little harm derives from the effect of obscene materials on the normal adult. The normal adult, in the first place, does not normally go looking for such things. To be sure, a typically conventional husband and father, away from his family on a trip, may buy a stag magazine to pass a dull evening at his hotel. A younger single man, facing an evening without female companionship, may find vicarious release in the arms of a *Playboy* playmate. And if middle-aged men find a bang in filthy pictures or prurient paperbacks, who ordinarily is harmed by it? The realistic answer is that no one is harmed—grievously harmed—by such private researches in sexual illusion.

The greater and more serious damage, it is said, results from the effect of obscene materials upon young people. They are naturally curious about sex. Should not they be protected especially from books that exploit or degrade the sexual relationship? Judge Bok raised the question and answered it effectively in the *Gordon* case.

It will be asked whether one would care to have one's young daughter read these books. I suppose that by the time she is old enough to wish to read them she will have learned the biologic facts of life and the words that go with them. There is something seriously wrong at home if those facts have not been met and faced and sorted by then; it is not children so much as parents that should receive our concern about this. I should prefer that my own three daughters meet the facts of life and the literature of the world in my library rather than behind a neighbor's barn, for I can face the adversary there directly. If the young ladies are appalled by what they read, they can close the book at the bottom of page one; if they read further, they will learn what is in the world and in its people, and no parents who have been discerning with their children need fear the outcome. Nor can they hold it back, for life is a series of little battles and minor issues, and the burden of choice is on us all, every day, young and old. Our daughters must live in the world and decide what sort of women they are to be, and we should be willing to prefer their deliberate and informed choice of decency rather than an innocence that continues to spring from ignorance. If that choice be made in the open sunlight, it is more apt than when made in shadow to fall on the side of honorable behavior.

Children ought not to be protected too much, says the case against censorship. While every effort is made, through home and church, to mold character totally, including an honest and decent regard for the role of sex in every man and woman's life, we fall into error in attempting to shield the adolescent from the tempering influences of the everyday world. So a boy of fourteen or fifteen surreptitiously buys a nudist magazine, slips it under his mattress, and looks at the pictures in secret—and a parent catches him at it. What then? Tears and recriminations, harsh punishments, stern lectures on lust? How much better it would be to treat such matters casually, disarmingly, teasingly; how much better to seize upon such opportunities to speak to a growing boy of the beauty and love of sex.

In their 1953 statement on "freedom to read," the librarians and book publishers put it this way:

> To some, much of modern literature is shocking. But is not much of life itself shocking? We cut off literature at the source if we prevent serious artists from dealing with the stuff of life. Parents and teachers have a responsibility to prepare the young to meet the diversity of experiences in life to which they will be exposed, as they have a responsibility to help them learn to think critically for themselves. These are affirmative responsibilities, not to be discharged simply by preventing them from reading works for which they are not yet prepared.

One final point. Attempts to clean up the newsstands, so that children will not be subjected to smutty books and magazines, can have the effect of depriving adults of material that, in all seriousness, causes such inconsequential harm—if indeed it causes harm at all—

that it should be left undisturbed in the name of a free and tolerant society. In most towns and cities adult reading already is limited by factors having nothing to do with obscenity censorship: libraries have limited budgets, local bookdealers have limited stocks, active men and women have little enough time to read under the best circumstances. To limit their opportunities further, by driving from retail outlets all those books that might offend children, is to reduce the community reading level to me Tarzan, you Jane. So thin and tasteless a diet must contribute to an intellectual anemia, in which the people suffer—whether they know it or not—for want of the occasional healthy shock, the sudden stimulation, of a lusty work of grown-up fiction.

3. THE CASE FOR CENSORSHIP

Very well. Let one or two things be said at the outset of a statement in behalf of the case *for* censorship. The proponents here, taking the affirmative side in this debate, are aggrieved at the abuse they have been receiving from the liberal team. They are weary of being depicted in the grim garb of the late Mr. Volstead; the hat doesn't fit. They are becoming increasingly resentful of the role in which the disciples of free expression would cast them, as prudes, bluenoses, Comstocks, crackpots, fuzzy threads on the lunatic fringe. They have had the contemptuous question thrown at them often enough: "What right do *you* have to judge of the literature to be read in a community?" Speaking as a legion of decent, normal, unashamed citizens and parents, they throw back a blunt reply: "Our right as free men to speak freely."

They are angry, these decent and normal people. The publisher or editor who mistakes this anger deceives only himself. They are angry at the obscene filth that, all unwanted, floods into their homes with the stench of a stopped-up toilet; they are angry at what they conceive to be the corrupting effects of pornographic literature; they are angry at the imputation that they are somehow poorer Americans than, say, the ex-pimp author of some paperback book or the cynical publisher of a nudie magazine. Of course, they agree, an author has rights. But what of the community? Does the community have no rights? Does freedom of speech exist only for the writer, publisher, and peddler of salacious books? Or do those who object to filth have some freedom of expression also?

The proponents of obscenity statutes have not the slightest hesitation in responding to the principal arguments of their opponents.

Their rebuttal merits a fair hearing. These are their principal contentions:

1. Of course laws punishing obscenity are constitutional; it is absurd to contend they are not constitutional.

In one unbroken chain of cases, extending from *Jackson*[88] in 1878 to *Smith*[175] in 1959, the Supreme Court of the United States consistently has upheld the power of both the Congress and the states to punish the dissemination of obscene materials. "The only question for our determination relates to the constitutionality of the [Comstock] Act," said the court in *Jackson,* "and of that we have no doubt."

"We have held that obscene speech and writings," said the court in *Smith,* "are not protected by the constitutional guarantees of freedom of speech and of the press."

It is an idle intellectual exercise, say the proponents, to argue questions of broad constitutionality. In this country, for good or ill, the Constitution is precisely what a majority of the Supreme Court says it is, on any given Monday morning. In theory it may be that the Constitution ought to be what the states say it is—or more definitively, what the people, acting as they always act politically, through their states, say it is—but in practice this is not so. The Supreme Court alone fixes the supreme law of the land, and until its constructions of the Constitution may be disturbed by (1) constitutional amendment, (2) an overriding act of the Congress, or (3) the appointment of new justices with different opinions, such constructions stand. These rulings fix the Constitution; these *de facto* are the Constitution.

On this hard and realistic rock the flimsy barks of academic argument crash and sink. "We hold that obscenity is not within the area of constitutionally protected speech or press." That is what the court said in *Roth-Alberts,* and in 1960, as this book is written, that is the final, unyielding answer to the opponents' claim upon the Bill of Rights.

The proponents are prepared to buttress their case. Judge Charles S. Desmond of New York, writing in the *Marquette Law Review,* long ago concluded that the First Amendment never was intended to sanction the publication of obscenity. It was intended, in his view, only to cover freedom to express opinion, to expound ideas, to treat those significant issues that truly are essential to the functioning of democratic government within the American republic. In Delaware, for example, the state constitution of 1782 extended freedom of the press only to those "who undertake to examine the official conduct of men acting in a public capacity." The Maryland constitution of 1776 went to freedom of speech and debates on proceedings in the legislature. The authoritative Judge Cooley wrote that the object of the amendment was to insure "such free and general discussion of public matters as seems essential."

Mr. Justice Brennan, in the *Roth* opinion, made this exception clear:

> It is apparent that the unconditional phrasing of the First Amendment was not intended to protect every utterance. . . . At the time of the adoption of the First Amendment, obscenity law was not as fully developed as libel law, but there is sufficiently contemporaneous evidence to show that obscenity, too, was outside the protection intended for speech and press.
>
> The protection given speech and press was fashioned to assure unfettered interchange of ideas for the bringing about of political and social changes desired by the people. . . .
>
> All ideas having even the slightest redeeming social importance—unorthodox ideas, controversial ideas, even ideas hateful to the prevailing climate of opinion—have the full protection of the guaranties, unless excludable because they encroach upon the limited area of more important interests. *But implicit in the history of the First Amendment is the rejection of obscenity as utterly without redeeming social importance.* [Emphasis supplied.]

Is this not clear from the public expressions of the framers and adopters of the First Amendment? The proponents suggest that doubters return to Jefferson, to Mason, to Madison, to the great men of the revolutionary period who fought so bravely to cast off the rule of Britain. Is it to be supposed that their object was to provide freedom for the inspired political ideas set forth so nobly in:

Then Wayne came back. "I've done all the work so far," I said. "You take off my panties." And he did, and let me tell you that felt like nothing in the world, having Wayne Whitney take off my panties. I mean it was a lovely feeling. . . .

This is what is meant by the great American ideal of freedom of the press? Freedom for this?

"Perhaps the most widespread and popular form of perversion," Cardinal Spellman once remarked, "is the perversion of 'freedom.' When hypocrites apply this sacred term to contemptible schemes in order to prey upon the weaknesses of unformed characters under the banner of 'freedom of speech' or 'freedom of the press,' they are not only victimizing our children, but endangering our nation's treasured heritage. . . ."

Those who imagine that, in drafting the First Amendment, the founding fathers intended to protect obscene and profane writings mistake both the law and the mores of that day. Judge Desmond has pointed out that for more than sixty years prior to ratification of the First Amendment the publication of an obscene book, picture, or article was a common-law offense in England. And far from repudiating the English common law, such states as Virginia made it the cornerstone of their own law. The strong rock of the First Amendment was intended to be a bulwark of liberty; it never was conceived as a shield for the merchant of filth.

The explicit terms of the First Amendment, ratified in 1791, reached only to the Congress. For more than a century thereafter, until the Supreme Court of the United States began writing one of its own amendments into the Constitution, the states were free to limit the press as they wished. They also were free, throughout this long period, to legislate largely as they pleased within the broad limits of their police power. In time it was held that the Constitution prohibited the states as well as the Congress from making any law that might abridge the freedom of the press, but this line of decisions left the states' basic police power untouched. It is important that this be understood. The power of the Congress to legislate upon obscene materials arises, somewhat uncertainly, from the power to establish post roads, and still more uncertainly, from the power to regulate commerce among the states. The states do not need to search for an affirmative statement of their political power; their reserved powers, under the Tenth Amendment, reach to the very limits of the prohibitions of the Fourteenth. Judge Harlan said this, in upholding the conviction of David Alberts under California law:

> In judging the constitutionality of this conviction, we should remember that our function in reviewing state judgments under the Fourteenth Amendment is a narrow one. We do not decide whether the policy of the state is wise, or whether it is based on assumptions scientifically substantiated. We can inquire only whether the state action so subverts the fundamental liberties implicit in the Due Process clause that it cannot be sustained as a rational exercise of power.

It follows from this that the states are entirely within their constitutional prerogatives in adopting a wide variety of statutes intended to regulate and to punish the traffic in obscene materials. Some of these statutes may not be wise; some of them may not be effective—it is not the court's function to decide. Such statutes are constitutional, and as such, they are entitled to the respect that is owed other laws equally within the constitutional structure.

Mr. Justice Frankfurter, to cite one final authority, has no doubt of the constitutional validity of state laws in this field. His concurring opinion in *Smith* v. *People,* the California case decided in December of 1959, sounds a recurring theme:

> The Court accepts the settled principle of constitutional law that traffic in obscene literature may be outlawed as crime. . . . It ought at least to be made clear that the Court's decision in its practical effect is not intended to nullify the conceded power of the state to prohibit booksellers from trafficking in obscene literature. . . . The constitutional protection of nonobscene speech cannot absorb the constitutional power of the states to deal with obscenity. . . . [The Court's requirements as to *scienter*] cannot be of a nature to nullify for all practical purposes the power of the state to deal with obscenity. . . . As a practical matter there-

fore the exercise of the constitutional right of a state to regulate obscenity will carry with it some hazard. . . .

True enough, no adjudications by the Supreme Court as to the constitutionality of anything may be viewed as permanent. The Southern states, in their maintenance of racially separate schools, were unanimously within the Constitution at noon on that May 17, and unanimously outside the Constitution at one o'clock, the Constitution not having been altered by a comma during the lunch hour. Are motion pictures entitled to the guaranties of free speech? In 1915, when McKenna wrote *Mutual,* a unanimous court said no. In 1959, when Harlan wrote the decision on *Lady Chatterley,* a unanimous court said yes. Same Constitution. It is sometimes hard to adjust to these things. But this phenomenon aside, the constitutionality of obscenity laws must be viewed, as this book is written, as certain, definite, and unshakable. The courts demand only that obscenity statutes meet the same general requirements laid down for other criminal laws.

2. The term "obscenity" is no more vague or elusive than many another concept of law; objections on this score are captious.

It is often said, generally with some solemn wagging of judicial heads, that obscenity law is a very delicate and difficult field of jurisprudence. Sometimes this is expressed in the superlative: it is the "most delicate" or "most difficult" field of them all. The standards are "vagrant breezes to which the mariner must ever trim his sails."[113] Nothing is fixed; nothing is definite. That which was obscene yesterday is not obscene today, and so on.

To these arguments the defenders of obscenity statutes answer simply, bosh! In their view truly precise criminal statutes are the exception, not the rule. For every sharp and cleanly delineated law, such as the law on honest weight, or the laws on speeding, or the laws that divide petit from grand larceny at the fifty-dollar mark, they cite a dozen statutes in which a jury's judgment, discretion, and flexible interpretation spell the difference between guilt and innocence. What constitutes justifiable homicide? What constitutes nonnegligent manslaughter? How is "consent" proved in a rape case?

These are all questions of judgment. And on the civil side of the law a thousand discretionary questions depend entirely upon the opinion of the twelve good men and true. What is simple negligence? What is gross negligence? Due care? The prudent man? Reasonable doubt? The chancery and appellate courts daily must feel their way into questions of testamentary intent, tax avoidance in anticipation of death, the four corners of an inconsistent will. What of the ten thousand individual and particular issues of due process? What constitutes a fair trial? How long may a prisoner be questioned prior to arraignment? It would be wonderfully convenient if appellate courts had some convenient thermometer, measured in degrees of inflammatory oratory, by which the reversible passions of a summation speech could be read.

The law of obscenity is not different. The word "obscene" is a word of common usage. Jurors know what it means, precisely as they know what other elusive terms of the law mean—*to them*. And if an obscenity law cannot be drafted as neatly as a speed-limit law, one ought not to complain excessively.

"I confess I see nothing absurd or benighted about leaving the law in such a state," Judge Desmond commented tartly. "No book has a brother, and it is, I think, beyond human ingenuity to devise a legal text for obscenity so precise that it can be laid alongside a book for comparison with an automatic mathematical result made instantly available. The law does not claim to be an exact science. It is a set of behavioral rules applied by human judges to human acts. Even theologians differ."

The Supreme Court itself accepted this view in the *Roth* case. Many decisions, said the court, citing cases,[165,117,230] have recognized that the terms of obscenity statutes are not precise. But what of this? The Constitution does not require impossible standards. All that is required is that the language of a statute convey "sufficiently definite warning as to the proscribed conduct when measured by common understanding and practices." The state and federal statutes at issue in *Roth-Alberts,* said the court, fully met this test. They gave adequate warning of the conduct proscribed, and marked boundaries sufficiently distinct for judges and juries to comprehend them. No more than this reasonably can be asked of any law intended to cope with obscene material that necessarily must be weighed in some subjective degree.

In a 1959 case in Pennsylvania, Judge Musmanno, still smarting, upbraided his brothers for suggesting that the word obscene is vague. "It is about as vague as the word 'cat,' " he said. "I doubt that there is a newspaper reader, radio listener, or television watcher, no matter how meager his education, who does not know the meaning of the word 'obscene.' "[41.1]

3. *A causal relationship between obscene materials and antisocial behavior may not be susceptible to statistical proof—by its very nature, the relationship is unprovable—but the common sense of mankind, supported by the opinions of experts, holds strongly that such a relationship exists.*

The proponents of obscenity statutes are entirely willing to meet Judge Bok, Judge Frank, and the philosophers of the Civil Liberties Union on this crucial question of causal relationship. Bok's proposed requirement of "clear and present danger" seems to them as unfair as it is unrealistic; many other fields of the law recognize the evils of a gradual or continuing social ill. The smog laws, for example, do not rest upon the theory that one belch of smoke, from one chimney, causes grave damage to the public welfare; it is the smoke of many chimneys, mixed together, that adversely affects the public welfare. Neither does the law, in other fields, insist upon a chain of cause and effect that runs from A to B only; the law recognizes that C and D may be gravely, if indirectly, affected also.

The first contention of proponents is that the precise relationship between pornography and antisocial behavior is simply unknowable. No one ever has contended that obscene materials are the *entire* cause of juvenile delinquency, or the *entire* cause of adult perversion either; the most that is contended is that obscene materials are a contributory factor toward inciting behavior that society has every right to suppress. To demand, as Judge Bok demanded, that one demonstrate evidence of immediate and direct incitement to overt acts—evidence of readers who lay down their dirty books and rush to the streets for a night of satyriasis—is to lay upon the proponents of obscenity statutes a burden not required elsewhere in the law.

Obscenity does not operate with the immediacy of a cyanide pellet, but with the imperceptible slowness of leukemia. Father Terence J. Murphy, speaking before a Loyola University Law School symposium, remarked that in demanding empirical-statistical evidence of such a causal relationship the followers of Judge Bok and Judge Frank demand the impossible.

They call for evidence produced by experiments which would require thousands of persons to be isolated from all erotic visual material over a number of years. And then their behavior pattern would have to be compared to that of a group of similar psychological make-up, influenced by the same environmental factors, but subjected to controlled exposure to obscenity. This demand by the men who know only of one method is completely unrealistic. The practical difficulties of carrying out such experiments in our society are readily evident.

The best one can do, in attempting soberly and realistically to appraise the dangers of the obscenity racket, is to apply common sense to known social ills and to weigh the testimony of experts. One such social ill, by general acceptance, is the appalling increase in juvenile delinquency. Between 1948 and 1957 juvenile court cases increased by 136 per cent while the under-seventeen population was increasing by only 27 per cent. FBI reports show a shocking increase in juvenile prostitution. The divorce rate has more than tripled since 1900. Plainly enough, something is wrong with national patterns of moral behavior, especially among adolescents and young adults, and doubtless a hundred factors have contributed in one degree or another to this disturbing picture. But our inquiry here goes to the effect of one factor only.

Said Monsignor George H. Guilfoyle, of New York, before the Granahan Committee of the House: "Without exception, it is the experience of the directors and staffs in [youth] programs, that the damage caused to children by obscene publications and pornography is readily noticeable, affects the entire personality and values of the person, and is extremely difficult and at times practically impossible to correct."

Dr. George W. Henry, professor of clinical psychiatry at the Cornell University College of Medicine, appeared before the Kefauver Committee of the Senate in 1955. He examined a book of sado-masochistic drawings offered as an exhibit in the hearings. This colloquy ensued:

MR. GAUGHAN: I ask you, Doctor, specifically, can you see any purpose for this publication other than the one purpose to cause erotic stimuli by showing acts of sexual perversion?

DR. HENRY: No, the sole purpose is to stimulate people erotically in an abnormal way.

MR. GAUGHAN: Doctor, I ask you, could children be sexually perverted by looking at, by studying, and by dwelling upon photos of this nature and the contents of this book?

DR. HENRY: Yes.

CHAIRMAN KEFAUVER: Doctor, is it a very unwholesome influence, this sort of thing?

DR. HENRY: It is.

CHAIRMAN KEFAUVER: In your opinion the increase in sex crimes, deviations, that we are having—does that increase result in part at least from the reading and looking at magazines and pictures of this kind by children?

DR. HENRY: I would think that was an important factor in the increase.

The Kefauver Committee also heard from William Deerson, dean of discipline at Haaren High School in New York. He was asked about pornographic material he had confiscated among the two thousand male students. Did such material in any way affect the juvenile delinquency rate of the students? He replied: "There is definitely a connection between the juvenile delinquency rate and the reading of this material. I feel that the material when read excites the young man; it stimulates him and may lead to some overt act."

Dr. Benjamin Karpman, chief psychotherapist of St. Elizabeth's Hospital in Washington, D.C., testified that pornographic literature draws a boy "into all sorts of gang life, which later discharges itself as juvenile delinquency." He found a "very direct relationship between juvenile delinquency, sex life, and pornographic literature."

Such testimony could be extended at length. Both the Kefauver

Committee and the Granahan Committee also developed examples of specific crimes apparently directly attributable to the influence of pornographic or sado-masochistic magazines. One such case occurred in Florida, where a seventeen-year-old boy, nude, was found fatally suspended from a bondage device copied from a fetish publication.

The evil effects of the obscenity traffic are not confined to the customer's end of the commerce. If a causal relationship is being sought between the sale of a filthy magazine and some antisocial consequence, one may well ponder the supplier's end of the business also. As the racket grows, a steady stream of teen-age girls must be attracted into nude modeling, perversion, and prostitution. Boys must be tempted into the sordid business of serving as sex partners, photographers, film processors, and salesmen. And inexorably, as the racket swells toward new records of annual take, it attracts those overlords of crime and corruption who do not hesitate to work upon police and legislative bodies.

Nor are adolescents and young people the only ones harmed by steady subjection to obscene materials. In a Delaware trial in 1952 Dr. M. A. Tarumianz, state psychiatrist, was asked about the effect of obscene movies on others. He testified: "I have found that such films are not only detrimental to the youth, but detrimental to any human being who has normal endowments and is not peculiarly psychopathically inclined. It creates various deviations of thinking and emotional instability in regard to sex problems. A happily married individual who is considered a mature adult individual, seeing such films, becomes seriously concerned with whether he is obtaining the necessary gratification of his sex desires from his normally endowed and inclined wife. It may deviate him in accepting that there is something which arouses him to become interested in an abnormal type of sex satisfaction which he has had perhaps from this picture. So it is unquestionably detrimental to adults."

But it is hardly necessary for one to be a psychiatrist, a psychologist, a police officer, or a priest to form an opinion on the consequences of prolonged exposure to obscenity. The common experience of mankind provides eloquent examples of the manner in which antisocial patterns develop from perhaps harmless beginnings. Such patterns may not be plotted exactly; expert evidence in the form of tidy statistical charts, tabulated to the second decimal point, never can be compiled. The question of cause and effect may be debated endlessly.

"I say that we can no longer afford to wait for an answer," J. Edgar Hoover said in 1959. "What we do know is that in an overwhelmingly large number of cases sex crime is associated with pornography. We know that sex criminals read it, are clearly influenced by it. I believe pornography is a major cause of sex violence. I believe that if we can eliminate the distribution of such items among impressionable school-age children, we shall greatly reduce our frightening crime rate."

4. It is no more futile to combat obscenity than it is to combat other social evils that may gain allurement from the fact of their suppression.

Police officials and decent-literature committees are well aware that existing statutes have not wiped out the obscenity racket. Postal authorities are convinced, indeed, that the racket is growing vastly larger. But they do not see these trends as evidence of the futility of their efforts. If this complaint were valid most criminal statutes would be equally subject to repeal. The drunk driver is still on the road; the narcotics peddler still goes about his evil trade; embezzlers daily find the temptation of easy money more than they can resist. No laws ever have been wholly successful in curbing man's predilection for sin. The churches are still doing business; so are the jailers.

The proponents do contend this: where obscenity statutes have been effectively enforced, the volume of seriously offensive material has been greatly reduced. They contend also that the familiar analogy between bootleg liquor and bootleg smut is more apparent than real. The man who is determined to have booze will find it. His craving is immediate and urgent, and it can be easily satisfied by the illicit sale of an otherwise licit item; bellhops do not customarily deal in moonshine put up in Mason jars, but in legal whisky legally bought. The ordinary male in search of a sexy magazine, however, is not so aggressive; he will settle for whatever reading matter is at hand, and ordinarily his wants can be sidetracked. In smaller towns and cities the number of newsstands, terminals, and drugstores is limited, and the number of such retail outlets deliberately dealing in prurient stuff is more limited still. Obscenity statutes, it is contended, indeed can be effective in reducing the total volume of obscene material in such communities and in making it harder to find.

There is this argument also, that even where such laws may not be relentlessly enforced, their very existence on the statute books accomplishes two desirable ends: the statutes reflect community censure upon a social evil, and they do provide a deterrent to dealers in hard-core items who otherwise could engage freely in their ugly traffic. And if one effect of an obscenity statute is to make forbidden fruit seem sweeter, and to run up the price on dirty pictures, that is too bad, but it would be a strange sort of morality that would sanction immorality at bargain prices.

Postmaster General Summerfield responded to Morris Ernst's proposal for an open market in pornographic items in a strong address before a women's conference in Washington in the spring of 1959:

> What is likely to happen if we do not rid ourselves of this social cancer? First, we may as well concede that the obscenity business, with its vast revenue, will be taken over by organized crime to a far greater extent. It will become a gigantic organized racket, with millions more of our children its principal victims. The undermining of the moral fiber of the nation's children will spread; with the poisoning of increasing millions of minds. Sex crimes will be a spreading blight on our society, and will become far more prevalent than they are today. And overall, we could expect an ultimate breakdown of order and decency in this country.

Judge Desmond wraps up the proponents' case on this point in two sentences:

> Obscenity, real, serious, not imagined or puritanically exaggerated, is today as in all past centuries, a public evil, a public nuisance, a public pollution. When its effective control requires censorship, I see no reason why democratic government should not use democratic processes on a high administrative level, under the control of the courts, to suppress such obscenity.

5. Yes, education is of course the ultimate answer to the obscenity racket, but ultimate solutions need to be supplemented by more immediate remedies.

On the fifth point of disagreement one finds no disagreement. In all of its publications the National Office for Decent Literature emphasizes affirmative and constructive reading, even as it censures the magazines and paperbacks that seem to its readers obscene. Americans for Moral Decency advances a nine-point program "on the positive side," in which the organization urges parents to cultivate in their children a love of good books, to support public libraries, and to foster the development of home libraries. The Citizens for Decent Literature, perhaps the most militant of the clean-up associations, hopes in time to launch a positive program, but attorney Charles H. Keating, Jr., founder of the CDL, is a realist. He says:

> In some families good, solid training may offset the lure of these publications, but I'm afraid they are in the minority. The plain fact is that this pornography, contrived by photographers and writers who know all the tricks of their trade, is deliberately designed to appeal to youths for whom a great curiosity about the human body is a normal thing. There is a vicious slickness about these publications. It is absurd for us to expect youths to resist these enticements, and then call them delinquents when they do not.

In the view of proponents the vice of obscenity, especially as young people may be caught in it, is not one that yields readily to education or home instruction. It is a secret sort of thing, operating upon the mind, not readily detectible. The young man who experiments with alcohol or narcotics soon enough evidences some physical reaction; his excesses can be detected early, and no lasting consequences may develop. The sex thing is another matter. In testimony before congressional committees, psychiatrists have emphasized the terrible lifelong effects that obscene materials—especially materials that emphasize perversion and homosexuality—can have on boys and girls in the impressionable years of puberty. Sex attitudes can be fixed at this age, so deeply that no parental affection or discipline can ever alter them, and if an attitude is built up of casualness, coarseness, brutality, and sheer carnal satisfaction, damage is done that cannot be undone later on. The high-school student who takes too much to drink will be all right the next day, but the seventeen-year-old who witnesses a stag movie in which men and women engage like animals in wanton copulation will find the image burned upon his subconscious. "The mind that becomes soiled in youth," Mark Twain once remarked, "can never again be washed clean." And when a youth accepts the idea of sex without love he is stained inside.

That is the viciousness of this racket, that it stains. The worst of the obscene magazines and books are engaged in a perverted educative process of their own. Keating speaks from a prolonged study of the field when he says:

> The magazines are not just amoral. They are openly and avowedly anti-Christian. It is not a question of depicting sin as virtue. Believe me, our problem would not be so complicated if these magazines merely contained too much unadorned flesh and indecent language.
>
> These magazines attack morality by ridiculing virtue, chastity, fidelity or restraint. Anyone who lives by a code of virtue is laughed at as a victim of outmoded hypocritical prudery. To have any scruples about free sexual indulgence is to be neurotically repressed.
>
> Instead of the Christian concept of love and marriage, the magazines advocate a pagan, libertine life.

Thus the case for the proponents. They conceive their war upon obscenity as a duty they owe society and as a responsibility they hold as parents and good citizens. They are deeply alarmed by what seem to them the manifest evil consequences of the traffic in pornography, and they are determined to put down these consequences as best they can. And on two main fronts they propose to carry their battle to the enemy. They are proceeding, that is to say, through private action and through public law.

4. PRIVATE ACTION

Anthony Comstock's New York Society for the Suppression of Vice grew out of a committee of the Y.M.C.A. in 1873. An annual report at the close of 1881 showed that in the society's first eight years Mr. Comstock had confiscated 203,238 obscene pictures and photographs, destroyed 27,584 pounds of books, seized 7,400 microscopic pictures for charms, knives, and the like, confiscated 1,376,939 circulars, catalogs, songs, poems, etc., seized 27 obscene pictures, framed on walls of saloons, and picked up mailing lists having 976,125 names and addresses. Mr. Comstock, we may suppose, counted every one of them.

The New England Watch and Ward Society came into existence in Boston in 1876. In 1907 it kept Mary Garden from playing in *Salome;* in 1908 it launched a famous prosecution based upon Elinor Glyn's *Three Weeks.*[42] The Rev. J. Frank Chase was its moving spirit for many years. H. L. Mencken sued both Chase and the society in 1926, over the Watch and Ward's effort to ban sales of the April issue of *American Mercury,* and won a resounding verdict from Federal Judge James M. Morton, Jr., in United States district court.[7.1] Mr. Chase had gone about Boston warning newsdealers that he would bring charges against them if they attempted to sell the issue. Judge Morton strongly condemned this sort of private censorship. The result of such officious interference with a publisher, he said,

is the same, whether that judgment be right or wrong; *i.e.,* the sale of his magazine or book is seriously interfered with. Few dealers in any trade will buy goods after notice that they will be prosecuted if they resell them. Reputable dealers do not care to take such a risk, even when they believe that prosecution would prove unfounded. The defendants know this and trade upon it. They secure their influence, not by voluntary acquiescence in their opinions by the trade in question, but by the coercion and intimidation of that trade, through the fear of prosecution if defendants' views are disregarded. . . . In my judgment, this is clearly illegal.

Thirty years later, in October of 1956, Editor John Fischer of *Harper's* leveled almost exactly the same charges against Monsignor Thomas Fitzgerald and the National Office for Decent Literature (NODL). Founded in 1938 by the Catholic Bishops of the United States, the NODL was created "to devise a plan for organizing a systematic campaign in all dioceses of the United States against the publication and sale of lewd magazines and brochure literature." Its original aims were to arouse opinion against pornography, to seek rigorous enforcement of obscenity laws, to promote strict legislation in this field, to prepare monthly lists of objectionable publications, and to persuade dealers not to sell such publications. In various dioceses canvass teams were created to call upon retailers; seals of approval were devised to be awarded co-operating merchants, and for a considerable time, it seems apparent, some NODL groups employed the weapon of boycott against any dealers who failed to comply with their demands to remove publications regarded as objectionable.

Fischer denounced these tactics in a stinging essay, "The Harm Good People Do," in which he began by charging that a little band of Catholics was engaged in a "shocking attack on the rights of their fellow citizens." He condemned the boycott technique as thoroughly un-American, accused the NODL of engaging in "literary lynching," and urged that the organization stop its campaign of threats, blacklisting, and boycott.

By every indication Fischer won his war with this single blockbuster. Not long afterward Monsignor Fitzgerald issued a clarifying statement, denying that the NODL ever had recommended or encouraged "arbitrary coercive police action," and emphasizing that its activities were limited solely to the censure of comic books, magazines, and pocket-size books judged objectionable *for youth*. The latter point is often misunderstood by NODL's critics. The NODL makes no attempt to judge reading material that might be objectionable for adults.

Today the NODL, a national successor to the New York and New England Societies, remains the largest and most active organization in the field of private action against obscenity. Its monthly listings of objectionable paperback books and magazines go out not only to Catholic societies across the nation but to hundreds of other individuals and organizations also. The NODL states categorically that its lists are "not to be used for purposes of boycott or coercion." In many cities of substantial Catholic population there is no question of the NODL's influence upon the sale and distribution of paperbacks and magazines; and because many dealers are unwilling to stock certain titles for sale to adults only, the effect of the NODL's monthly listing, for good or ill, is to block the offering of many publications for youths and adults alike.

The NODL lists as objectionable reading for youth those publications which (1) glorify crime or the criminal, (2) describe in detail ways to commit criminal acts, (3) hold lawful authority in disrespect, (4) exploit horror, cruelty or violence, (5) portray sex facts offensively, (6) feature indecent, lewd, or suggestive photographs or illustrations, (7) carry advertising which is offensive in content or advertise products which may lead to physical or moral harm, (8) use blasphemous, profane, or obscene speech indiscriminately and repeatedly, or (9) hold up to ridicule any national, religious, or racial group.

Comic books are reviewed every six months by a committee of approximately 150 mothers, divided into thirty teams of five each. A negative vote of four out of five on a team is required before a comic book is placed on the "objectionable" list; an affirmative vote of ten mothers is required for an "acceptable" listing. Magazines are reviewed every six months by a committee of six reviewers, all of whom must find the magazine in violation of the code before it is listed as objectionable. Paperback books are reviewed month by month on the same general basis.

Operating under these standards and procedures, the NODL has found hundreds of paperback books objectionable for youth, among them novels by Ayn Rand, William Faulkner, James M. Cain, James T. Farrell, Somerset Maugham, John O'Hara, C. S. Forester, Ernest Hemingway, James A. Michener, Christopher Morley, Ben Ames Williams, John Dos Passos, and François Mauriac. It is acknowledged that even though these listings apply only to works regarded as objectionable for youth, the effect may be to deprive adults of them, but adults are encouraged to put the protection of adolescents above their own personal interests.

The NODL does not attempt to operate on a basis of national uniformity. Its policy is to encourage the formation of autonomous local committees, nonsectarian in nature, which will represent not only Catholic interests but a number of social, fraternal, and religious groups also. A plan of organization suggests how such committees may be brought into being for effective action. Copies of typical local constitutions and bylaws may be obtained from the NODL office at 33 East Congress Parkway, Chicago 5, Illinois.

Once formed, the committees are encouraged to organize neighborhood territories on a systematic basis. Every establishment selling comic books, pocket-size books, and magazines is to be visited every two weeks, generally by two-man teams who will be assigned three dealers each. These committees are to leave copies of the NODL monthly ratings with each dealer, discuss with him the need for protecting the ideals of youth, and examine publications offered for sale. Where no objectionable titles are found, the committee is asked to commend the owner or manager. Where objectionable titles are found, the committee should "courteously recommend that the manager or owner remove such publication from sale." If the dealer complies, favorable publicity should be given him; but if co-operation is refused, the committee workers should silently leave. "Little is ever gained by argument, but silence can often be most effective."

In his 1957 statement of policy Monsignor Fitzgerald emphasized the NODL's view that final decisions on obscenity lie with the courts. He hoped also to see intelligent laws devised that would "restrict the worst of the objectionable publications without placing undue hardship upon the adult reader." But he also said this:

While advocating the enactment of adequate and constitutional legislation to remove the worst of the offensive material from the neighborhood racks, NODL at the same time reaffirms the democratic right of any citizen to protest in a legal manner against the sale of publications he considers objectionable for youth. Further, NODL defends the right of parents, teachers, pastors of souls and others charged with the welfare of youth to counsel and direct their families, their students and their flocks in these matters. . . .

Our democratic way of life is based upon ideals of patriotism, family integrity, justice, honesty, respect for law and for the rights of others. These ideals must be inculcated in youth if they are to be practiced in manhood. If they are destroyed in our youth during the formative years and replaced by motives of perversion, violence, brutality, disregard for law, property and country and contempt for family responsibilities, then future generations of Americans face an unhappy and chaotic life.

All these vile and repulsive traits of character are glorified in certain publications on neighborhood racks today. Were one to read many passages from these publications on radio or to show some of their pictures and cartoons on TV, he would be immediately cut off the air. Yet these same passages and pictures are sold to youth with impunity. NODL urges its critics to be realistic about this danger, which is a serious threat to the future security of our country.

Legislation cannot solve the problem in its entirety. It can only rid the stands of the worst of the material. A good reading program and good recreational facilities for youth will answer part of the problem, but again not all. NODL is endeavoring to fill a void.

Also seeking to fill that void are the local chapters of Citizens for Decent Literature, Inc., a group set up first in Cincinnati in 1957. By the time of its second national conference in February of 1960 CDL knew of two hundred affiliated committees and could report inquiries from three hundred more communities. CDL makes no bones about its aggressive policies. Chairman Keating, himself a lawyer, believes in going to court. Though the NODL and the CDL maintain a completely cordial relationship, the Citizens for Decent

Literature do not use any sort of book list. "We don't want to set up a censorship," Keating says. "We want the newsstand dealer to use his own conscience and obey the law."

The story of CDL's clean-up campaign in Cincinnati, known as Operation Newsstand, has been told by Kay Sullivan in *Catholic Digest*. The drive began among a small group of business and professional men who shared Keating's deep concern at the volume of pornography in local retail outlets. They invited opportunities to speak before school groups and women's clubs, and simply by displaying and quoting from material freely available in Cincinnati won an outraged response from parents. Local police, assured of community support, began to descend upon newsstands dealing in "really lewd publications," Within the next two years, seven cases were brought successfully against retailers. Then police arrested a large distributor, confiscated sixteen thousand copies of magazines, pictures, and books, and brought him to a bitterly contested five-day trial before Judge John W. Keefe. Among the prosecution witnesses was Professor Arthur F. Bills, head of the University of Cincinnati's psychology department, who testified to the obscene nature of the seized material:

> I made a thorough study of all the magazines, their pictures, their text. I was shocked. At the university we have textbooks on abnormal psychology which we keep under lock and key. Only students of advanced classes may use them. But here were books and magazines containing stories and pictures of abnormal sex practices that far outdid anything in our reference books—and they lay on public newsstands, available to anyone, child or adult.

With the defendant's conviction (he was fined $400 and given a suspended jail sentence), CDL might have counted its battle won and retired from the field. But across the country scores of other communities, hearing of Cincinnati's clean-up, were seeking help in organizing their own committees. Since then CDL's offices at 3901 Carew Tower, Cincinnati, Ohio, have become a busy GHQ in the war upon obscenity.

CDL recommends that a community interested in suppressing pornography begin as the Cincinnatians began, with a core of ten or twelve individuals who will volunteer as speakers before receptive audiences. J. Patrick Conroy, a member of the executive committee, suggests that these individuals "should be convinced in order to be convincing, but not overly zealous which may create an objectionable approach." Among the core group should be at least one lawyer, prepared to advise on questions of law and legislation. Secretarial assistance also will be required; high-school students often make willing assistants.

In Cincinnati some highly effective work was done through organization of a city-wide women's division. By systematic labor an army of nine thousand volunteer workers was assembled; in one hectic day of doorbell ringing they signed up seventy thousand women in general support of CDL's program. That is the sort of impressive backing, CDL leaders remark, that carries a political impact; it is the sort of pressure that distributors, druggists, newsstand dealers, and police officials can feel.

A third organization actively in the field is the Churchmen's Commission for Decent Publications, created in the spring of 1956 as the outgrowth of a meeting called in Washington, D.C., by O. K. Armstrong, a former member of Congress from Missouri. Its headquarters in 1960 were at 1405 G Street, N.W., Washington, D.C. An informative newsletter is published by a research committee headed by the Rev. Ralph A. Cannon, 113 Franklin Village, Spartanburg, South Carolina. The Churchmen's Commission makes the same general recommendations for local action that other groups make, to study suspected magazines carefully in the light of obscenity laws, to give retail dealers an opportunity voluntarily to clean up their stands, and, that failing, to "present all facts to the prosecuting attorney who is under obligation to bring proceedings against the dealers."

A fourth organization, Americans for Moral Decency (AFMD), urges a largely constructive program to raise community moral standards. Its headquarters are at Room 1105, 173 West Madison Street, Chicago, Illinois. In the view of AFMD leaders, the answer to the evil of obscene matter lies primarily in the good of decent literature. Hence parents are asked to take a hand in encouraging their children "to take advantage of the excellent, the good and the amusing titles that are easily available to them at a nominal cost." Community groups are asked to sponsor book fairs, book reviews, and other programs intended to advance good reading generally. However, AFMD emphasizes that every citizen enjoys "the right to protest publications objectionable for youth." It is a right to be exercised with restraint; citizens should "make sure the material is objectionable youth reading" before making courteous request of a retailer to remove the publication: "The owner has a legal right to sell it until a court rules otherwise. It is only an interest in the youth of the community that can prompt him to comply with your request." AFMD suggests that communities look to their obscenity laws, to make certain these conform to new requirements, but "a community should never expect to solve this problem entirely by law." Public opinion, directed toward raising community standards, is viewed as a more effective tool than criminal prosecutions.

In addition to these four organizations, working nationally in the field of decent literature, a number of Parent-Teacher Associations, 4-H Clubs, Junior Holy Name Societies, and church bodies have sponsored local campaigns. Among these is the Council of Churches of Detroit and Michigan, which in 1959 issued a notable statement of policy. The council reminded its members that "determination of the legality of a publication should be made by a judge or jury, and not by any agency of law enforcement." Moreover:

> Pressure by religious groups or citizens' committees on dealers to remove certain publications from sale is an improper procedure— if the publication is legal it should not be removed by any one interest group, and if it is illegal it should be challenged by the law authorities and ruled illegal by a judge or jury; unofficial censorship of one group's reading matter by another group may lead to misunderstanding and bad feelings.

The Detroit council believes that effective law enforcement in the field of obscene publications requires two kinds of legislation—a criminal statute clearly defining what is meant by indecent literature, and a corollary statute permitting civil proceedings, including injunctions and restraining orders, to adjudicate the obscenity of particular titles.

Finally, mention may be made of the statement approved in May,

1959, by the Board for Christian Social Action of the American Lutheran Church. Decent-minded Americans, said the board, "are growing increasingly incensed over the flood of sex-centered or violence-saturated products appearing on the magazine racks, bookshelves, and motion-picture screens." While corrective action is necessary, "sweeping condemnation of all magazines, books, and motion pictures is alike inaccurate, unfair, and unjust." Because much good material is intermingled among the bad, each case should be judged individually.

The Lutheran program calls for individual action first of all, in avoiding purchase of objectionable material and in seeking to influence public opinion against obscene publications. Individuals should not hesitate to have recourse to the courts in the enforcement of obscenity laws, but more may be accomplished through effort aimed at voluntary action by retail dealers. Community action also is recommended: "A citizens' advisory council on objectionable printed materials and motion pictures can be a valuable aid to conscientious public officials in evaluating materials." Positive rather than negative means should be used: "Lists of forbidden books, magazines, and motion pictures, especially those emanating from religious sources, should be avoided." However, lists of co-operating dealers pledged to standards of review, distribution, and sale could well be published, and emblems of participation given them for display. Parents and schools share a responsibility for seeing that young people receive a sound, sensible education in sex. Churches have an important role in warning of the evils in obscene publications. Through such a many-pronged attack the evil may be combatted:

> A community which provides wholesome and constructive, educational, leisure time, and occupational opportunities for its youth, good social, cultural, and economic conditions for its people, and genuine neighborly interest and companionship among its residents thereby provides at least a partial antidote to the poisons of pornographic and other morally objectionable materials.

Individual and community efforts of the sort recommended by the various decent-literature groups can be effective. Given some energetic leadership, and systematically organized, citizens' groups can succeed in ridding newsstands and drugstores of great quantities of reading material regarded as objectionable. The clean-up campaign in Coral Gables, Florida, described in the December, 1957, issue of *Reader's Digest,* is an example of such a concentrated effort. A Decent Literature Council, representing forty-six community organizations, succeeded not only in driving pornography from Coral Gables newsstands but also in persuading the Florida General Assembly to adopt a strong new anti-obscenity law. The American Legion Auxiliary, the State Federation of Women's Clubs, and the Florida Association of Juvenile Judges had an influential hand in the new legislation also.

In such concerted drives against obscenity the consequences are both good and ill. There are real and serious dangers in the excesses of private groups—the dangers of an organized intolerance, a sort of blindly humorless zeal for reform, that can overtake the best-intentioned group unless its leaders are careful to keep a clean-up campaign in bounds. When the desires of a citizens' committee get tangled with the power of a willing police chief or with the ambitions of men in public life, violence can be done to individual liberties. Two cases may be recalled, one in Ohio, the other in New Jersey.

The former case arose in Youngstown in 1953, when Chief of Police Edward J. Allen, backed by the Federated Women's Clubs of the city, launched an intensive drive against indecent books and magazines. Armed with a formidable list of 108 books—later raised, incredibly, to 335 books—he descended upon a local bookdealer with an implied demand that the books be removed if prosecution were to be avoided. In the course of time the New American Library of World Literature stormed into court with an indignant petition for an injunction against him: eleven of its titles were on the chief's blacklist, and seven of these were freely available at the Youngstown Public Library. District Judge Charles J. McNamee upheld the constitutionality of Youngstown's ordinance against the sale of obscene materials but he found nothing in the law that authorized Chief Allen or the Women's Clubs to serve as a censor of books.[112] "Arbitrary power inspired by good motives," said the court, "no less than that animated by evil intent, is an attack upon the supremacy of the law."

The second case arose in Middlesex County, New Jersey, in the spring of 1950, when a group of citizens formed a Committee on Objectionable Literature and called on the county prosecutor, Matthew F. Melko, with a request that he crack down on pornographic publications. The agreeable Mr. Melko assigned a detective, Bucko, to visit newsstands throughout the area, to bring back books he regarded as suspect, and to submit them to the committee for review.

Eventually this process resulted in a formidable list of publications thought to be obscene. Mr. Melko sent Bucko's index around to the dealers, with a declaration that the listed books "should be withdrawn from circulation." He added a pointed inquiry: "Will you please advise me what steps you will take in the matter?"

Among the proscribed books was Vivian Connell's *The Chinese Room,* a beautifully written if highly improbable novel, published in a paperback edition by Bantam Books. At the time the book fell into Detective Bucko's hands approximately 2,500,000 copies had been published, and Bantam had no intention of seeing the work censored in New Jersey. An injunction proceeding was brought against Mr. Melko in the Superior Court of New Jersey, and on March 31, 1953, Judge Sydney Goldman delivered himself of a long opinion, amounting to a critical essay on the evils of censorship, and emphatically granted the injunction.[14] He concluded that *The Chinese Room,* despite a few sexy passages, was a "rather poor and pale figure" beside Kathleen Winsor's *Forever Amber.* The court's principal objection, however, was to the approach adopted by the prosecutor in his zeal to satisfy the citizens' committee. This amounted to "a clear case of previous censorship in the area of literary obscenity." If booksellers are to be attacked, said Judge Goldman, they must be attacked through due process of law, that is, by arrest, arraignment, and by trial by jury under criminal law.

Citizens' groups, wishing to do a job that is at once both firm and fair, might profitably read the whole of Judge Goldman's opinion. The case is *Bantam Books* v. *Melko,* reported in 96 Atlantic Second at page 47. A reading of this opinion may take some wind from their sails, but it will give them a clear idea of the excesses to be avoided. Up to a point—and that point should be soberly pondered—citizens' committees can operate within the solid guarantees of the Constitution; they do no violence to minority rights in protesting, objecting, persuading, lobbying, swearing out warrants, seeking injunctions. These are their rights. The danger arises when private groups set themselves up, in effect, as public censors, and by tactics of intimidation seek to impose their views upon a community. A better approach, as both the CDL and the American Lutheran Church make clear, is to avoid check lists of "objectionable books," and to go into court on particular items whenever genuinely voluntary programs appear ineffective. This means reliance upon law at every level—federal, state, and local. It is important, therefore, that new trends in the writing of obscenity laws be recognized.

5. PUBLIC LAW

Few major changes are foreseen in obscenity law at the federal level. The Treasury Department, through the Bureau of Customs, stands ready to investigate complaints of obscene matter imported into the United States. The Justice Department, through the FBI, has responsibility for obscene matter transported in interstate commerce. The most active agency, of course, is the Post Office Department. Throughout the nation postal inspectors, relying chiefly on the established basic act of 1873, are equipped to advise the outraged citizen and to prepare cases for effective prosecution. Parents who may receive obscene matter in the mail are urged to get in touch with the inspectors at once, to preserve all envelopes and enclosures as evidence, and, alas, to be patient: the preparation of a Section 1461 case for trial is a tedious job, often requiring nationwide co-ordination, and there may be a dozen good reasons why the department, which can manage only so many cases at a time, delays a recommendation for prosecution. Nevertheless the circular received by a family in Brooklyn may be the last piece in a puzzle that will make a successful case in Kansas; the lewd photographs actually received in Minneapolis may well figure in a trial in Los Angeles, Detroit, or Birmingham. Or it may be that a particular mailing will clinch a departmental decision to launch "unlawful" proceedings.

On September 1, 1959, the House of Representatives adopted by an overwhelming vote a bill, H.R. 7379, sponsored by Mrs. Kathryn Granahan of Pennsylvania, to make three significant changes in Section 259b of the postal laws. Under the law sought to be amended, the postmaster general may impound for not more than twenty days all mail addressed to a person or corporation suspected of an unlawful mail-order operation; the Granahan bill was designed to extend this period to forty-five days. The old law limited such impounding orders to instances in which the postmaster general found it necessary to impound mail in order to support an actual "unlawful" order; the Granahan bill was intended to permit impoundings whenever the postmaster general regarded impoundings as desirable "in the public interest." A third amendment was designed to prevent Federal courts from dissolving the department's impoundment orders unless the orders appeared to be wholly arbitrary and capricious.

Ernest Angell, chairman of the board of directors of the American Civil Liberties Union, strongly attacked the Granahan bill in testimony before a House subcommittee. In his view the measure vested almost unlimited discretion in a postmaster general to censor the operations of mail-order houses, and even to drive them out of business entirely, before the questioned material ever had come before a court for adjudication as to obscenity. Such censorship would be bad under any circumstances, said Mr. Angell, but "it is especially so when it is to be exercised by a public official with as notoriously poor a record of judgment as this one." To leave it up to a postmaster general to decide what considerations "in the public interest" might justify the seizure for forty-five days of all mail addressed to a citizen not actually charged with any crime, was to impose a harsh and probably unconstitutional penalty upon a man presumed innocent until proved guilty.

Spokesmen for the Post Office Department warmly defended the Granahan bill as a necessary weapon against the elusive hit-and-run pornographers whose operations are most difficult to break up. In a typical case a merchant of filth may mail fifty thousand circulars on the first day of the month, under the name of ABC Films, at P.O. Box 1234. Under the luckiest circumstances it will be the fourth or the fifth day of the month before a circular comes into the hands of postal inspectors. By the tenth to the fourteenth day the great bulk of the cash has come back to the pornographer. Along about the twentieth day the pornographer fills the accumulated orders, counts his profits, and abandons ABC Films and P.O. Box 1234 altogether. The department's position is that in such a case it must be permitted to move at the earliest possible moment, just as soon as the operation is detected, if the quick-haul operator is to be thwarted. Unless mail can be impounded in this crucial period when returns are pouring in, subsequent "unlawful" orders are useless; and as often as not the material actually mailed by the dealer, in filling the orders, is not sufficiently obscene in itself to warrant prosecution under Section 1461. The racketeer has made his coup and placed himself beyond reach of the postal laws.

The Granahan bill was pending in the Senate as this manuscript was prepared.

A number of other proposals for federal action, apart from the Granahan bill, also have come before the Congress in recent years. Senator James O. Eastland of Mississippi has proposed a constitutional amendment, to say that "the right of each state to decide on the basis of its own public policy questions of decency and morality, and to enact legislation with respect thereto, shall not be abridged." An alternate resolution, sponsored in 1960 by Senators Kefauver, Eastland, and Herman Talmadge, proposed to add to the Constitution an amendment stating that "freedom of speech and freedom of press shall not extend to the publication, manufacture, sale, dissemination, or distribution of obscene material, and both the Congress and the states may enact legislation with respect to the prohibition thereof." Under the opposition of the ACLU, the American Book Publishers Council, and other respected critics, these proposed amendments died in committee. Other proposals, intended to toughen postal and commerce laws by increasing the penalties for mailing or shipping obscene materials, also have tended to fall by the legislative wayside.

The states have been far more active than the Congress in the field of obscenity legislation. With the Supreme Court's decisions in *Butler*,[31] *Roth-Alberts*,[3,166] and *Smith*,[175] wholesale changes in state laws became necessary across the nation. The trend of decisions as to motion picture censorship, beginning with *Burstyn*[29] in 1952, and extending through the *Lady Chatterley* case in the summer of 1959,[90.1] necessitated a host of new laws also. The state legislator, city councilman, or decent-literature advocate who interests himself in the drafting of new laws will find an interesting challenge in the contradictory problems before him. The object is to draft a law that will catch the pornographer without trapping the serious writer or artist. A law should be wide enough to take in the multiple forms of actual obscenity, and yet narrow enough to leave free room for works protected under our cherished principles of press freedom. Several guides to workable legislation, fair and firm at the same time, may be suggested.

1. The aim of a criminal statute must be to punish the commercial or public traffic in obscene materials, and great care must be taken to see that terms are clearly defined and that due process of law is assured at every step of the way.

An approved definition of obscenity now has been securely fixed by the Supreme Court. A thing is obscene which, taken as a whole, appeals to the prurient interest of the average person applying contemporary community standards. The term "obscene" may be further defined in the language of the American Law Institute's model statute—that is, "a shameful or morbid interest in nudity, sex or excretion, which goes substantially beyond customary limits of candor in description or representation of such matters."

Care should be taken to avoid loading a criminal statute with excess adjectives. Such terms as "indecent, immoral, lewd, lascivious, and filthy" add nothing of value to "obscene," and may cause a law to be voided for uncertainty.

The importance of a precise definition was demonstrated in Indiana on January 12, 1960, when Marion County Criminal Court Judge Richmond M. Salb acquitted eleven Indianapolis newsdealers who had been arrested in June, 1959, in raids sponsored by the Citizens Committee for Decent Literature. In the court's view the state law was unconstitutional and void for want of a clear definition of obscene literature.

On similar objections Federal Judge Robert L. Taylor in 1958 voided an ambitious ordinance of the City of Knoxville.[274] The law created a board of review with power to issue cease-and-desist orders prohibiting the sale of any publication that "prominently features an account of crime, or is obscene, or depicts . . . obscene actions and accounts, or the commission or attempted commission of the crimes of arson, assault with a deadly weapon, burglary, kidnapping, mayhem, murder, rape, robbery, theft, or voluntary manslaughter."

Judge Taylor commented that "a paramount duty of the state is to exercise its police power to minimize those things that are calculated to undermine the morals of its citizens and incite to crime," but this ordinance went too far. Literally construed, the law would have permitted a board of review to ban classics beginning with the kidnapping of Helen of Troy, and proceeding on through Cain's murder of Abel to the pickpocketing tricks of the Artful Dodger.

A provision that may desirably be included in an effective statute (though some students of the subject disagree) is a clause aimed at preventing tie-in sales by magazine and paperback distributors. Florida's statute, for example, makes it a misdemeanor for any distributor to require "as a condition to a sale or a delivery for resale of any commodity or thing, that the purchaser or consignee thereof receive for resale any article reasonably believed by the purchaser or consignee to be [obscene]."

In drafting an effective criminal statute, care should be taken to avoid weaving a net to catch more than the lawmakers truly wish to haul in. To prevent misunderstandings, and to free librarians from unwarranted harassment, it is desirable that some exemptions be written into the law. The American Law Institute suggests three actions that might well be excluded: (a) dissemination, not for gain, to personal associates other than children under sixteen; (b) dissemination, not for gain, by an actor below the age of twenty-one to a child not more than five years younger than the actor, and (c) dissemination to institutions or individuals having scientific or other special justification for possessing such material." The language of Washington's act of March 23, 1959, is possibly simpler:

> Nothing in this act shall apply to the circulation of any such [obscene] material by any recognized historical society or museum, the state law library, any county law library, the state library, the public library, any library of any college or university, to any archive or library under the supervision and control of the state, county, municipality, or other political subdivision.

A list of obscene items, intended to be proscribed, may be as long or as short as a competent drafter cares to make it. The American

Law Institute's model statute takes in "any obscene writing, picture, record, or other representation or embodiment of the obscene," with an additional ban on "any obscene play, dance, or other performance." By contrast a bill approved in January, 1960, by the Virginia House of Delegates proposed to embrace "any obscene manuscript, writing, paper, leaflet, pamphlet, brochure, magazine, newspaper, book, booklet, picture, motion picture, painting, photograph, negative, film, slide, printing, drawing, sketch, design, figure, object, recording, transcription, play, drama, show, entertainment, exhibition, exposition, tableau, scene, incident, or mechanical, chemical, or electrical reproduction." Other state laws use such additional terms as article, instrument, image, circular, catalog, comic book, storybook, story paper, pictorial representation, graphic art, auditory device, novelty device, model, stimulant, periodical, written matter, and printed material. The Virginia law, incidentally, was much condensed before its final approval in March, 1960. As adopted, several of its provisions approach a model enactment.

In general, it may be suggested, a statute should attempt to proscribe printed or visual materials in one class, recordings and transcriptions in a second, novelty devices and objects in a third, and possibly live theatrical performances and exhibitions in a fourth.

The choice of verbs available to a drafter is scarcely less extensive than his choice of nouns. The Virginia proposal earlier mentioned reached to every person who "writes, composes, designs, draws, sketches, engraves, paints, prints, makes, copies, produces, reproduces, publishes, sells, rents, lends, transports, distributes, exhibits, carves, casts, cuts, molds, manufactures, prepares, advertises, stages, presents, directs, manages, carries on, participates in, displays, posts, or keeps for sale, rental, loan, distribution, or exhibition," any obscene material. Perhaps half of these would appear to suffice.

In most states the preparation, manufacture, and sale of obscene materials are treated, at least on first offense, as misdemeanors, ordinarily punishable by a fine of up to $1,000 and a year in jail. In a number of states—the statutes of Arkansas, California, Delaware, Massachusetts, and Michigan are typical—the law provides for a prison term on second offense. Ohio's maximum of seven years' imprisonment is the severest penalty provided by any state.

2. If it is desired to define an offense in terms of minors, care must be taken to treat such provisions as a class to themselves.

By common agreement the greatest evil of the obscenity racket lies in the impact of obscene materials upon juveniles. It is generally agreed that the probable damage to adults, in many borderline cases, is not sufficient to justify a suppression of individual expression, whether in art or in literature. The Supreme Court has warned that the door against censorship, especially as to adult reading, must be kept tightly closed, and opened only on particular occasions when truly obscene matter, lacking the slightest redeeming social importance, may be proscribed.

The court's view as to young people is somewhat different. In 1944, in *Prince* v. *Massachusetts*,[154] Mr. Justice Rutledge said:

> The state's authority over children's activities is broader than over like actions of adults. . . . A democratic society rests, for its continuance, upon the healthy, well-rounded growth of young people into full maturity as citizens, with all that implies. It may secure this against impeding restraints and dangers within a broad range of selection. . . . It is too late now to doubt that legislation appropriately designed to reach such evils is within the state's police power. . . .

What is "legislation appropriately designed" to reach such evils? The Supreme Court of Rhode Island spoke on this point[180.1] in December, 1959, in unanimously upholding an act of 1956 in which the state had made it a felony for any person knowingly to sell or distribute commercially to any person under the age of eighteen

> any pornographic motion picture, or any still picture or photograph or any book, pocket book, pamphlet or magazine the cover or content of which exploits, is devoted to, or is principally made up of descriptions of illicit sex or sexual immorality, or which is obscene, lewd, lascivious, or indecent, or which consists of pictures of nude or partially denuded figures posed or presented in a manner to provoke or arouse lust or passion.

In the view of Rhode Island, one of the states most active in the war upon obscenity, the distribution to minors of obscene material is "a contributing factor to juvenile crime, a basic factor in impairing the ethical and moral development of our youth and a clear and present danger to the people of the state." The Rhode Island Supreme Court concurred with this view.

A precisely opposite opinion on a similar statute was rendered on January 19, 1960, in the Baltimore County Superior Court by Judge Reuben Oppenheimer. In 1955 the General Assembly of Maryland had adopted a law that began with a recital of the Assembly's finding that in recent years there had been "a serious and tremendous increase" in Maryland in the number and variety of comic books of an obscene nature. In the Assembly's view children under eighteen, "being of susceptible and impressionable character," were likely to be incited to commit certain crimes, "in good part through the influence of these vicious and corrupt publications." The Assembly therefore made it a crime (surprisingly, in view of the act's formidable preamble, no more than a misdemeanor carrying a maximum punishment of a $200 fine and six months in jail) for any person to sell to a child below the age of eighteen any publication "principally composed of pictures and specifically including but not limited to comic books, devoted to the publication and exploitation of actual or fictional deeds of violent bloodshed, lust or immorality, or which, for a child below the age of eighteen years, are obscene, lewd, lascivious, filthy, indecent or disgusting, and so presented as reasonably to tend to incite a child below the age of eighteen years to violence or depraved or immoral acts against the person."

Judge Oppenheimer ruled the law unconstitutional on two principal grounds: first, that the provisions of the law were too vague, citing the *Winters* case of 1948;[275] and secondly, that the effect of the law was to prohibit circulation to the general public of material deemed unsuitable for minors. On this point he cited the *Butler* case from Michigan, in which Mr. Justice Frankfurter had expressed the objection of a unanimous court to a state law that effectively prevented anyone, adult or child, from reading John Griffin's *The Devil Rides Outside*. It was in that case that the court warned against laws, intended to protect children, which burned a house down to roast the pig.

In the Maryland case Judge Oppenheimer acknowledged the right of the General Assembly to enact laws protecting children, but he emphasized that due process extends to children no less than to adults: "The right of young persons to read what they will, within the limits of permissible state or federal action, is vital not only to them but to all our citizenry. The exclusion of obscenity from protected utterances does not carry with it the right to obscure, from young or old, facts or events, however unpleasant, disturbing or violent."

Within these ground rules statutes making it a separate, severable offense to sell obscene materials to minors probably will be upheld. Florida has experimented with such a law, applying to children under seventeen, with a maximum punishment of three years in prison. The state of Washington makes it a gross misdemeanor to exhibit within the view of any minor an obscene item. In its model statute the American Law Institute suggests that a judge or jury, in determining the obscenity of a particular article, should judge the article with reference to ordinary adults, "except that it shall be judged with reference to children or other specially susceptible audience if it appears from the character of the material or the circumstances of its dissemination to be specially designed for or directed to such an audience."

Even Morris L. Ernst, who has spent his life warring upon censorship in every form, suggested in *To the Pure* that it might be tolerable to adopt laws prohibiting the exhibition or sale of pornographic material to persons under eighteen, except by teachers, doctors, or parents. He proposed to limit "pornographic material" to "any matter or thing exhibited or visually representing persons or animals performing the sexual act, whether normal or abnormal." No state appears to have adopted Mr. Ernst's model statute.

3. It is now vitally important that the element of scienter *be provided for in any criminal statute.*

On December 14, 1959, the Supreme Court of the United States handed down an opinion that caused some agitated concern among citizens' groups and decent-literature committees around the country. This was the court's opinion reversing the conviction of Eleazar Smith, a Los Angeles bookdealer, under a Los Angeles city ordinance making it unlawful for any person to have an obscene book in his possession "in any place of business where ice cream, soft drinks, candy, food, school supplies, magazines, books, pamphlets, papers, pictures or postcards are sold or kept for sale."[175]

Some of the reasoning in the court's opinion was exceedingly far-fetched, but the concern expressed both in the press and in Congress was largely unwarranted. The court voided the Los Angeles ordinance for one reason only, that the law failed to require as an element of the criminal offense that a defendant *knowingly* possessed an obscene book. A number of hasty critics felt that the high court had done grave damage to law enforcement and had opened for the merchants of filth a fine new loophole. In point of fact, the *Smith* case did no such thing.

A requirement of *scienter* is an entirely familiar requirement both in obscenity law and in criminal law generally. It is the element that protects an innocent person, to offer one example at random, from prosecution for unknowingly passing counterfeit money. The Post Office Department has lived with *scienter* from the days of the first Comstock Act. As far back as 1887 a district court in Virginia dismissed an indictment against a woman, charged with mailing an obscene pamphlet, because the government inadvertently had failed to charge that she put the pamphlet in the mail "knowing it to be obscene."[259] To this day the basic postal statute (Title 18, Section 1461) punishes only those who "knowingly deposit for mailing or delivery anything declared by this section to be nonmailable, or knowingly take the same from the mails for the purpose of circulating or disposing thereof." Section 1462, dealing with the importation or obscene literature, says the same thing: "Whoever knowingly takes from such express company or other common carrier," etc.

In the Los Angeles case the charge against Smith was simply that he had in his store a copy of a book, *Sweeter Than Life,* by Mark Tryon. Smith's defense was that he had never read the book, and if the book were obscene, he did not know it to be obscene. He complained that if a law were to be upheld that imposed an absolute criminal liability on a bookdealer—a law that punished a bookdealer for unknowing possession of obscene books—the dealers would find themselves in an impossible position.

The Supreme Court, speaking through Justice Brennan, agreed.

The elimination of *scienter* in an ordinance such as this one, in the court's view, could have the effect of "inhibiting the freedom of expression, by making the individual the more reluctant to exercise it." The ordinance would penalize booksellers "even though they had not the slightest notice of the character of the books they sold." In the lower court the state had pressed an analogy with pure food and drug laws. Such laws contain no element of *scienter* and punish distributors of contaminated food whether or not the distributors have any idea of the contamination. But Justice Brennan thought the argument not analogous at all: "There is no specific constitutional inhibition against making the distributors of food the strictest censors of their merchandise, but the constitutional guarantees of the freedom of speech and of the press stand in the way of imposing a similar requirement on the bookseller." The court continued:

By dispensing with any requirement of knowledge of the contents of the book on the part of the seller, the ordinance tends to impose a severe limitation on the public's access to constitutionally protected matter. For if the bookseller is criminally liable without knowledge of the contents, and the ordinance fulfills its purpose, he will tend to restrict the books he sells to those he has inspected; and thus the state will have imposed a restriction upon the distribution of constitutionally protected as well as obscene literature. . . . And the bookseller's burden would become the public's burden, for by restricting him the public's access to reading matter would be restricted. If the contents of bookshops and periodical stands were restricted to material of which their proprietors had made an inspection, they might be depleted indeed.

In passing, it may be suggested that the court's language here is the chaff from which straw men are made. In point of fact every newsstand and bookshop is subject to some limitation, if only the physical limitation of shelf space; "the public's access to forms of the printed word" depends upon a thousand considerations having nothing to do with obscenity statutes or a bookdealer's reading habits.

Speaking for the court, Brennan said:

It is argued that unless the *scienter* requirement is dispensed with, regulation of the distribution of obscene material will be ineffective, as booksellers will falsely disclaim knowledge of those books' contents or falsely deny reason to suspect their obscenity. We might observe that it has been some time now since the law viewed itself as impotent to explore the actual state of a man's mind. . . . Eyewitness testimony of a bookseller's perusal of a book hardly need be a necessary element in proving his awareness of its contents. The circumstances may warrant the inference that he was aware of what a book contained, despite his denial.

We need not and most definitely do not pass today on what sort of mental element is requisite to a constitutionally permissible prosecution of a bookseller for carrying an obscene book in stock; whether honest mistake as to whether its contents in fact constituted obscenity need be an excuse; whether there might be circumstances under which the state constitutionally might require that a bookseller investigate further, or might put on him the burden of explaining why he did not, and what such circumstances may be.

These various elements and requirements of *scienter* remain to be worked out by the states, but the problem is not likely to give great trouble. Most state laws have contained this requirement right along (California's state obscenity law, as distinguished from the voided Los Angeles ordinance, requires that *scienter* be proved). And for the sort of common-sense approach to *scienter* that is likely to be upheld, a 1959 decision in the United States District Court in Milwaukee offers a handy example.[226] There the government brought charges against one Samuel R. Hockman for receiving, by common carrier, some obscene books for sale in his bookstore. It was brought out that Hockman was a college graduate; that he was an experienced dealer; and that he himself had selected the books in question—*The Sex Factory* and *Virgins Come High*—from a New York wholesale house. In overruling Hockman's motion for a directed verdict, on the grounds that the government had failed to prove that Hockman "knowingly" shipped obscene books by express, the court commented that "the jury might have considered that the titles and the illustrations in the books are such as to put an intelligent and experienced person on notice of the type of books which they were."

A somewhat similar comment came from the New York Court of

Special Sessions in January, 1960, in upholding the conviction of five Times Square bookdealers for selling obscene paperbacks at five dollars a copy. The dealers pleaded the *Smith* case—they didn't *know* the books were obscene—but the court held that any dealer selling something called *Garden of Evil,* or *Bloomer Boy,* or *Succulent* at five dollars a copy had reason to be generally aware of the contents of the books. In July, 1960, however, the Appellate Division in Brooklyn reversed the conviction of a distributor on a charge of handling *Gent* magazine. Four of the five judges agreed the issue in question was obscene, but they felt *scienter* had not been proved. Judge George L. Beldock, dissenting, said "casual inspection" by the defendant would have put him on notice of the magazine's character.

4. In addition to criminal statutes, laws may be considered creating public bodies charged with some responsibility in the field of obscene materials.

Three states, Oklahoma, Massachusetts, and Georgia, have passed laws to create state commissions with some authority to recommend prosecution of materials found to be obscene, and Rhode Island has created a State Commission to Encourage Morality in Youth. The Oklahoma commission never was activated. The Massachusetts Obscene Literature Control Commission came into being in January, 1959, under an act directing it to recommend to the attorney general that appropriate action be taken whenever it appeared to the group that a violation of obscenity laws had occurred. The commission consists of seven members, of whom one is to be an educator, one a Protestant, one a Catholic, and one a Jew. During its first year of operations, Chairman William J. McCarthy advises, the commission devoted its efforts primarily to the organization of local decent-literature committees in such urban areas as West Springfield and Beverly. He feels the commission has been "very successful, indirectly," and that the local groups, without using "hard pressure, boycotts, or lists of books," have obtained much voluntary co-operation from dealers. The Rhode Island Commission, under steady bombardment from the Providence *Evening Bulletin* and the Rhode Island American Civil Liberties Union, has been subjected to much criticism for using a censor's blacklist, instead of law-enforcement channels, to back up its proscriptions. In the spring of 1960 four publishers (Bantam, Dell, Pocket Books, and New American Library) brought suit against the Rhode Island commission in an effort to have the agency declared unconstitutional.

The one state commission with a record of discreet and effective action over a period of years is Georgia's State Literature Commission. Created in 1953, the commission at first had power directly to "prohibit the distribution of any literature . . . [found] to be obscene." In 1958 the law was rewritten to leave any final determination of obscenity entirely within the hands of state courts. The commission's procedure, under the amended law, is to receive complaints, to make investigations, and to hold hearings on items that appear to warrant hearings. If the commission determines that a publication "contains evidence of being obscene," it forwards its file to the attorney general for appropriate action and simultaneously publishes its findings in a monthly newsletter to wholesale and retail outlets. In only one case, involving the paperback novel *Rambling Maids,* has the commission exercised its power to seek an injunction on its own motion.

In practice, the Georgia commission's monthly notices have had the effect of achieving voluntary co-operation from local newspapers. A typical month may see perhaps a dozen magazines and two or three paperback novels set for hearing and found obscene. In between the commission's meetings Secretary Hubert L. Dyar gently disposes of complaints regarded as failing to meet the standards of the *Roth* decision. Complaining citizens are advised politely that material "must be considered as a whole," and objectionable as a few passages may seem to be, the challenged material probably would not meet the criteria established by the commission. These criteria require the commission, in every case, to make eight inquiries: (1) what is the general and dominant theme? (2) what degree of sincerity of purpose is evident? (3) what is the literary or scientific worth? (4) what channels of distribution are employed? (5) what are contemporary attitudes of reasonable men toward such matters? (6) what types of readers may reasonably be expected to peruse the publication? (7) is there evidence of pornographic intent? (8) what impression will be created in the mind of the reader, upon reading the work as a whole?

5. A law providing for civil proceedings against a suspected book, to adjudicate its obscenity subject to restraining order or injunctive decree, offers many advantages.

The eight inquiries required in Georgia substantially parallel the criteria recommended in a model statute prepared by Professors William B. Lockhart and Robert C. McClure of the University of Minnesota Law School. Messrs. Lockhart and McClure are this nation's leading authorities on the law of obscenity censorship; their article in the *Minnesota Law Review* of March, 1954, frequently quoted by the Supreme Court of the United States, is the most definitive survey of this difficult subject ever put together. Their recommendations carry the weight of profound study; their recommendations merit the deepest respect. And when they submit that the field divides itself roughly into three broad classes—the hard-core items, about which there is little disagreement; the clothbound books, about which there is little disagreement; and the paperbacks and magazines, about which there is much disagreement—their comments deserve to be listened to. What they propose, in brief, is that dealers in hard-core items be prosecuted under familiar obscenity laws; that the publishers of trade-edition books be left substantially alone (there is truly no problem here, and assuredly no problem seriously affecting juveniles); and that the one perplexing and difficult field of paperback novels and magazines be handled through what amounts to an *in rem* procedure; that is, a proceeding against the thing itself.

Their recommendations make great sense. Police officials ordinarily are totally unequipped, by temperament or training, to act intelligently upon material in this field. This is no reflection upon the police; all men have their areas of competence and their areas of inadequacy. When it comes to enforcing an obscenity ordinance the police do handsomely on the hard-core items; beyond that point they often are reduced to reliance upon someone's prepared list of objectionable books, or they are tempted to ignore the law altogether.

At the same time, newsstand operators and drugstore proprietors are almost equally unequipped, by reason of time and opportunity, to watch over their magazine racks. Every few days a distributor's truck arrives bringing quantities of new magazines and paperbacks. These cannot possibly be read critically; even if the retail dealer were interested in reading them, his day is not long enough to read all of them. When a committee comes around from the local Holy Name Society his inclination is to surrender without a struggle. Why offend good customers? Or alternatively his inclination is to get his back up: who do these birds think they are? Then come the police, and he has to hire a lawyer, make bond, and risk a jail sentence.

"Wholesale distributors and retail dealers of books and magazines," say McClure and Lockhart, "need protection against the indiscriminate use and abuse of obscenity laws. For they are reputable businessmen of their communities and have no practicable means of knowing the nature and content of the books and magazines they handle or of determining whether a particular book or magazine is legally obscene. They should be held criminally responsible *only after a book or magazine has been properly adjudicated obscene and they have received notice of the adjudication.*"

Toward this end—and in order to accord both the procensorship and the anticensorship groups a fair hearing before a qualified and impartial tribunal—Professors McClure and Lockhart recommend a proceeding by which the obscenity of a publication may be determined judicially without going through the embarrassments and difficulties of a criminal trial. The model law they recommend has been approved, in its essence, by the American Law Institute. In abbreviated or modified form the idea has been adopted in Virginia, Georgia, New York, Ohio, Florida, and Washington. Each of these states now authorizes an injunctive procedure aimed at determining the obscenity of a publication without recourse to the criminal trial of a retail dealer. The Ohio law, for example, permits any county or city attorney to maintain an action for injunction in a common pleas court to prevent the distribution or sale of an article the attorney believes to be obscene. The Florida law permits the state attorney general or any local prosecuting attorney to institute a proceeding "for a declaratory judgment to determine whether such periodical or printed matter is, in fact, obscene." The law in Washington State is similar. In each case the statute requires a prompt determination of the issue.

The advantages of such a procedure become apparent upon a moment's reflection. A conscientious and reputable druggist or newsstand operator does not want to sell material that is unlawfully obscene; neither does he want to deny his more sophisticated customers the reading material they are constitutionally entitled to have if they want it. Police do not want to bring a criminal charge against a reputable merchant, with all the attendant risk and embarrassment such a charge entails. The more responsible decent literature committees, while they want to eliminate obscenity, recognize a need for tolerance toward adult tastes. And the more responsible defenders of civil liberties agree that they are hard put to defend the worst of the pulp paperbacks and lewd magazines.

Each of these interests may be served by a law that permits a declaratory judgment, or a temporary restraining order, or an injunction of some sort directed against the sale of a particular book or books. Under the McClure-Lockhart bill a proceeding is brought through a petition directed against the printed matter by name. Both publisher and seller are invited to answer to the proceeding; prompt hearings are required. If no answer is filed the court determines the obscenity of the publication according to the broad requirements of *Roth-Alberts*. If the case is contested the court is instructed to receive evidence, including the testimony of experts, upon (1) the class of persons for whom the publication is intended, (2) the manner of publication, advertisement, distribution, and sale, (3) the predominant appeal of the publication considered as a whole, (4) the artistic, literary, scientific, and educational values of the matter, and (5) the intent of the author and publisher in writing and publishing the printed matter. At the conclusion of such a trial the court is required to reduce its findings to writing, to declare the publication either obscene, not obscene, or obscene only for particular classes of readers, and to enter judgment accordingly. Notice of such judgment, served upon retail dealers, charges them with knowledge of the book's standing. And if a publication has been thus adjudicated obscene, only the fact of sale need be proved in a criminal prosecution. The act adopted by Virginia in 1960 follows this pattern.

The McClure-Lockhart approach has been endorsed both by the Council for Independent Distribution, representing the paperback and magazine wholesalers, and the American Book Publishers Council. Chief Justice Warren, in a brief dissenting opinion, instinctively objected to the procedure in the *Kingsley* case:[90] "The New York law places the book on trial. . . . The personal element basic to the criminal laws is entirely absent. . . . It savors too much of book-burning." Mr. Justice Brennan also objected in this case that the absence of a right to a jury trial in such proceedings "is a fatal defect." Nevertheless it may be submitted that the McClure-Lockhart procedure, embraced in new state laws, properly submitted to the high court, would be found wholly in accord with the rulings of respected courts over a period of many years. It is true that for a time courts refused to consider evidence of the literary values in a suspected book.[124, 142] Massachusetts would not hear of this in the *An American Tragedy* case[129] nor would California in the matter of Edmund Wilson's *Memoirs of Hecate County*.[147] But the trend is indisputable. In the trials of Joyce's *Ulysses*[252] and Flaubert's *November*[136] and in many other leading cases[145,237,144] this rational and common-sense approach has been approved. As far back as the Marie Stopes cases[251,254] it was agreed that works of genuine medical value should be exempted. The *Parmelee*,[117] *Popenoe*,[273] and *Life* magazine[134] cases have confirmed this view. Since Voltaire's reputation was examined in the *St. Hubert's Guild* case[78] in 1909, most courts have agreed that authors of established literary standing deserve special consideration not accorded fly-by-night hack writers of pulp fiction. And though a few courts have refused to hear the evidence of literary critics, psychologists, and other expert witnesses,[176] the recent trend has been to admit such testimony gladly.[47,54.1,55.1,138,165.1]

This approach, in which the author, publisher, distributor, and dealer are protected by due process every step of the way, should be acceptable to police, to decent-literature committees, and to civil libertarians alike. Its consideration is earnestly recommended to them.

6. MOTION PICTURES

The censorship of motion pictures, like the censorship of books and magazines, also operates under both private and public aegis, with this difference: where books and magazines have been subject only to subsequent punishment, after publication, motion pictures have remained subject to a wide variety of prior restraints before their exhibition. As the decade of the 1960's began, four states still maintained official state censor boards, with power to prohibit the exhibition of any unapproved film, and Pennsylvania was experimenting with a new statute permitting injunctive proceedings against any film after a single showing. In at least twenty cities, ranging from Atlanta to Tacoma, municipal censorship boards or officials were operating under a formidable array of statutes, most of them unconstitutional.

The opening of the decade marked a difficult time for the motion-picture industry. In 1928, when there were 22,300 movie houses in the country, the industry had 834 releases. By 1955 the number of releases had been cut in half and so had the number of the theaters. Paid admissions had dropped from eighty million a week to forty-eight million. In the succeeding four or five years the number of total releases increased somewhat, but fewer than half of the new films represented films made in the United States. In 1958 a significant milestone was reached: for the first time the domestic industry counted more than half of its gross revenue from foreign countries; of $590 million in worldwide revenues $290 million came from viewers within the United States, $300 million from moviegoers in other countries, chiefly in England, Italy, France, Germany, Japan, and Brazil.

The industry's economic problems stemmed from a series of changing habits and attitudes that probably were beyond the movies' power to influence one way or another. There was the villain of television, which wrought great mischief, but there were other villains also: prodigious increases in production costs; some ruinous federal and local taxes on admissions; the mounting expenses of maintaining year-round theaters (as distinguished from the 4,700 seasonal drive-ins); and more than anything else, the subtle change in the movie-going audience from every-week family attendance to a far more selective and discriminating choice of film fare.

In a desperate effort to stay alive the industry began to break away from old patterns of self-imposed restraint. As far back as 1925 a committee of producers had attempted to set up some rules on morality, but the scheme had failed. In 1930 came the first Motion Picture Code of the Motion Picture Association of America (MPAA), in which the producers set forth three general principles to which all members of the association were to be bound:

1. No picture shall be produced which will lower the moral standards of those who see it. Hence the sympathy of the audience shall never be thrown to the side of crime, wrongdoing, evil, or sin.

2. Correct standards of life, subject only to the requirements of drama and entertainment, shall be presented.

3. Law, natural or human, shall not be ridiculed, nor shall sympathy be created for its violation.

These principles were supplemented by a number of guides: "The use of firearms should be restricted to essentials." "The treatment of bedrooms must be governed by good taste and delicacy." The code contained a number of flat prohibitions also: "Pointed profanity and every other profane or vulgar expression, however used, are forbidden." "The illegal drug traffic, and drug addiction, must never be presented."

This first formal code also failed to accomplish much, and it was not until the Catholic Church established its Legion of Decency in 1934 that the industry rushed Joseph L. Breen to the scene and sat down to strict enforcement under a Seal of Approval plan. In 1938 and 1939 the MPAA supplemented its code of 1930 with some clarifying resolutions, but it was not until December, 1956, that any significant amendments were authorized. It is often forgotten that these liberalizations of 1956 came with the advice and consent of an unlikely body, a sub-committee of the United States Senate. In March of that year, following a series of sympathetic hearings, the subcommittee adopted a report suggesting that the code of 1930, while its principles were sound, contained restrictions "not in keeping with the social changes that have transpired since it was written." The subcommittee felt that in the past "the framework and administration of self-regulation had been overly moralistic." A screen maturely performing the functions of mass communication demanded a wider orientation and a greater flexibility to deal with many phases of various social problems.

Thus encouraged, the MPAA directors set promptly about some liberalizations of the old rules. The three general principles of 1930 were retained intact, but some of the former inhibitions and prohibitions upon films dealing with miscegenation, for example, and the drug traffic, were abandoned. In the next few years film audiences began to hear words they never had heard from the screen—"rape," "sperm," "pregnant," "bitch"—and to see themes of race relations, homosexuality, adultery, narcotics, and sexuality explored.

Prior to the *Paramount* antitrust case in 1948[255] enforcement of the Production Code was a relatively simple matter. Every major producer belonged to the MPAA; moreover the producers controlled the theaters. They could effectively prevent the exhibition of any film not bearing the Seal of Approval. But the breakup of the industry was followed within a few years by significant changes in movie production: independent producers and foreign producers, not members of the MPAA and thus not bound to compliance with the Code, came into new prominence; they began to risk censure from the Legion of Decency and local censor boards by releasing films that did not carry the Seal of Approval. *The Miracle* was such a film. So was *La Ronde*. In 1953 came *The Moon Is Blue,* and later *I Am a Camera* and *Room at the Top.* As the decade of the sixties began an estimated 90 per cent of all films released for domestic exhibition still were carrying the Seal of Approval, granted under the tolerant and rather easy-going enforcement of the code's administrator, Geoffrey Shurlock, an English-born Episcopalian who had worked directly under Joe Breen. Subjects that would have been viewed as entirely too controversial for earlier production began to be treated with increasing boldness. And notably, the Legion of Decency, in an understanding gesture toward the industry's bid for more sophisticated audiences, revised its classification system to add to its Class A, covering "unobjectionable" films, a new category: "unobjectionable for adults." The Legion also adopted a plan of listing certain films, such as *Suddenly Last Summer,* in a special classification; the Legion described the picture as "moral in its theme and treatment" but urged that exhibitors take pains to restrict viewing to a serious audience capable of mature reaction to the theme of perversion.

The Production Code of 1956 carries a special interest for students of the law of obscenity censorship. It will be recalled that the Supreme Court of the United States, in reversing New York's ban in 1959 on *Lady Chatterley's Lover,* pointedly refused to consider whether the controls that may be imposed upon motion pictures "are precisely coextensive with those allowable to newspapers, books, or individual speech." The MPAA itself has considered the question, and historically has *not* contended that its freedoms of expression should be coextensive with those of newspapers, books, or stage plays. In a formal statement of "reasons supporting the code," the industry has emphasized since 1930 that theatrical motion pictures "are primarily to be regarded as entertainment." Movies are an art form, to be sure —indeed they are the "art of the multitudes"—but art can be both morally good and morally evil; the industry has recognized a high responsibility to see that moral evil is avoided. The industry's own statement says this:

> This art of the motion picture, combining as it does the two fundamental appeals of looking at a picture and listening to a story, at once reaches every class of society. By reason of the mobility of a film and the ease of picture distribution, and because of the possibility of duplicating positives in large quantities, this art reaches places unpenetrated by other forms of art. Because of these facts, it is difficult to produce films intended for only certain classes of people. The exhibitors' theaters are built for the masses, for the cultivated and the rude, the mature and the immature, the self-respecting and the criminal. Films, unlike books and music, can with difficulty be confined to certain selected groups.

The latitude given to film material cannot, in consequence, be as wide as the latitude given to book material. In addition, a book describes; a film vividly presents. One presents on a cold page, the other by apparently living people. A book reaches the mind through words merely, a film reaches the eyes and ears through the reproduction of actual events. . . . Hence many things which might be described or suggested in a book could not possibly be presented in a film. This is also true when comparing the film with the newspaper. Everything possible in a play is not possible in a film.

The MPAA's statement contains a note that the practice of limiting patronage at a general theater to adults only for a particular film "is not completely satisfactory and is only partially effective." A better approach, in the association's view, lies in the establishment of a special type of theater, catering exclusively to adult audiences, where films with "problem themes" may be viewed. "Maturer minds may easily understand and accept without harm subject matter in plots which do young people possible harm."

From the earliest days of the motion-picture industry both state and local governments have recognized the very distinctions and dangers acknowledged by the MPAA itself, but with the passing of years and the rulings of the Supreme Court, local censorship by prior restraint has been almost abandoned. In the fall of 1959 inquiries to some twenty cities listed by *Film Herald* as having prior-restraint censorship turned up only a few localities, such as Atlanta, in which the work is done systematically; elsewhere censorship operates informally, erratically, good-naturedly, and for the most part unconstitutionally.

In Geneva, Illinois, for example, local censors arrange with the town newspaper to publish ratings from the Green Sheet of the Film Estimate Board of National Organizations, and generally let their duties go at that. The Green Sheet, available from the Film Estimate Board's offices at 28 West Forty-fourth Street in New York, carries appraisals of current motion pictures by viewers representing eleven national groups, among them the DAR, American Association of University Women, American Jewish Committee, American Library

Association, National Congress of Parents and Teachers, and the Protestant Motion Picture Council. Their monthly ratings indicate a film's suitability for viewing by adults only, by mature young people, by young people, by families, and by children unaccompanied by adults. The Geneva Censor Board occasionally asks the local exhibitor not to book a picture, such as *Blue Denim,* and now and then asks local ministers to view a film "and we more or less rely on them for an opinion as to whether or not it shall be shown." The Geneva ordinance of 1938, creating the board, is patently unconstitutional in the light of the *Gelling* case[69] in its effort to ban all films not "to the best interest of the community."

The ordinance of San Jose, California, is equally vague; it directs a local entertainment commission "to prevent offenses against public morality and decency and to encourage and foster peace and good order in the showing of motion pictures." In Bellingham, Washington, a local board of review fixes its own rules and regulations; the town ordinance states only that no film shall be exhibited "unless the same shall have been approved by the board." The Detroit ordinance of 1934 flouts due process more severely still; it directs the commissioner or superintendent of police to inspect all movies, "and if in his judgment they are indecent or immoral, he shall reject the same." The neighboring city of Highland Park has a remarkable ordinance, but police sensibly pay no attention to it; the law says flatly: "No moving picture depicting the commission of crime shall be exhibited in the City of Highland Park. The chief of police shall have power to censor or suppress any immoral or questionable moving picture, plates, plays, films or exhibitions." In Little Rock a fifteen-man board of censors operates under an ordinance giving it sweeping authority to effect the closing of any motion picture or play, or to ban from sale any paper, magazine, book, or other publication "which they find violates the public sense of decency, morals, and propriety, or which might lead those under legal age into delinquency." This authority has been used in recent years only on the book and the film of *Lady Chatterley's Lover.* The City of Sacramento in 1932 created a motion-picture censor board, to be composed of the police chief and the city manager, with authority to ban any movie they felt might offend public morality and decency, but the ordinance no longer is enforced. Portland, Oregon, also has dropped enforcement of a 1953 ordinance vesting censorship powers in the local police chief, except as to stag or smoker films dealing in hard-core pornography. The Tacoma Censor Board, created in 1954, banned only one film (*The Outlaw*) in the succeeding five years. In Oklahoma City a Mayor's Advisory Committee on Censorship was called in but twice in a twelve-year period, once to delete a scene from an Ingrid Bergman movie, and again to view *Baby Doll*. The committee could find nothing particularly offensive in the latter.

Motion-picture censorship is taken more seriously in Atlanta, possibly, than in other cities. Substantial parts of the city's ordinance of 1953 are now plainly in violation of the Constitution. The censor is to view films and to determine if they are obscene "or will in his opinion adversely affect the peace, health, morals and good order of the city." If so, "he shall thereupon order a deletion of such scene or scenes or dialogue." Operating under this ordinance, a city censor, Mrs. Christine Smith Gilliam, regularly alters a number of films offered for local exhibition and bans some films entirely. Her decisions are subject to appeal to the board of trustees of the Atlanta Public Library, and then to the courts.

Over a representative two-year period, extending from October, 1957, to October, 1959, Mrs. Gilliam required these deletions:

Illicit Interlude   Several cuts for nudity.

Woman in a Dressing Gown   Cut word "bitch."

Green Eyed Blonde   Cut scene of Negro girl being kissed by white girls.

Lost Continent   Several close-ups of nude breasts.

And God Created Woman   Four cuts listed with exhibitor.

A Farewell to Arms   Cut of extreme labor pains; two short cuts of baby in Caesarian operation scene.

Lost Paradise   Cuts for close-ups of women's nude breasts.

Passionate Summer   Cuts of close-ups of birth of kid.

Wild Is the Wind   Cuts of close-ups of birth of lamb.

Walk into Hell   Two cuts of close-ups of nude breasts.

Girls on the Loose   Two cuts on details of murder.

Manhunt in the Jungle   Two cuts of close-ups of nude breasts.

Mark of the Hawk   Cut of white man dancing with Negro woman.

No Sun in Venice   Cut of scene of man bathing woman; cut of man caressing woman's breast and body.

The Night the Heavens Fell   Two close-ups in bullfighting scene.

The Defiant Ones   Cut lines of man telling Negro to spit; Negro spitting; Negro smoking cigarette, then handing it to white man.

The Sorcerer   Cut scene of nude woman in swimming.

The Light Across the Street   Cut of nude swimming scene; cut of Bardot running hands over her bosom.

In this same two-year period the Atlanta censor refused permits to *Fire Under Her Skin, Fruits of Summer, Nana, Cop Hater, The Flesh Is Weak, Adam and Eve, Teenage Doll,* and *Smiles of a Summer Night.*

Prior-restraint censorship by full-time state boards continues only in Virginia, Maryland, New York, and Kansas. They stay busy, viewing from five hundred to a thousand films a year, but the board members are painfully aware of their limited authority. In New York the 1960 fiscal year saw eliminations ordered in only 35 of 1,094 films examined; only one was banned in toto. Said Louis M. Pesce, director of the state's film censorship program: "In the last few years the eliminated material involved almost exclusively scenes with some erotic elements which alluringly portrayed sexually immoral situations, exploitations of nudity in situations other than those permitted in documentaries on nudism or in films depicting primitive societies. Other eliminations involved use of obscene dialogue or obscene gestures usually occurring in certain types of dance routines."

The future of state and local movie censorship seems largely a political question, in the broadest sense of that phrase. The motion-picture industry, if it felt the effort politic, doubtless could make a frontal assault upon the remaining prior-restraint laws and ordinances and have the lot of them declared unconstitutional. But in Atlanta, for example, such an assault might win the exhibitors more freedom than they really would like to have. So long as prior-restraint censorship operates with a light rein, the industry may well take the view that the small price it pays in terms of freedom may be worth the gain it derives in public relations. The remaining censors may be a nuisance but they are not ordinarily a large nuisance; they are a sort of housefly nuisance, less trouble to tolerate than to swat.

PART IV

THE MIDDLE GROUND

Above all stands the realization that we deal here with an area where knowledge is small, data is insufficient, and experts are divided.

JUSTICE JOHN MARSHALL HARLAN
concurring in Alberts v. California, 354 U. S. 376 (1957)

This is in the nature of an author's afterword. I write it toward five o'clock on a winter's afternoon, with the thin cutting edge of a March wind prying at the office windows and the radiators gurgling with a sudden activity. Across the hall, on the *Times-Dispatch* side of the building, the morning side reporters are coming on the job; my own *News Leader* city room lies deserted, the typewriters dust-covered. In a few hours we too will be caught up in the wonderfully recurring miracle by which a daily newspaper is brought into being.

I mention these things—the far-off thump and chatter of an AP printer, the faint hiss of the pneumatic tubes, the dangling pennants of some galley proofs—only to suggest the world I live in. It is a newspaperman's world; it is the only world I know; and it depends for its very survival upon the vitality of the great constitutional principles embodied in the First Amendment. Because of this, my every inclination in the conflict between writers and censors is to side with the forces that speak for freedom of the press. I live under the protection of this principle every working day of the world, and though I am not much given to Miltonian epitaph I expect I willingly would die for it. I can't think of many other things I willingly would die for. To those of us in the business of writing and publishing, freedom of the press is every most cherished possession, and I would not see it diminished.

But it seems to me that this conflict is grossly oversimplified when it is viewed only as a battle between those who are for press freedom and those who are against press freedom. Properly seen, it is not that at all. It is too easy to choose up sides, between the Philistines and the literati, as Douglas put it, or between the Comstocks and the Ingersolls, or the Chases and the Menckens, or the Summerfields and the Bryans. If I have learned anything at all from these past six months it is that both sides have some merit in their positions. Both sides exaggerate and both sides minimize, and when it comes to intolerance they finish in something close to a dead heat.

On the matter of exaggeration, I think the Philistines regularly tend to overestimate the social damage that may be caused by some of the materials they undertake to suppress. The NODL's February newsletter came in the other day and I counted the number of paper-back books listed as disapproved for youth; there were 241 of them. Alphabetically cheek by jowl were *Tortilla Flat* and the Fabian Books' *Turbulent Daughters,* and in another place, *Lady Chatterley's Lover* and something called *Lady Was a Man,* and up at the beginning of the list, Ayn Rand's *Atlas Shrugged* and a classic work put out by Bedside Books known as *Anything Goes.*

Now it seems to me, even acknowledging that the NODL's list deals only with books objectionable for youth, that the Philistines, if Monsignor Fitzgerald will forgive me, fall into error in this sort of undiscriminating approach. Indeed there is double error here, both as a matter of tactics and as a matter of fact. From the tactical point of view, in this choosing up sides, the February listing offers a great advantage to warriors of the literati. Ninety per cent of February's 241 titles may be trash, pure pulp pornography, utterly without redeeming social importance, but any spokesman for the Civil Liberties Union can run his eye down the list just as I did and say, "Look! Steinbeck! Lawrence! Ayn Rand!" And the whole list is discredited.

Wholly apart from these questions of tactics, I believe, some serious questions of literary merit—even for youth—need to be pondered more deeply by the NODL reviewers. I happen to think *Lady Chatterley's Lover* a very bad book; how any man could have written so beautiful a work as *Etruscan Places,* to recall only one of Lawrence's books I have loved, and still have written this stiff and clumsy piece of fiction is almost beyond me. What can Lawrence's defenders say of that scene, toward the end, where Lady Constance and her sister are riding toward London? Lady Constance makes some pedestrian remark, whereupon: "Hilda drove in silence for some time after this unheard-of insolence from that chit Connie." Ye gods! The book just happened to fall open on page 295. If there is any scene more ludicrous in all English literature than that Burpee's garden of adultery, in which the lovers entwine themselves in forget-me-nots, campion, bluebells, columbines, new-mown hay, oak tufts, honeysuckle, woodruff, creeping Jenny, and hyacinth, until "he sneezed, sneezing away the flowers from his nose and his navel," I should like to know of it. Under rules of appraisal that I happen to believe in, I would be forced to say, reluctantly and with a great many doubts, that *Lady Chatterley* perhaps is not legally obscene. The reputation of the author, the reputation of the publishers, the circumstances of publication, the methods of advertising and promotion —all these might incline me unwillingly to express an opinion that the book is not dirt for dirt's sake; and I agreeably would accept Justice Harlan's view, expressed in *Roth,* that in any event *Lady Chatterley* ought not to be banned from the country as a whole.

I cannot for the life of me understand why Steinbeck's *Tortilla Flat* and Ayn Rand's *Atlas Shrugged* should have warranted a place on the NODL's Index. Few juveniles are likely to read the Steinbeck; no juveniles are likely to tackle *Atlas,* and I would take oath that no seventeen-year-old who read either one of them from start to finish would have his moral values corrupted in any significant degree. When the NODL places such works as these on its list the action lessens one's confidence in every other title on the list. As for *Lady Chatterley,* which is a highly exceptional case, not likely to recur in any similar context any time soon, my suggestion would be that General Summerfield and the NODL let this one pass as a work of doubtful literature, and trust that parents exercise some sort of discipline in banning it, if they choose, on their own accord.

On the matter of minimizing important considerations, it seems to me that the Philistines regularly underestimate the sincerity, the conviction, and the sound position of persons who genuinely plead for freedom of expression and freedom to read. "Freedom! Liberty! They are always crying freedom and liberty," Mr. Comstock complained a long time ago. General Summerfield, Cardinal Spellman, and the chairmen of a hundred decent-literature committees all tend to regard this defense against censorship as nothing more than a specious excuse for licentiousness. I believe they are wrong in this, but I believe it is understandable that they should be wrong. Both the ideal and the reality of press freedom are remote from their everyday lives. They cannot wholly comprehend the seriousness with which writers and editors and publishers view an encroachment upon our right to get into print. I wish it were possible in some way to indoctrinate them in the meaning of press freedom, so that in any doubtful case their inclination would be to side with freedom and not with suppression.

It is this inability to discriminate, on the part of the Philistines, that has caused me so much trouble. The same unreasoning illogic that alphabetizes *Tortilla Flat* and *Turbulent Daughters* side by side in an NODL list sees a work of D. H. Lawrence, a dirty picture from Roy Oakley, and a contraceptive device all brought to bar under the same Section 1461. This makes no sense to me, and with the friendliest feelings toward the Philistines, I do wish devoutly that General Summerfield would not weaken their position by delivering edicts as to a Goya painting and a Lawrence novel; I wish he would look the other way. The public interest would not suffer.

It seems to me that some of the literati exaggerate, too. I listen to their caterwauling about the long dark night of suppression and the horrible excesses of the puritans and the Comstocks, and I am minded to say, seriously, now, stop that blubbering, and let me see where you're hurt. As Judge Bryan pointed out in the *Lady Chatterley* case, the Lawrence novel was only the second major work by a serious author to be attacked under federal law in a quarter of a century. The other was Joyce's *Ulysses* in 1934, and that was admitted to customs just as *Lady Chatterley* was admitted to the mails. That seems to me not so awful a record of abuse and excess on the part of the contemporary Comstocks. Two major novels in twenty-five years, and both acquitted! What is all the hollering about? If the administration of justice set so admirable a record in any other field of the law it would be a marvel of jurisprudence. Those on the literati side are as urgently in need of perspective and moderation as the Philistines.

I believe some of the literati are guilty of exaggeration also in their bland and hoity-toity certainty that obscene materials really cause no social damage. This is a matter of believing, not of knowing. It is a proposition not susceptible to any sort of demonstrable proof.

"We deal here," Harlan said in his dissenting opinion in *Alberts,* "with an area where knowledge is small, data is insufficient, and experts divided." My researches in recent months persuade me that most of the experts on the literati side are academicians, lady psychologists, book publishers, and lawyers of the ACLU; and most of the experts on the side of the Philistines are juvenile judges, criminal psychiatrists, and cops. For my own part, and my opinion is worth not one ounce more than anyone else's opinion, I am persuaded that prolonged subjection to obscene matter *can* have a profound influence on sexual attitudes and social behavior not only of adolescents but of adults also, and not only of especially susceptible adults but of tolerably normal adults too. There is a horrible fascination in these things. They put in motion all sorts of carnal desires far better left quiescent, and it requires no very vivid labor of the imagination to perceive a delayed cause-and-effect relationship between the nudie magazine, the filthy photograph, the hard-core movie, and the act of adultery or rape. What is involved, or so it seems to me, is a slow rotting of the social fabric, and I believe the states and the localities, moving with the utmost care under due process of law, have every right to protect their society from this sort of slow corruption. If this puts me on the side of the Philistines, I may be a little uneasy at the alliance, but there it is.

It is not a novel thought with me but I keep coming back to it: this problem, like so many problems of law, is the familiar one of weighing conflicting values. The rights of freedom of speech and of the press are not absolute rights; valuable as they are, they always have been subject to some occasional superior right of society as a whole. In this regard, the field of obscenity law does not seem to me so very different or unusual or difficult. I have a right to publish; society has a right to protect itself from overt obscenity. At what point do my rights and society's come in conflict? Courts and legislatures grapple with precisely such questions every day of the world, and with the assistance of juries, politicians, pressure groups, prosecuting attorneys, defense counsel, editors, parsons, cab drivers, and barbershop lawyers, the questions are roughly resolved. Ours is still the freest country on earth.

I keep coming back to Harlan's dissenting opinion too. It seems to me he sees the conflicting values better and clearer than anyone else I have read on the subject. It is important to remember that he dissented in *Roth,* and concurred in *Alberts,* because the former was a federal case and the latter a prosecution under California law. He made the point that the Congress has no substantive power over matters of sexual morality; the Congress (and by extension, the Post Office Department and the Justice Department and the Bureau of Customs) has only those powers that may be drawn necessarily and properly from the power vested in the Congress to establish post roads, to regulate commerce, and to control goods imported into the country. The federal authority thus is attenuated, and "the dangers of federal censorship in this field are far greater than anything the states may do." The fifty states, under our federal union, provide fifty experimental laboratories, in which legislative bodies may experiment in different ways with the treatment of social problems. Different states, said Harlan,

> will have different attitudes toward the same work of literature. The same book which is freely read in one state might be classed as obscene in another. And it seems to me that no overwhelming danger to our freedom to experiment and to gratify our tastes in literature is likely to result from the suppression of a borderline book in one of the states, so long as there is no uniform nationwide suppression of the book, and so long as other states are free to experiment with the same or bolder books.

Because Harlan's views seem to me so sound and rational, I myself would urge the Post Office Department to redouble its vigilance against doubtful prosecutions; in every such case the department ought to let the scales tip in favor of the author, the publisher, the magazine editor. So esoteric a publication as *Big Table,* which kicked up a row in Chicago, cannot be expected to cause more than infinitesimal damage to the body politic. How many persons would read it? In such a case it seems to me far better to risk this probably imperceptible damage, and to risk also the setting of some precedent that might later cause trouble, than to ban *Big Table* from the mails throughout the United States. I hope the advisory committee created by Mr. Summerfield late in 1959 will provide some effective guidance to the Postmaster General on this score.

At the same time I would view with equanimity the prosecution of *Big Table* under a state law or local ordinance. If the publication were banned from the bookstalls of Schenectady the people could drive to Albany for it. If the State of Georgia sought to ban it from local newsstands (though the State of Georgia has better sense) the literati of Atlanta could pick up a copy in New Orleans or New York, or order it by mail. The editors of the magazine would not suffer grievously; neither would the state of public enlightenment; neither would our constitutional liberties. And if the states and localities provided for *in rem* proceedings in these doubtful cases, in which the Philistines and literati could scrap out the issue of a book's obscenity before a judge or jury, under fair rules of evidence, I would sit on the front row spurring them on. Spurring *both* of them on.

If I were a card-carrying Philistine, which I am not, I would urge my brothers toward tolerance, forebearance, and a rational, realistic appraisal in each particular case of the values of suppression, against the values of free press; the damage to society, compared to the damage done to individual liberty. And if the damage to society seemed small I would ask them to side with free press and liberty every time. Such counsel, in most instances, is not particularly warranted: the Philistines as a group are more lenient, tolerant, sensible, and ready to listen than the literati as a group.

And if I were a certified subdeacon among the literati, which I am not, I would urge my more sophisticated brethren to emerge from their lofty towers, acquaint themselves with some ugly realities, and learn what this obscenity racket is all about. I would suggest that they accept, as a fact, that for every postal case involving a *Lady Chatterley* or a "Naked Maja" there are a thousand cases involving hardcore pornography of a viciousness that might shake even their urbane attitude. Weighed against the total number of books, magazines, and motion pictures brought into being, the number of successful obscenity prosecutions is minute; and if this penny's worth of censorship has served as any real deterrent to writers who would write about sex, I cannot conceive that their liberties have been seriously infringed.

Back in 1942, when New York's Mayor Fiorello LaGuardia was warring upon the burlesque houses, a case arose in which the Gaiety Theater sued for a license to reopen. The trial turned into a *cause célèbre*. Morris L. Ernst and Alexander Lindey were on the theater's side, and the Citizens Committee on Decency was supporting LaGuardia. It was a lusty fight. In the end Judge Aaron J. Levy concluded that the burlesque promoters were "habitual and confirmed vendors of smut," and he refused to order the license granted. He said:

> The criticized action [refusal of the Gaiety's license] is not a sporadic or isolated attempt at societal regulation. Viewed in its historical aspect it appears to be only another episode in society's uninterrupted campaign for self-protection. Quite naturally, the regulatory power is a restraint upon the free action of the individual, compensated, however, by the advantages each derives from public services. Self-preservation is as much a function of social organization as it is of each of us. The natural irritation and resistance of the individual to restraint resulting from surrendered freedom and its regulation are a guarantee against excess in the exercise of the power. Irked though we may be, experience teaches that the alternative is social anarchy and oppressive license. Thus, in our frontier days, each could, as an individual concern, condone and even enjoy the excesses of the hell holes of vice and immorality. Yet history records the perennial struggle against all influences tending to corrupt and incite to vice and crime upon the established principle that otherwise the reservoir of social life is poisoned. . . .
>
> While each of us may feel rightly or wrongly immune to the indicated harmful effects of the proscribed entertainment, that however is not only an unsafe criterion for judgment, but a clear invitation to disorder and anarchy. True, morality is not amenable to legislative fiat, but we must either surrender some area of freedom to the regulatory power of organized society or yield up the advantages of all its manifold protections. Thus the criterion of reasonableness and validity here is the lesson of the experience of society in its constant vigil to keep the reservoir clean.

"To keep the reservoir clean!" That is the only valid purpose the advocates of censorship may pursue, but it is a purpose the opponents of censorship ought not to reject out of hand. Few persons ever would agree on what should be meant by "clean," and fewer still would agree on acceptable methods for controlling pollution. But the effort is worth making, to find a rational answer to this ancient problem, and a free society should find nothing inconsistent with its freedom in seeking to keep from its reservoirs the merchants of filth.

TABLE OF CASES

LAW REVIEW ARTICLES

Alpert, *Judicial Censorship of Obscene Literature,* 52 Harv. L. Rev.

Desmond, *Censoring the Movies,* 29 Notre Dame Law. 27

Desmond, *Legal Problems Involved in Censoring the Media of Mass Communication,* 40 Marq. L. Rev. 38

Grant, Angoff, *Massachusetts and Censorship,* 10 Boston L. R. 36

Kupferman, O'Brien, *Memphis Blues,* 36 Cornell L. Q. 273

Mackay, *Recent Developments in the Law of Obscenity,* 32 Canadian B. Rev. 1010

Marks, *What Is Obscene Literature Today,* 73 U. S. L. Rev. 217

Moskin, *Notes on Inadequacy of Present Tests as to What Constitutes Obscene Literature,* 34 Cornell L. Q. 442

Paul, Schwartz, *Obscenity in the Mails,* 106 U. of Pa. L. Rev. 214

INDEX